Third World Debt

Third World Debt
The Search for a Solution

Edited by Professor Graham Bird
Department of Economics, University of Surrey

Edward Elgar

Published by
Edward Elgar Publishing Limited
Gower House
Croft Road
Aldershot
Hants GU11 3HR
England

Gower Publishing Company
Old Post Road
Brookfield
Vermont 05036
USA

British Library Cataloguing in Publication Data

Third world debt: the search for a solution
   1. Developing countries. External debts
  I. Bird, Graham
  336.3'435'091724

  ISBN 1-85278-162-9

Printed in Great Britain by
Billing & Sons Ltd, Worcester

To my mother

Contents

Notes on Contributors

Graham Bird is Professor of Economics at the University of Surrey and Head of the Department of Economics. He has been Visiting Professor of International Economic Affairs at the Fletcher School of Law and Diplomacy, Tufts University, and an adviser to both the World Bank and the Commonwealth Secretariat. His previous books include *The International Monetary System and the Less Developed Coutries*, *The Quest for Economic Stabilisation* (with Tony Killick and others), *World Finance and Adjustment*, *International Financial Policy and Economic Development*, *International Macroeconomics*, and *Managing Global Money*. His recent research has covered various aspects of Third World debt policy including debt-equity swaps, interest rate caps, and commercial bank provisioning.

Benjamin J. Cohen is William L. Clayton Professor of International Economic Affairs at the Fletcher School of Law and Diplomacy at Tufts University in the United States having previously taught at Princeton University. He has also been a Ford Foundation, Rockefeller Foundation and Council on Foreign Relations Fellow. His previous publications include *Balance of Payments Policy*, *Organising the World's Money*, *Banks and the Balance of Payments* and *In Whose Interest? International Banking and American Foreign Policy*. He has recently completed a major study into the political economy of developing country debt.

Mike Faber is currently a Professorial Research Fellow at the Institute of Development Studies at the University of Sussex having previously been its Director. He has been an adviser to many developing countries and international agencies. A frequent commentator on many of the problems faced by developing countries, Professor Faber has recently taken a keen interest in Third World indebtedness and has published a number of articles arguing the case for debt buy-backs.

Stephany Griffith-Jones is Reader at the Institute of Development Studies at the University of Sussex. She has acted as an adviser to the World Bank and the United Nations, as well as to the commercial sector. Her publications include *The Role of Finance in the Transition to Socialism*, *Latin America and International Finance*, *The Crisis of International Debt and National Development* (with O. Sunkel) and *Managing World Debt*.

Ingrid Iversen is an economist with Amex Bank. She has had considerable practical experience of debt rescheduling from the viewpoint of the commercial banks.

Tony Killick is Senior Research Fellow at the Overseas Development Institute in London, where he was Director until 1987. An adviser to numerous developing country governments and international agencies, he was President of the Development Studies Association from 1986 to 1988. Since 1988 he has been an Honorary Visiting Professor at the University of Surrey. His previous publications include *Development Economics in Action*, *Policy Economics*, *Adjustment and Financing in the Developing World*, *The Quest for Economic Stabilisation* and *The IMF and Stabilisation*.

Bahram Nowzad is editor of *Finance and Development*, an international journal published jointly by the IMF and the World Bank. Prior to this he was on the staff of the IMF and has considerable experience of the Fund's involvement with indebted developing countries. He is the author of a number of journal articles, as well as a Princeton Essay in International Finance which deals with *The IMF and its Critics*.

Miguel A. Olea was at the time of writing his chapter General Co-ordinator for Economic Affairs at the Mexican Ministry of Foreign Affairs. In this capacity he is particularly qualified to discuss the developing-country debt problem from the perspective of the governments of the indebted countries.

Philip Suttle is currently with the International Division of the Bank of England. Formerly he worked on the statistical analysis of debt at the Institute of International Finance in Washington. His previous publications include a survey of debt projection models which appeared in the *Oxford Review of Economic Policy*, Winter 1985.

Preface

There are many signs that Third World debt is becoming more, rather than less of a problem. Hopes that it would be solved by economic expansion in the industrial world or by a combination of adjustment within the indebted nations and rescheduling have not been realized.

This book is based on papers contributed to an international conference held by the Economics Department at the University of Surrey in England in Spring 1988, although it also contains some contributions from an earlier conference held at the Fletcher School of Law and Diplomacy, Tufts University, USA. As the search for a solution continues, the book focuses on a range of issues: the problem of forecasting debt difficulties; the risk of debtor default; the roles of the official and private sectors; the future provision of development finance; the political economy of debt policy; and the arguments for and against different approaches, contrasting, in particular, centralized with market-based reform.

Every effort has been made to avoid merely bringing together a loosely related group of papers, but instead to provide an integrated analysis of the problem of Third World debt with the view of helping to find a solution.

In seeking to provide a non-technical treatment of one of the most serious problems currently facing the world economy, the book should be of interest to academics, students, practitioners and policy makers. It should be relevant to courses dealing with development, international and financial economics, as well as international relations and international political economy.

Those to thank include: Gioia Pescetto for overseeing the organization of the Surrey conference; Liz Blakeway for doing much of the organizational work and for supervising the preparation of the book; Michael Foot, Christopher Johnson, Charles Larkum and Jorge Navarrete for creating a lively and informative panel session; Lance Taylor and Jeff Sachs for the views they expressed at the Fletcher School conference, which it is hoped find expression in this book; and to all conference participants.

1 Introduction

Graham Bird

This chapter sets out to examine three main questions: why do debt problems arise; how have they been handled in the past; and how might they be handled in the future? These questions imply an assessment of the adequacy of existing techniques for dealing with the debt problem along with some comment on alternative techniques.

By discussing the three questions listed above, this introductory chapter attempts to put the following chapters into some form of perspective.

THE CAUSES OF DEBT PROBLEMS

While it is tautological to say that the acquisition of debt is a precondition for the emergence of a debt problem, it is important to note that debt acquisition need not lead to problems. Indeed, in many respects, the taking on of debt is an entirely rational and welfare-enhancing activity representing an inter-temporal redistribution of living standards. Provided that the rate of discount exceeds the rate of interest, welfare will be raised by borrowing now and repaying later. The underlying logic of debt acquisition is reinforced by theories of life-cycle consumption, where an individual or household may maximize the welfare derived from a given lifetime income by going into debt at certain stages in the life cycle; it is much the same for developing countries.

Borrowing increases the financial and real resources currently available to the borrower. Whether it leads to problems depends largely on how these additional resources

1

are used. Basically, where the increase in current resources is used to enhance the availability of resources in the future, the acquisition of debt should be manageable and should not lead to problems in the sense of an inability to service the debt and to meet outstanding debt obligations.

In determining whether a debtor nation will be able to service its debt, three considerations are central. The first relates to the relationship between the marginal productivity of the resources borrowed and the rate of interest on the loan. For as long as the marginal productivity exceeds the rate of interest, the loan may be serviced and some contribution made towards repaying the principal. Where, however, the rate of interest on the loan exceeds its marginal productivity, there will be debt-servicing problems and the debtor may be forced to try to take on extra debt to meet existing obligations.

The second consideration relates to domestic saving. Borrowing may be viewed as a way of closing a domestic savings gap, i.e. the gap between the savings required to finance the investment which is itself needed to achieve a targeted growth rate, and the actual amount of domestic savings. If borrowing is necessitated by a deficiency of domestic saving, it follows that, to service and repay debt, there will have to be an excess of domestic saving over and above that needed for financing domestic investment. A crucial factor here will be what is happening to the domestic savings ratio. If the marginal propensity to save exceeds the average propensity to save, the savings ratio will rise. Other things remaining constant, a rising savings ratio will offer a better prospect that the debtor will be able to meet its obligations than if the ratio were falling.

However, it is not enough that additional domestic savings are generated. Since borrowing will have been conducted in foreign exchange, excess savings have to be converted or transferred into additional foreign exchange. Inasmuch as borrowing is undertaken to close a foreign exchange gap, i.e. the gap between the foreign exchange needed to buy the imports that are in turn needed to achieve development and the foreign exchange earned through exporting, the repayment of the related debt requires that the borrowing country reverses this gap and moves into a current account surplus.

The third important consideration is therefore what is happening, and what is likely to happen to export earnings and import payments. Where a debtor faces deteriorating income terms of trade, it is more likely to encounter debt problems than where its terms of trade are improving.

The significance of export performance *relative* to changes in interest rates is revealed by most simple debt models. Assume, for example, that current account deficits are financed by taking on extra debt such that

$$M - X - rD = \Delta D$$

where M is imports, X is exports, r is the rate of interest and D is external debt. Allowing k to stand for the debt–export ratio (D/X), $\dot{x}$ for the growth of exports and $\dot{k}$ for the change in the debt–export ratio, it follows that

$$(M - X)/X = k(\dot{x} + \dot{k} - r)$$

This formula suggests that where the interest rate is higher than the growth rate of exports, a trade surplus will be required if the debt–export ratio is to be prevented from increasing. At the same time, with export growth greater than the interest rate, a constant proportionate trade deficit will not raise the debt–export ratio and, in these circumstances, a potential borrower will be encouraged to continue to acquire debt. The problems for the management of debt are aptly illustrated by the above formula inasmuch as $\dot{x}$ and r are unlikely to be invariant over time, and changes in them cannot be perfectly predicted.

Timing, indeed, constitutes another aspect of potential debt difficulties. For, while in the long run a country may be solvent in the sense of being able to meet all its debt obligations, it may be unable to do so in the short run or at any particular moment in time. The time pattern of export earnings may, for example, fail to match the time pattern of debt obligations. The debtor country may then face a *liquidity* problem rather than a *solvency* one. As will be seen later, this distinction is useful since, to the extent that it can be made operational, it helps in identifying appropriate debt policies both at the individual country and global levels.

Up to now, the factors affecting the incidence of debt problems have been presented almost as if they are beyond the control of the debtors. This is far from the truth. Governments may, in principle, be able to influence the productivity of investment, through domestic economic and social policy, the domestic savings ratio, through taxation and interest rate policy, and exports and imports, through domestic macro-economic and micro-economic policy as well as through exchange rate policy. Extending this argument somewhat, it may also be noted that both the savings and foreign exchange gaps are *ex ante* concepts. In effect, they can be closed *ex post* by means of countries simply failing to achieve their aspired growth rates. This would seem to suggest that, having once acquired debt, governments can avoid servicing problems provided only that they are prepared to pursue the necessary (deflationary) policies. But will they be willing to do so?

The question of the willingness, as opposed to the ability, of debtor countries to meet their debt obligations is still broader than it appears from this. Even where full servicing of debt would imply relatively little in the way of restrictionary domestic policy, there may be pressures on debtor governments not to pay and instead to default on their debt or repudiate it.

The calculus of debt default is, in principle, quite straightforward, and simply involves comparing the probable costs and benefits of such action. Where there appears to be a net benefit from default then a rational debtor should repudiate its debt. In practice, the decision is more complicated. This is more to do with problems associated with calculating the costs of default than the benefits. The latter will rise with the volume of the debt and with the rate of interest, or, more generally, the severity of the terms. The costs, however, depend crucially on certain behavioural responses which it may be difficult to predict with any degree of precision. How will creditors, for example, respond to default? It is perhaps reasonable to suppose that a defaulting country would lose access to new credit, including trade credit, for some period of time; might induce sanctions from the international community of creditors; and might encourage internal debtors to reconsider whether they should continue to meet outstanding obligations. But how significant would the responses be? If the defaulter were to lose access to international capital markets, for how long would the exclusion last?

Given the uncertainty surrounding the costs of default, it may be assumed that a government's propensity to default will depend significantly on its degree of risk aversion. A risk-averse government will tend to put a relatively high probability on there being relatively high costs and the calculus will therefore be biased against default.

Moreover governments may feel a moral obligation to meet outstanding commitments and may value an international reputation for honesty; this will also discourage default.

Even so it needs to be recognized that anything which is perceived by the debtors as reducing the costs of default relative to the benefits will raise the probability that it will occur.

Just as it was noted above that the distinction between solvency and liquidity problems is sometimes difficult to sustain, so too the distinction between the ability and the willingness to service debt can become clouded, since in many cases the ability to pay exists if sufficient domestic sacrifice is made. In practical terms it seems likely that ability and willingness will be positively related. If, in fact, governments only become unwilling to meet their debt obligations as the size of the required sacrifice becomes unacceptable, then this suggests that policy designed to avoid default should concentrate on keeping the sacrifice of debtors (or the burden of adjustment) below this critical level. If, on the other hand, governments are actively seeking the optimal moment to default from the point of view of maximizing net benefits, then global anti-default policy needs to concentrate on maintaining, and indeed raising, the perceived costs of repudiation.

The above discussion identifies some of the factors that might lead to a specific volume of debt becoming less manageable or to its giving rise to a greater incidence of debt problems. In some of the literature these factors have been reclassified as being either internal (endogenous) or external (exogenous). Internal factors include the mismanagement of the debt itself, or the mismanagement of the economy through the selection of inappropriate microeconomic and macroeconomic policy. Proxies for internal causation have included the fiscal deficit and the real exchange rate.

The external causation line of argument suggests that debt problems have not been caused, or at least have not been primarily caused by domestic mismanagement but rather by exogenous factors beyond the control of domestic governments. External factors include deteriorating income terms of trade caused by falling growth in the demand for primary products, and rising interest rates caused by the stance of macroeconomic policy in the industrial countries.

Again the distinction between internal and external factors is a somewhat cloudy one. For example, excessive domestic inflation, which tends to result in currency overvaluation, may be caused by excessive fiscal deficits and monetary expansion, or by an increase in import prices. Until the cause of inflation is discovered, it is rather ambiguous as to whether the related debt difficulties are of internal or external derivation. However, putting the problem of classification to one side, it is interesting to ponder, as much of the debt debate has done, on whether endogenous or exogenous factors lie at the heart of the debt problems that have visibly faced the world since 1982.

Initially there is strong support for external causation. First, is it realistic to assume that a number of debtor countries fairly simultaneously but independently began to mismanage their economies? Second, evidence during the early 1980s shows that the real rate of interest increased dramatically and that export receipts for the developing world dipped. These developments combined to increase the debt–service ratio for developing countries from 18 per cent in 1980 to 25 per cent by 1982. There is then ample evidence to suggest that debtor nations faced a deteriorating world economic environment.

But this is not the whole story. Taking negotiations over debt rescheduling as a proxy for the existence of a debt problem, it emerges that not all the heavily indebted countries encountered debt problems as a result of the deteriorating environment. The most notorious example is Korea which, whilst holding the third largest amount of debt amongst the developing countries, was able, unlike many of the Latin American developing countries, to avoid debt rescheduling. Why is it that not all indebted nations appear to have been similarly affected by external factors?

One potential answer is clearly that some might have been more insulated from them than others because of the structure and pattern of their trade, as well as the structure of their debt. Yet this explanation finds little empirical support.[1] The alternative explanation, for which empirical support does exist, is that the non-problem countries adapted better to the changing environment and pursued policies that were better suited to the new set of global economic conditions.[2] If this is indeed the case, the conclusion emerges that although external factors were the underlying or initiating cause of debt problems in the early 1980s, the extent to which these factors actually resulted in the renegotiation of debt commitments depended crucially on internal factors. As econometric evidence confirms, neither internal nor external factors may be excluded from the explanation of debt problems during the 1980s.[3]

HOW THE DEBT PROBLEM HAS BEEN HANDLED

Once debt problems have arisen, whether caused by internal or external factors or a combination of the two, the question of how to cope with them has to be answered. Basically there are four broad global approaches to dealing with the problem of debt.

1. The market solution

This approach, which appears to have been much favoured in some political circles particularly before the Mexican debt crisis in 1982, says that market forces should be allowed to operate. If debtors cannot meet their obligations then the market will penalize both the debtors and creditors. Debtors will find it harder to gain access to loans in the future and creditors will incur losses. The market will thereby police both overborrowing and overlending.

The problem with this approach arises if, for some reason, the market fails. A conventional cause of market failure relates to externalities, and a market solution to the debt problem will indeed involve such externalities. The external costs will fall on the populations of debtor countries that encounter debt problems, and also, quite possibly, on the populations of other highly indebted countries as their creditworthiness is adversely affected. For the international banking system, the failure of banks that might result from either formal or informal default could have far-reaching consequences, with, ultimately, the stability of the system itself being threatened, which could have adverse consequences for creditor countries. It was the eventual acceptance of the undesirability of some of these externalities which pushed the world away from fully implementing the market solution to the debt problem.

2. Economic adjustment in debtors

In principle, adjustment may take a number of forms. Where its purpose is to free foreign exchange which may then be used to meet debt obligations, the options are either to expand exports or to contract imports. Although governments may, through appropriate policy, stimulate export growth, the extent to which this will occur will be constrained by the state of the market for developing countries' exports. If the governments of industrial countries are pursuing anti-inflationary policies which restrain the growth of demand in their economies and, at the same time, are pursuing protectionist measures to limit imports and avoid payments deficits; then the environment will not be conducive to export expansion by the debtor nations.

In these circumstances, and where debtors are under international pressure to turn their own balance of payments around over a relatively short time span, there is little effective option open to them other than to reduce imports either by deflating domestic demand or by imposing their own controls on imports.

Such an adjustment strategy, however, raises a number of further issues. First, there will again be externalities associated with it. Living standards or, at best, the rate of growth of living standards in the debtors will fall, and there may be limits on the domestic acceptability of this. One possible externality is, therefore, social and political unrest within the debtor countries which could result in the undermining of democracy. Second, rapid adjustment is unlikely to induce the structural changes which may be required and it may therefore be anti-developmental. Here, it needs to be recognized that economic growth within the debtors provides the greatest opportunity for them to be able to meet their debt obligations. An inter-temporal inconsistency can easily arise between measures that are pursued in the short run and those that are required in the long run. Creditors may well be anxious to observe that governments are prepared to make domestic sacrifices to service their debts. On the other hand, they will not be pleased to see a scenario for the debtors which involves falling economic growth and declining export prospects due to shortages of required imported goods. Thus, while deflationary adjustment programmes may increase the confidence of creditors in the short run they will probably fail to raise confidence in the long run unless the growth of output and exports picks up. And this may itself be made less likely by a deflationary programme of adjustment.

The third issue associated with deflationary or protectionist adjustment in the debtor countries relates to the causes of the problem. Is it reasonable to expect debtor countries to shoulder the burden of adjustment if it may be demonstrated that it was, in substantial part, policies in industrial countries which caused the debt problem in the first place? Simple macroeconomic theory suggests that the simultaneous rise in world interest rates along with a decline in the demand for developing countries' exports, as was observed in the early 1980s, may be explained by the pursuit of contractionary monetary policy in a number of important industrial economies at that time.[4] If this explanation of events is accepted, not only would emphasis on adjustment within the debtors represent an inequitable distribution of the adjustment burden, but it would also be inefficient in the sense that it would fail to realize the world's productive potential.

3. Adjustment in other countries

For reasons implied by the above discussion, this appears to be an attractive alternative strategy for alleviating the debt problem. A policy of expansion across the industrial countries could, for example, reduce world interest rates and enhance the export prospects of debtor countries. But even here, things are not as straightforward as they might initially seem. First, a question hangs over the appropriate form of expansion: to what extent should it rely on fiscal or monetary policy? Clearly too much emphasis on expansionary fiscal policy could lead to rising interest rates, and this would not be to the advantage of the debtors. Second, if the expansion were to be uncoordinated, the benefits to different debtors would depend on their individual patterns of trade. Moreover, inasmuch as uncoordinated expansion results in exchange rate instability, this could be to the disadvantage of developing and indebted nations. Third, there remains the fundamental problem of how to put pressure on industrial countries to expand their economies, particularly in a coordinated fashion. Although the international economic system affords some opportunity to exert pressure on deficit countries to adjust — although even here not all deficit countries are uniformly treated — it has yet to come up with a satisfactory mechanism by which surplus countries can be encouraged to expand their economies.

4. Rescheduling

The main idea with rescheduling is to allow debtor countries more time to service and repay their debt by spreading out their existing obligations. With a relatively high discount rate in debtor countries, rescheduling serves to reduce the present value of a given stock of debt obligations. However, the principal appeal of rescheduling exists if the debt problem is of the liquidity type. In this case it is time that is the problem, and it is time that rescheduling provides.

Where the problems are more fundamental and are more of an insolvency nature, the benefit from rescheduling depends crucially on how the time provided is used. Where rescheduling enables appropriate structural adjustment to be carried through, it can clearly make an important contribution towards solving an insolvency problem. Much rests on the superiority of gradualism and structural adjustment programmes over 'shock' short-run adjustment programmes. Indeed, if it can be argued that a short, sharp shock is what is needed, then it follows that rescheduling, which enables such policies to be avoided, is undesirable.

From this menu of choice, options 1 and 3 have been largely, though not totally, rejected. Banks have suffered some losses as a result of their lending to developing countries and have not been completely insulated from the market; moreover, in 1984, economic expansion in the USA enabled some Latin American debtors to increase their export earnings — although US policy also had the effect of keeping interest rates high. But, in the main, the debt problem has been handled by a combination, and usually a formal combination of adjustment in the debtor countries and rescheduling. The adjustment has normally been conducted under the auspices of the International Monetary Fund, but with the World Bank taking on an increasingly significant role in policy conditionality. Although elements relating to the supply side have crept into some Fund-supported programmes, the conventional emphasis on demand restraint and devaluation of the exchange rate has been maintained. After an initial period of strictness, rescheduling terms have gradually been liberalized across a number of areas.

Whether one assesses the approach that has *de facto* been adopted as a success or as a failure depends very much on the particular perspective adopted. Certainly, mass default and the collapse of the international banking system has been avoided. Indeed, it could be argued that the banks have had to undertake relatively little adjustment and have made relatively few sacrifices. From this perspective the approach has worked. However, from the perspective of the debtor countries, where it might be supposed greater attention will be focused on domestic living standards rather than the stability of the international banking system, it might appear somewhat different.

In any event, the question arises as to whether techniques that have been used in the past will prove adequate in the future. It is to a consideration of the future that we now turn.

RECENT TRENDS: A DEEPENING PROBLEM?

In order to provide a background against which the adequacy of existing techniques for dealing with debt may be assessed, it is useful to identify some recent trends in the evolution of Third World debt. Of course, any summary statistics are open to criticism. There may, for example, be many exceptions to any general trend that is observed. Moreover, differences may exist depending on the sources of data used and on the time period studied.

Acknowledging these statistical problems, Table 1.1, which is extracted from the most recently published World Debt

Table 1.1 Debt indicators for and economic
performance of highly indebted countries

	1980	1981	1982	1983	1984	1985	1986
Debt service ratio (%)	18.1	20.0	25.0	24.7	23.1	26.1	29.0
Interest to exports ratio (%)	8.8	10.3	14.3	15.0	15.0	17.1	18.7
Net transfer (US $ billion)	8.8	18.4	3.8	-7.5	-17.5	-26.1	-24.9
GDP % real increase	5.7	0.4	-0.6	-2.9	2.3	2.9	2.9
Investment % real increase	9.3	1.3	-14.9	-20.5	0.3	4.9	2.7
Exports % real increase	3.8	-1.1	-5.0	1.7	12.3	-0.5	-2.7
Imports % real increase	10.9	6.1	-14.3	-20.2	-2.4	0.1	-0.7

Source: World Debt Tables, 1987–88, World Bank, 1988.

Tables produced by the World Bank, reveals a number of interesting features concerning both the size of the debt problem, and the economic performance of highly indebted countries. The first two lines of the Table examine a couple of conventional debt indicators; the debt–service ratio and the interest to exports ratio. In both cases there has been a very significant deterioration in the period 1980–86, with the most pronounced change coming in 1980–82. In the case of the DSR some small decline (improvement) took place between 1982–84 before it continued to rise to 29.0 per cent in 1986. In the case of the interest to exports ratio the rise was more persistent throughout the entire period.

With the implied increase in debt–service payments it is unsurprising to see that, at the same time as these indicators were showing a deterioration in the debt situation of highly indebted countries, the net transfer of financial flows turned negative. Having been +$18.4 billion in 1981, net transfer was –$26.1 billion in 1985. There was some reduction in this negative flow in 1986 because of a limited number of large debt renegotiations which involved new financial inflows and reduced current outflows. Although the data in Table 1.1 refer only to the highly indebted developing countries, a similar overall pattern emerges both for Latin American debtors and for the poorer debtors of Sub-Saharan Africa.

One weakness of the Table is that the data only run up to 1986, and there is some evidence from other sources to suggest that things improved somewhat in 1987. Even so it would be too early to argue that the trends revealed in Table 1.1 have been reversed.

The rest of the data in the Table show the implications for economic performance of the deteriorating debt situation revealed in lines 1–3. The pursuit of adjustment programmes has implied a sharp decline in the rate of economic growth in highly indebted countries (HICs). With rates of population growth in excess of economic growth rates, per capita GDP has, in many cases, fallen quite dramatically. Line 5 shows that investment has not been insulated from adjustment, with a cumulative fall of over 35 per cent during 1982–83. When the key role of investment in economic growth is remembered, this feature of the 1980s is particularly worrying.

Lines 6–7 provide data on the balance of payments. Although the negative net transfer seen in line 3 provides a clue that many debtor countries have managed to run payments surpluses, these have tended to occur at lower levels of trade. Line 6 shows that apart from 1984 (and 1983 to a much lesser extent) real export growth has been negative during 1981–86, falling overall by almost 5 per cent. This, however, has been more than matched by a fall of over 31 per cent in real imports. Apart from again illustrating the impact of adjustment programmes in the highly indebted countries, these data give rise to some concern about the future. Inasmuch as imports are needed to facilitate economic development, and as inputs into exports, the prospects for future growth in output and exports, which are the avenues through which debt obligations may be met in the longer term, look rather bleak.

Bearing in mind the discussion of the sources of debt problems undertaken earlier in this chapter, Table 1.1 provides little cause for optimism. Interest rates continue to be relatively high in comparison with both the marginal productivity of resources and the growth of exports. Domestic savings are being channelled into the servicing of existing external debt rather than into the financing of domestic investment which provides the basis for future economic growth. The rise in exports relative to imports has been achieved not through export expansion but through a larger fall in imports than in exports. Furthermore, this form of adjustment has brought about a significant decline in living standards and growth rates. But what about the future? Again there is cause for concern.

First, as noted above, net transfers have turned negative since 1983. In other words, debtor countries are now paying back more in the form of servicing old loans than they are receiving in the form of new ones. This is true not only of private sector loans but also of loans from the IMF. Although, in one sense, anybody that takes on debt must anticipate a negative net transfer at some time in the future, the turn-round in the case of the major borrowers has come too quickly for them to be able to cope with it and as noted above has been achieved at the cost of domestic investment that holds the key to future growth. There has simply been too little time for their economies to develop sufficiently for both economic growth and net repayments to the rest of the system to be sustained. Indeed where economic growth is sacrificed this implies that the net transfer from the debtors will not be sustainable in the longer run.[5] Moreover, negative net transfers increase the incentive for debtors to default, since what they gain, in the form of the avoided debt service payments, is greater than what they lose in the form of new loans. At present there are, in any case, very few new loans to lose. It is hardly surprising therefore that countries such as Peru, and more recently Brazil, have limited their debt–service payments. The economics of debt repudiation predicted that they would.

Second, falling growth rates and living standards in debtor countries raise pressures on debtor countries to default. These falling rates reflect the sacrifices that have been made to release foreign exchange as well as the inability to pursue the less painful means of economic adjustment through export expansion which has been frustrated by slow growth in industrial countries and by rising protectionism. If the costs of complying with the rules of the game rise, there is greater incentive to abandon the game. There must be some doubt about how far demand deflation as a means of stabilization can be taken. In any case, as already noted, while reducing consumption may be a necessary element in economic adjustment, the capacity of countries to service their debt in the future will not be enhanced by reduced rates of investment and economic growth. Nor, of course, will their creditworthiness with the banks be improved.

Third, but in conjunction with the above, there seems little prospect of the debtors being able to climb on the back of a world expansion. Indeed the IMF and the World Bank have been adjusting downwards their growth forecasts for the OECD. Talk of trade wars and further protectionism offers little comfort to the heavily indebted nations. In addition to these general trends other more recent developments have given an extra twist to the already knotty problem of Third World debt.

Greater provisioning by the banks against their developing country exposures, which has resulted in global loan loss reserves rising to an estimated $70 billion or more will, by effectively taxing them, make new loans less easily available. Moreover, it has created tension between the banks where it is perceived by some as having been used by others as a predatory and aggressive weapon of competition. Furthermore, the smaller banks that have unwillingly participated in new money packages now see less incentive for them to lend in future, since they perceive the larger banks as being in a stronger financial position. In this way the bargaining strength of the debtors may have been raised, and with a reduced prospect of new loans, default again becomes more likely.

In addition to the greater tensions amongst banks, there is also a significant gulf between the perceptions of the banks and of the official sector. The banks see new loans as going to support net repayments to the IMF and feel that they have made greater concessions than have the multilateral agencies, the Paris Club and the export guarantee agencies. The official sector feels that the banks have been too unwilling to accept their share of the blame for the debt problem and have not gone far enough in offering relief.

Taking these various factors together, there is little reason to believe that the debt problem will simply evaporate. Instead there are many reasons for believing that it will get worse. So what needs to be done?

THE SEARCH FOR A SOLUTION: QUESTIONS FOR THE FUTURE

The remaining chapters of this book examine some of the questions that need to be asked in attempting to find a solution to the problem of Third World debt. The book does not, however, claim to have found the solution.

A prior question is, 'What is the size of the debt problem and is it possible to forecast it with any degree of accuracy?'

Debt simulation models can give a rather false sense of accuracy, and can tempt the uninitiated to see things in over-simplistic terms. It becomes relatively easy within the context of such models almost to assume the problem away, since its size is revealed as being quite sensitive to the assumptions or projections made concerning export growth and interest rates. Even relatively small changes in projected export growth can have dramatic consequences for the anticipated size of the problem. The difficulty is, of course, that it is hard to predict global economic growth and interest rates with any large measure of confidence, and uncertainties relating to these factors impinge on the confidence with which debt projections can be treated.

In any case, as Philip Suttle argues in Chapter 2, there are deficiencies in the information available on the size and structure of external debt, such that those involved in formulating policy may not know the precise nature of the problem. In some instances the information may be in-sufficient, while in other cases there may be too much conflicting information coming from different sources such as the World Bank, the Bank for International Settlements, and now the Institute of International Finance.

Suttle also stresses that greater sophistication is required in understanding the subtleties of the debt problem, as well as the scope that governments have for coping with it. Clearly there is a strong case for refining techniques of country risk analysis, the inadequacies of which were fairly clearly under-lined in 1982 when their use largely failed to predict Mexico's debt difficulties.

However, while acknowledging the difficulties in fore-casting debt problems, the indicators used in this chapter point to a deterioration in the situation. An interesting question relates to how debtors might conduct themselves in this changing environment. Will they continue to accept programmes of domestic stabilization which carry with them significant political implications, or might they be en-couraged to consider and use the default option? Does the reluctance of the debtors to default in the past mean that they will continue to be reluctant to do so in the future? Does a repudiation paradox exist in the sense that countries

will only be forced to think about repudiation at a time when
they are short of foreign exchange and therefore need
trade credit, and will only be able to cope with the loss
of trade credit when they have adequate foreign exchange
and therefore do not need to default? These important
issues are covered in Chapters 3 and 4 by Stephany
Griffith-Jones and Miguel Olea respectively.

Debtors might be more reluctant to default if the adjustment programmes favoured by the major multilateral
agencies, especially the IMF and the World Bank, were
regarded by them as being appropriate. This raises a series
of questions relating to adjustment in indebted countries
and the role of the institutions in facilitating and encouraging
it. Tony Killick in Chapter 5 examines in detail the spread
of obligatory adjustment and discusses the issues to which
this gives rise. Chapter 6 by Bahram Nowzad provides a
succinct and somewhat contrasting view from within the
Fund as to what its role has been and should be in addressing
the problems of financing and adjustment.

Certainly during the 1970s and 1980s the IMF played a
relatively small part, in a direct quantitative sense, in
financing payments deficits in developing countries. Now
somewhat notoriously, it was the private international banks
that took over this role. Yet it has become a role that they
are anxious to relinquish. In Chapter 8, Ingrid Iversen
examines the scope for maintaining a commercial bank
involvement via various new lending options and for expanding the role of foreign investment in financing economic
development. She also describes the proposals put forward by
her own bank for alleviating the debt problem, although
these are rather unrepresentative of the typical banker's view.

Many bankers have up until quite recently tended to
favour a rather passive approach to the debt problem. However, moves to convert debts into equity and to set aside
larger provisions against loans to developing countries reveal
some change in these attitudes.

Benjamin Cohen in Chapter 7, and in what is essentially
one part of a trilogy on the political economy of developing
country debt, argues that activism is required to solve the
debt problem. He maintains that while there are positive net

benefits to be gained through cooperation between debtors and creditors, such a solution is unlikely to emerge spontaneously, but will need to be formulated and promoted.

Graham Bird, in Chapter 9, continues on a similar theme by assessing alternative approaches to solving the debt problem. In particular a contrast is drawn between centrally designed 'strategies' or 'plans' and solutions which emerge from the market place.

Finally in Chapter 10, Mike Faber surveys the growing terminology of Third World debt. His argument is that semantics are important and that words can influence attitudes and decisions about the future.

While the above chapters make no claim to have produced, in any sense, a definitive solution to the problem of Third World debt — indeed they suggest that such a solution probably does not exist — it is hoped that they do make a useful contribution towards the ongoing search for some solution by identifying and analysing some of the crucial issues that need to be tackled.

NOTES AND REFERENCES

1. See, for example, Jeffrey Sachs, 'External Debt and Macroeconomic Performance in Latin America and East Asia', *Brookings Papers on Economic Activity*, vol. 2, 1985; and Peter Nunnenkamp, *The International Debt Crisis of the Third World*, Brighton, Wheatsheaf Books, 1986.
2. See Sachs; and Nunnenkamp, op. cit.
3. For a concise report on one piece of econometric investigation see Donal Donovan, 'Nature and Origins of Debt Servicing Difficulties', *Finance and Adjustment*, December 1984.
4. For a fuller discussion of this see Graham Bird, 'The World Economy in 3-D: Debt, Deficits and Dollars', mimeographed, 1988.
5. It is illuminating to note that external surpluses have not been achieved by increased saving and that the 'strengthening' in the debtors' current account balance of payments (excluding interest payments) has been matched by an almost exactly equivalent reduction in investment.

2 The problem of forecasting debt servicing difficulties

Philip Suttle *

This chapter addresses some of the problems of forecasting debt-servicing difficulties, or (semantic problems aside) country risk analysis. Perhaps I should begin by noting what this chapter does not cover. I have not reviewed the statistical literature based around discriminant or logit analysis. Not only is this covered adequately elsewhere,[1] but it is also largely irrelevant to the practising country risk analyst. I have tried to look at the more immediate problems facing analysts, and to do so I have divided the chapter into two main sections.

In the first section, I have considered the general areas on which analysts should focus in assessing country risk. Of importance here is the analysis of domestic financial and exchange rate policies. Expansionary budgetary and monetary policies tend to have very rapid (and predictable) effects in small, open macroeconomies. The problems in developing countries can be particularly acute since the weakness of capital markets makes governments reliant on either the domestic banking system or the international capital markets to finance a budget deficit. An appreciating real exchange rate weakens both the current and capital accounts. However, governments may contribute to debt-servicing difficulties in other ways. Debt management policies

*The author is with the International Division, Bank of England. This chapter reflects the views of the author, and not those of the Bank of England or The Institute of International Finance. The author benefited greatly from spending two years at the IIF, and the helpful comments of Horst Schulmann and Greg Fager on this chapter were much appreciated. Of course, all errors remain the author's responsibility.

may be weak and uncontrolled, and structural policies may foster a concentration of resources in particular sectors leaving the country vulnerable to external shocks.

The external environment may endanger debt-servicing capabilities in two ways. General macroeconomic conditions may deteriorate, leading to a loss in the demand for exports, a loss in the terms of trade, or a rise in the interest rate payable on external debt. Creditor confidence may also adjust sharply, and particular attention should be paid to both the creditor and maturity distribution of external debt.

In the second section, I have turned to the sources and uses of data. My experience at the Institute of International Finance (IIF) brought home to me the difficulties of finding and using data on developing countries.[2] A considerable amount of judgement is required to turn the fragments of information which are available into a coherent picture of an economy's performance. There is no substitute for experience in collecting and interpreting data on the domestic economy. The danger with using standardized, international sources is that the data will be neither timely nor necessarily accurate. Data on external performance are more widely available. On debt, there is now almost an embarrassment of riches. However, here too there are problems. It is difficult to reconcile debt stocks with capital flows without reconstructing the traditional capital account of the balance of payments. There are also many overlaps between, and weaknesses in, publicly available debt data.

This chapter was not intended to come to a series of conclusions. Rather, it has been written to highlight the areas of concern for a country risk analyst. However, one conclusion is implied by the detail that follows: that country risk analysis involves a lot more than looking at a series of debt ratios and awarding points on the basis of whether they have exceeded a particular value.

FACTORS AFFECTING DEBT-SERVICING CAPABILITIES

At the risk of oversimplification, it is possible to break the factors which influence a country's ability to meet its foreign exchange commitments into five categories. These are: domestic financial policies, debt management policies, structural (or supply-side) policies, the external economic environment and the behaviour of creditors (in particular, developments in international banking and capital markets). Mistakes or adverse developments in any one of these areas are unlikely to cause debt-servicing difficulties. However, difficulties are likely to emerge rapidly when there are weaknesses in all five of these factors. Above all else, country risk analysts should have learned this from the developments of the early 1980s.

Domestic financial policies

There is a clear bias among country risk analysts to concentrate their attention on the external accounts of the economy. This is understandable for two reasons. The external accounts present the direct evidence of a looming foreign exchange shortage. They are like a speedometer warning of a prospective speeding ticket. Also, they are often the most easily available and understood type of data. However, it is vital to look behind the external accounts if a serious effort is to be made to forecast debt-servicing difficulties, as distinct from warning of imminent danger when the loans have already been committed and the exposure run up.

In any country, domestic financial policies are of great importance to the performance of the economy. Under this heading I include monetary, fiscal and exchange rate policies. In developed countries, it is often possible to separate monetary and fiscal policies. For example, the Federal Reserve enjoys complete autonomy and the US Treasury finances the budget deficit independently through bond sales. In most developing countries, capital markets are insufficiently established to permit this separation and the consequent reliance of the public sector on credit from the banking system means that monetary and fiscal policies are tightly linked.

The budget deficit is an important factor to consider for

two reasons. First, it is a measure of the demand injected into the economy by fiscal policy. The higher the deficit, the more the public sector is expanding demand and the more likely the current account is to deteriorate. Second, there may be problems of financing the budget deficit. In the absence of a well developed domestic capital market, financing must be obtained either from the domestic banking system, or from abroad. Borrowing from banks (often the central bank) inflates the money supply and tends to impart a further expansion to demand. Borrowing from abroad not only adds directly to the stock of external debt but also leaves the authorities, whose own income will accrue in local currency, with the difficulty of raising foreign exchange in the future to service the debt.

When analysing the macroeconomic impact of the public sector, it is important to be aware of the institutional make-up of that sector. Typically, analyses of fiscal policy concentrate on the central government. In some countries this is wholly appropriate since the role of local authorities, social security funds and public enterprises is limited. However, in many cases it is not and these sectors may accumulate large deficits, and thereby bloat the public sector borrowing requirement, even though the accounts of the central government are under control. In the period 1981–83, the Portuguese general government deficit averaged about 11 per cent of GDP. However, the PSBR amounted to about 18 per cent because of the large deficits run up by public enterprises. These were a result of a reluctance to pass on higher import prices to consumers and were, in effect, subsidy payments boosting the real incomes and spending in the private sector. Another problem to be alive to is the degree of control exercised over the branches of the public sector by the central government. In Turkey, the public sector accounts have weakened significantly in the past three years because the municipalities have increased sharply both current and investment spending, and have turned to international capital markets in response to central government efforts to limit their domestic borrowing.

A large and persistent budget deficit usually leaves the monetary authorities with a series of difficult choices. If it is to meet the demands of the public sector while maintaining monetary growth within reasonable bounds, then it must squeeze credit to the private sector. It may do this either by maintaining domestic interest rates at a level which is sufficient to choke off demand from the private sector, or by allocating credit directly by a series of reserve requirements and other controls. From the fiscal authorities' point of view, the former option has clear disadvantages. A squeeze on the private sector is likely to fall heavily on the traded goods sector and would threaten the supply of foreign exchange the government needs to service its own external debt. It would also raise the cost of credit to the government itself. Therefore, there is a tendency to rely on the latter option. Of course, in some cases there is also a tendency to allow monetary growth to rise to meet the credit demands of both the public and private sectors.

This mix of monetary and fiscal policies is a significant threat to a country's debt-servicing abilities. A lax fiscal policy is likely to cause the current account to deteriorate. At the same time, credit controls on the private sector may lead to a misallocation of saving, weakening a country's export potential over the medium term. Repressed domestic interest rates discourage domestic saving and encourage the purchase of foreign exchange assets (commonly referred to as 'capital flight'). Rapid monetary growth fuels inflation and further enhances the attractiveness of goods and foreign assets.

In the 1970s there were a number of attempts by developing countries to use a fixed exchange rate as a means of correcting the inflationary impact of loose monetary and fiscal policies. The most notable example of this policy is that of Chile. Without exception, this policy was disastrous. It led to an appreciation of the real exchange rate, thereby imposing a very tight squeeze on the traded goods sector and promoted capital flight. For all developing countries particularly those operating under the monetary–fiscal policy mix described above, it is vital to maintain a competitive exchange rate.

To summarize, an analysis of domestic financial policies is an important baseline for the assessment of debt-servicing capability. Ideally, budget deficits should be maintained under control. This does not necessarily mean that budgets should balance. Many developing countries have high savings ratios which can support modest deficits. However, when they rise much above 2–3 per cent of GDP the net stimulus to demand and the associated financing difficulties may be too much for other sectors of the economy to bear over the medium term.

Debt management policies

For any given set of financial policies, a country is more likely to experience debt-servicing difficulties if it has poor debt management policies. Debt management policies can be divided into three categories: monitoring, advice and guidance, and controls.

Monitoring the accumulation of external debt seems a rather obvious thing for a country to do, but it is surprising how few countries had a true picture of total national indebtedness until the conclusion of rescheduling agreements. In some cases, most notably that of Nigeria, we may never know the true amount of total external debt taken on up to 1983. Since 1956, the World Bank has required borrowing countries to maintain a loan by loan database of credits extended to the public sector or to the private sector with public guarantee.[3] This has been extremely valuable in monitoring the path of debt in countries with large state sectors. However, in those countries with large and active private sectors (e.g. Nigeria, Chile and Venezuela) the external debt of the private sector may be substantial. Tracking private sector debt is usually achieved through the system of foreign exchange controls; borrowers must register loans (usually with the central bank) to be eligible to buy foreign exchange to service the debt.

In some cases foreign exchange controls do not cover all debt. For example, short-term debt in the form of suppliers' credits and inter-bank lines are often excluded. In these circumstances, it is important for both debtors and creditors to monitor all other forms of data, including monetary data and creditor reporting systems. Short-term credit facilities often remain open to countries for some time after medium-term credits have dried up, so their exclusion can seriously understate the growth in debt during critical periods.

Advice and guidance should also be extended by the central bank — where the expertise on international capital markets is likely to reside — to prospective borrowers. Guidance should extend to the choice of currency instrument, maturity and timing. The last is particularly important in avoiding the externalities associated with overborrowing in a single market or attempting to raise finance in a market which is temporarily weak.

Foreign exchange controls often stipulate that borrower must obtain explicit central bank permission before obtaining a foreign credit. There are clear advantages and disadvantages to this type of control. The advantages include the ability of the authorities to check a build-up in debt by the private sector. This may be necessary when a loose fiscal policy is offset by the monetary authorities, either through credit controls or interest rate policy. In these circumstances borrowing abroad might be attractive to domestic enterprises particularly if the authorities were simultaneously squeezing inflation by holding the exchange rate unchanged. The disadvantages include the likelihood that the controls will be circumvented and the debt incurred in a different form (e.g. with a shorter maturity) than would have been the case without controls. Such controls may also promote the misallocation of resources, in the same fashion as controls on domestic credit.

Ideally, a country should have a debt management system which monitors closely the evolution of total external debt within the pattern of total financing in the economy. The central bank should be actively involved in the negotiation and arrangement of foreign credits, but should not be reliant on foreign exchange controls to allocate foreign credits.

Structural policies

In an accounting sense, a country's current account deficit – which is the counterpart to the accumulation of external debt – is the excess of domestic absorption over domestic supply. Financial policies help shape the path of domestic absorption, but have a longer-run effect on aggregate supply. However, structural, or supply-side, policies can have a significant effect on output even in the short run in developing countries. Among structural policies which are most likely to affect output in developing countries are trade and agricultural policies.

In the 1960s and 1970s, policies of import substitution were followed in many countries. Inefficient industries were subsidized behind high tariff walls, and the pattern of comparative advantage was distorted. In the presence of high tariffs the exchange rate was also supported at higher levels than would otherwise have been the case. More recently, a number of countries have moved towards more open trade regimes. These moves have been combined with a reorientation of exchange rate policy to that of export promotion. Such policies enhance aggregate supply by releasing resources from protected industries to those which can compete in export markets. The latter are helped by a more adequate supply of both labour and financial resources, a more favourable exchange rate and, possibly, lower input prices of imported goods. Perhaps the best example of these policies in recent months is that of Mexico, where local manufacturing industry has been given a considerable spur by the reform in trade policy. In the first 10 months of 1987, exports of manufactures were 44 per cent higher than in the same period in 1986.

Agriculture remains the main source of export revenues for many lower-income developing countries. Despite this importance, agriculture is often subject to heavy taxation. This may take the form of low purchase prices offered to farmers by national marketing boards. As well as financing government activities, this helps maintain food prices at low levels, which is popular in urban areas where political power and influence often reside. In the medium term, these policies tend to reduce agricultural supply, but when reversed can have dramatic stimulative effects on production. For example, Ghanaian cocoa production fell steadily from the mid-1960s (when Ghana was the world's largest producer) to a drought reduced low in 1983–84. A shift in policies contributed to a 22 per cent increase in production in 1985–86, compared to modest increases or falls in neighbouring countries.

In the medium term, agricultural policies should be oriented towards diversification and away from reliance on single crops. This does not necessarily insure against a dramatic loss in export earnings since a drought may damage all crops. It does insure against the danger of a sudden collapse in the world price of that commodity. Of course, this risk is not limited to agricultural exporters; concentration of export earnings in any single commodity – oil, copper or coffee – is an important factor contributing to country risk.

The external economic environment

Among the external variables which most affect a country's debt-servicing capabilities are: the interest rate payable on floating rate loans, the world price of exports and imports, and the rate of growth of export markets. In general, the first and last of these variables will be given to the country analyst from elsewhere. The rate of growth of export markets is usually defined as a weighted average of the rates of growth in import volumes of partner countries. Since the industrial countries account for about 75 per cent of world trade, developments in those countries tend to shape the overall pattern of growth in world trade. It is far from straightforward to forecast changes in market share. Important factors would include competitiveness (which is not easy to measure in countries with high inflation and volatile terms of trade) and the pressure of demand in the domestic economy (high demand tends to dampen export growth). Wherever possible, attention should be given to the limitations imposed by the spread of non-tariff barriers to trade. In sectors such as textiles, vehicles and electrical products, importing countries may impose limits on annual import volumes; these limits may bite particularly hard on producers of low value-added manufactured goods.

Adverse movements in trade prices can have a swift and devastating effect on external performance, particularly when export earnings are concentrated in a single commodity. This was seen most recently in the case of oil-exporting countries, when the oil price fell by about 44 per cent in dollar terms in 1986. The best way to identify the likelihood of such an occurrence is to construct a commodity balance, which combines data on supply, demand and global stock-building.[4] This approach does not give explicit price forecasts, but does highlight potential shortfalls and excesses. As for manufactured goods, the export prices of developing countries follow those of developed countries closely. In periods of dollar depreciation, dollar unit values of manufactures rise sharply: in 1986, the world price of manufactured exports was about 20 per cent above 1985, even though consumer prices in the main industrial countries rose by only 2.4 per cent in the same period. Such price rises can add to the squeeze on primary-producing countries whose export prices are already falling in dollar terms. In 1986, the fall in the real oil price (which is the nominal price deflated by the world price of manufactured exports, and is more like the terms of trade of oil exporters) was about 55 per cent.

Creditor behaviour

At the IIF, it was found convenient to divide creditors into five categories: IMF, multilateral (official sector) organizations, bilateral official sector, commercial banks and other private creditors (mainly unguaranteed suppliers' credits, bond issues and foreign exchange deposits). Our emphasis was based on exposure, so that lending by one creditor guaranteed by another was attributed to the latter. We also redesigned the capital account presented in the *Balance of Payments Manual* to reflect this creditor breakdown. Thus, each IIF country study takes an explicit view on who is financing the current account deficit.[5]

A specific financing role should be attributed to each creditor only after consideration of the factors shaping that creditor's behaviour. In the case of the IMF, a formal programme is normally required. This usually carries conditions which should be (explicitly or implicitly) met in any forecast

if sustained disbursements are projected. Also, IMF programmes often unlock disbursements from other sources.
Multilateral development banks have typically financed
projects, so that disbursements in the short term are related
to commitments made in the recent past. More recently,
the World Bank has provided more fast-disbursing structural
and sectoral adjustment loans, but these are usually well
publicized and, therefore, easy to identify. In some cases,
the World Bank has also entered into co-financings with
commercial banks. Aside from the World Bank, regional
development banks are prominent lenders. Official bilateral
creditors are primarily export credit agencies (ECAs). These
agencies undertake two types of activity. In some cases they
make direct loans, while in others they guarantee credits,
either extended by the supplier or a third party (usually a
commercial bank). The former has the disadvantage of
appearing as a form of government expenditure so guarantees
have become the more important type of activity.[6]
Projecting the behaviour of these agencies is fraught with
uncertainty. However, there are a few simple pointers to
bear in mind. First, agencies tend to have fairly rigid cover
rules. A few years ago, these were very conservative and
ECAs were very slow to come back on cover following a
rescheduling. Although this attitude has softened, analysts
need to be careful to check whether the potential borrower
is eligible for new loans or guarantees, and on what maturities
these are available. Second, agencies exist to promote the
exports of the lending country and new credits are not
available as general-purpose finance. Therefore, in countries
where imports remain compressed, the potential for
attracting net new credits is limited. Third, ECAs are not
limited to developed countries. Some middle-income developing countries have agencies which have substantial credits
outstanding. In highly competitive world markets, the trend
will be towards rather than away from this type of export
promotion in developing countries.

Commercial bank behaviour is notoriously difficult to
forecast. It seems appropriate to characterize the excessive
lending of the early 1980s as evidence of herd behaviour.
Developments since then have highlighted the difficulties in

encouraging banks to return to the pattern of voluntary lending which would surely be to their mutual benefit. However, it would also be a mistake to treat commercial banks as a homogeneous group when dealing with the prospects for countries still active in international capital markets. One important distinction to be made is that of size. Smaller regional banks are generally pulling back from international lending although larger banks remain active. Related to this is a shift in the type of business. Large, syndicated general-purpose loans have become infrequent, but many banks continue to do business through trade-related activities. Perhaps a more important distinction is that of nationality. Japanese banks have taken over from American banks as the leading national grouping and are likely to have a significant presence in lending to all areas, especially where their exposure is currently limited. Unfortunately, it is difficult to identify these areas precisely since the Japanese authorities do not publish statistics on lending by country of borrowing agent.

Many of these arguments also hold for other private capital flows, although relatively few developing countries enjoy access to international bond markets. For some countries, foreign exchange deposits of nationals living abroad are an important source of foreign exchange. The flow of these will be partly conditioned by developments abroad (e.g. employment opportunities), but also by domestic financial policies which shape the incentives to remit funds.

SOURCES AND USES OF DATA

Economic data on developing countries vary enormously in both quality and quantity. There is no substitute for local knowledge if, for example, the traps of a country's budgetary accounts are to be avoided. Nevertheless, it is possible to develop a more robust dataset for analytical purposes if two simple principles are followed. First, efforts should be made to cross-check data from different sources: for example, debtor and creditor reporting systems and mirror-image trade statistics. Inconsistencies arising can sometimes be put down to reporting area differences, but more often will expose the inaccuracy and incompleteness of a particular data source. Second, economic data should be internally consistent. Stocks and flows should be reconciled, and it is very often this type of exercise which allows the analyst to decide on a preferred source of data. For example, it is difficult to have confidence in an external debt series which, when adjusted for exchange rate changes, implies inadequate external financing. This situation brings into question not only the level of a country's external debt but also its ability to measure and control the level of that debt.

Domestic data

Domestic data are usually most readily available in central bank publications. Such publications (usually at least quarterly) contain the most recent publicly available data on financial policies and performance. They may also contain conjunctural indicators of trends in the real economy. Because of the simplicity of the financial system in most developing countries, monetary statistics can be particularly useful since they record a substantial portion of the flow of funds. Thus, changes in net credit extended to the public sector can provide as up-to-date a view of the PSBR as is possible. Also a weakness in the demand for money relative to domestic credit expansion, and the consequent loss of net foreign assets by the domestic banking system, is one of the signs of forthcoming external liquidity difficulties. While monetary data are often available ahead of other types of economic data, there is often a considerable reporting lag before these data are published. Sometimes a subset of data is available early, and it has been suggested that attention should be focused on the central bank's balance sheet which is probably the first available.[7]

Alternative sources of data on domestic developments are the publications of the IMF: *International Financial Statistics (IFS)* and *Government Finance Statistics (GFS)*. These publications have the advantage of international comparability, since the IMF adjust the raw data provided by national authorities according to their own conventions.[8] However, in my judgement, they have two main shortcomings. The first is timeliness: there is often a considerable lag between the release of data and their appearance in *IFS*. This problem is even more pronounced for *GFS*. The 1987 *GFS Yearbook* (released January 1988) reported data on most developing countries to the end of 1985. (Incidentally, central government operations for the UK were also reported only to the end of 1985.) Second, the data are submitted on tape by national statistical authorities to the IMF's Bureau of Statistics, where they are handled by analysts working on a large, heterogeneous set of countries. This can result in the publication of series which may not be thought the most appropriate by independent experts on the various countries.

External data

External data — balance of payments flows and external debt stocks — are collected by international agencies, as well as reported in national publications.

The IMF produces the authoritative *Balance of Payments Yearbook*, which is compiled from national submissions. This source is adequate for monitoring current account developments, although it needs updating with local releases to ensure timeliness. The IMF also produces *Direction of Trade Statistics (DOTS)*, which provide the geographical breakdown of a country's trade. Where nationally produced data are scarce, or felt to be untrustworthy, mirror-image trade data produced by the OECD can be particularly useful. These are direction of trade data collected from OECD members, which can be added across the OECD countries to give the exports and imports of most countries with the OECD area. As a consistency check, the minimum requirement is that the OECD total is less than the world total reported in national sources. This is not always the case. When a country's real exchange rate is overvalued, there may be an underreporting of exports and overreporting of imports in national sources, although the flows are properly measured in the accounts of the partner country. There may be other reasons for systematic misreporting of trade flows. At the IIF, we discovered that the Cameroon was underreporting petroleum exports in the period up to 1985 (and beyond) in an effort to build up public sector reserves overseas. When the oil price fell, the authorities were able to maintain budgetary programmes and finance a higher current account deficit than would have been possible from official data.

Capital account data are usually more troublesome. According to IMF conventions,[9] capital flows are recorded by borrowing agent. Usually, a split is given between the resident official sector, domestic money banks and the non-bank private sector. However, in a world where most developing countries are finance-constrained it makes much more sense to look at capital flows from the point of view of who is doing the lending. As noted above, debt-servicing difficulties may arise from a shift in creditor behaviour, so it is vital to know what role creditors have played, and might be expected to play, in providing external finance. Unfortunately, there is no basic source of data on capital flows by creditor. Instead, a mixture of sources must be used: the *World Debt Tables (WDT)* of the IBRD provide some data on disbursements and repayments by creditor; some attempt can be made to link flows by debtor to flows by creditor (e.g. short-term inflows to domestic money banks might be assumed to be inter-bank credits); and debt stocks by creditor can be differenced and adjusted for exchange rate effects to provide an estimate of net lending by each creditor. At the IIF, we constructed historic capital accounts for each country using the last of these methods. Admittedly, the numbers so produced were approximations (but were cross-checked with all other available information), yet they provided an important insight into the pattern of external financing.

Forecasts of external financing by creditor should be even more detailed. Gross, as well as net, flows should be identified to produce what some bank economists call a sources and uses (of foreign exchange) table. This approach allows for an explicit identification of the effects of a rescheduling and the accumulation of arrears. For countries which retain market access, it also helps to highlight potential refinancing difficulties. Table 2.1 reproduces the

Table 2.1   Peru: External financing (millions of dollars)

	1986e	1987f	1988f
Current account balance	-1421	-1675	-1475
Non-debt-creating flows, net	116	40	35
External borrowing, net	*839*	*849*	*910*
IMF	*-13*	*59*	*67*
Disbursements	0	0	0
Repayments	-47	0	0
Due	-181	-139	-150
Unpaid	134	139	150
Interest arrears	34	59	67
Multilateral organizations	*139*	*167*	*93*
Disbursements	216	216	155
Repayments	-131	-111	-131
Due	-131	-208	-261
Unpaid	0	97	130
Interest arrears	54	63	69
Official bilateral	*124*	*303*	*295*
Disbursements	30	65	30
Repayments*	-257	-119	-123
Due	-638	-697	-706
Unpaid	380	578	583
Interest arrears	351	357	368
Commercial banks	*514*	*322*	*445*
Disbursements	15	0	0
Repayments	-42	0	0
Due	-595	-543	-739
Unpaid	552	543	739
Short-term credits, net†	156	-90	-25
Interest arrears	385	412	470
Other private	*75*	*-1*	*10*
Disbursements	120	20	10
Repayments	-68	-40	-20
Due	-194	-180	-205
Unpaid	127	140	185
Interest arrears	22	19	20
Resident lending abroad, net	-53	135	130
Errors and omissions	127	0	0
Change in reserves, net (- = increase)	392	650	400

*Includes reduction of medium- and long-term debt through commodity trades.
†Includes reduction of working capital debt through commodity trades.

Source: IIF country report on Peru, 28 December 1987.

IIF's external financing table for Peru. The numbers in italic correspond to net capital flows, as would appear in the IIF's presentation of the capital account. In 1986, the IMF was repaid $13 million net by the Peruvians. The IMF had expected to receive $181 million, but only $47 million of principal repayments were made before the Peruvian moratorium. Following the moratorium, $34 million of interest went unpaid, reducing the overall net outflow to $13 million. Aside from reserves, one use of foreign exchange which should not be overlooked is the increase in non-reserve assets (resident net lending abroad). This may reflect speculative outflows, but should also be linked to policies of export promotion through the provision of export credit.

There has probably been more effort put into the collection of external debt data than any other series on developing countries. Most countries now publish comprehensive data of their own, and these may be complemented with those of the major international agencies. The rationale for using the data provided by international agencies is twofold. First, although developing countries have improved their reporting of external debt significantly in recent years, most do not yet provide the types of breakdown — particularly debt by creditor — that analysts may prefer. Second, there are some circumstances where the local reporting system may be felt to be incomplete or incapable of capturing the true extent of external indebtedness. In this situation an independent source of data — one based on a creditor-reporting system — can provide a valuable insight. At the least, creditor reporting information should be used as a cross-check to the debtor reporting system of the country in question.

The main creditor-reporting systems are those of the IMF, the OECD and the BIS. Each has an obvious comparative advantage in the reporting of a particular type of claim: the IMF obviously records the use of IMF credit the OECD collects reports from 22 ECAs; and the BIS collects data on bank claims from a reporting area (as at April 1988) of monetary authorities in 18 industrial countries and 6 offshore centres (and the US reports the activities of US banks in a seventh: Panama). The IMF also

Table 2.2 External debt data

Source	Strengths	Weaknesses	Overlaps
National data	Usually covers some private as well as official debt. Often derived as part of picture of overall financing of economy	Usually excludes some private debt (especially ST). Rarely gives reliable creditor breakdown	Often close to IBRD DRS
IBRD (WDT)	Database built up on loan-by-loan basis. Gives some creditor split. Gives data on flows	Covers only public and publicly guaranteed loans reliably	Bilateral, suppliers, fin. mkts overlap with OECD and BIS data
IMF (IFS)[10]	Gives data on IMF credit (stocks and flows). IBS data give banks' claims and DMBs' liabilities	Breaks in IBS data and inconsistency with BIS data	Uses BIS QPR data
BIS (QPR)*[11]	Timely data on banks' claims	Reporting errors by banks. Includes guarantees. Changes may reflect write-offs, debt-sales or calling of guarantees. Treatment of securities varies. Treatment of arrears unclear. Limited reporting area (offshore centres report every 6 months). Exchange rate adjustments to obtain flows are estimates	Overlaps with WDT fin. mkts and OECD guaranteed
OECD (ECA data)†	Only available data on direct and guaranteed official claims	No split between direct and guaranteed. ECA reporting errors (do they report claims, commitments or even bids?) Problems with reschedulings (when claims sometimes disappear from ECA books without being picked up elsewhere). Limited reporting area	Overlap with WDT fin. mkts, suppliers and bilateral, and BIS data

*The US, UK, French, and German authorities publish their submissions to the BIS quarterly data in their respective central bank publications.
†The OECD also publishes an annual survey of total external debt, although these data are a combination of those from some other sources in the table.

collects data on banks' claims, although these are widely felt
to be less reliable than the data published by the BIS. Each
of these data sources has strengths and weaknesses (see Table
2.2). It is important to recognize that these will vary across
country, so that a source which may be reliable for one
country may not be appropriate for another. Somewhat of a
hybrid between the debtor and creditor systems are the
World Bank data, published in the WDT. World Bank
exposure is reported from the IBRD's own database, but the
claims of all other creditors are reported by the debtor. The
WDT is potentially a very valuable source of data, since it
reports debt stocks (and some flows) by creditor. However,
the database is comprehensive for only medium-term public
and publicly guaranteed debt. To identify short-term and
private debt, the WDT must be used in conjunction with
other sources.

When a number of different sources are used, care should
be taken to avoid double counting. One way to do this is to
combine data from sources that are known to be
independent. Thus, one could add the IMF's claims to those
of the multilateral agencies (WDT), and those of the banks
(BIS), and those of guaranteed suppliers (OECD). One could
even go one step further and split the BIS banks' claims into
unguaranteed (exposure) and guaranteed, using the OECD
data. This is essentially the approach taken by the OECD in
their annual publication on external debt. Unfortunately, this
approach has three difficulties: it rests on a presumption that
data in each of the sources is accurate; it does not include
loans extended by creditors outside the reporting area; and
it is not based on a picture of the external financing of the
economy. It is virtually impossible to combine most of the
WDT data with those from the BIS and OECD. For example
the BIS data will include credits in the WDT financial
markets category and credits not captured in the WDT data.
The OECD data will overlap with the WDT's financial
markets, bilateral and suppliers' categories, but may still
include credits that are guaranteed from the point of view
of the OECD bank or supplier, but not from that of the
developing country borrower. These overlaps cannot be
identified precisely.

There is no correct way to overcome these difficulties. At the IIF, analysts are very pragmatic, using national sources where possible and combining them with creditor estimates where necessary. In doing this, a joint requirement is imposed on the preferred series that it is consistent with an explicit picture of external financing, and that it can be reconciled with other estimates, and information on creditor behaviour.

In the light of the uncertainties outlined above, there is clearly a need for the major international agencies to come together, it is hoped with the authorities of developing countries, to produce authoritative international data. The International Debt Compilers' Group (made up of the IMF, IBRD, BIS, and the OECD) met between 1984 and 1988, and have recently reported publicly.[12] The group's major achievement has been to reach a 'core definition' of external debt, which all reporting agencies now aim to respect. However, most of the report is a repeat of what is already in the public domain about the respective reporting systems. Most fundamentally, the group failed to achieve a synthesis between alternative reporting systems, and, by and large, analysts are left with the bewildering mixture of overlapping and incomplete data illustrated in Table 2.2.

NOTES AND REFERENCES

1. See Heffernan, S.A. (1986), *Sovereign Risk Analysis*, London, chap. 2.
2. See Institute of International Finance (1987), *Annual Report*, Washington DC.
3. See Hope, N. (1985), 'Information for external debt management: the debtor reporting system of the World Bank' in H. Mehran (ed.), *External Debt Management*, IMF, Washington DC, chap. 12.
4. See IMF (1987), *Primary Commodities: Market Developments and Outlook*.
5. See Fager, G.B. (1987), *External financing and debt analysis*, IIF Staff Paper, Washington DC.
6. See IMF (1988), *Officially Supported Export Credits: Developments and Prospects*.
7. See Atkin, J.M. (1984), 'Country risk: what the central bank's

figures may be signalling', *The Banker*, London, November (43–50).

8. See, for example, IMF (1986), *Manual on Government Finance Statistics*.

9. International Monetary Fund (1977), *Balance of Payments Manual*, 4th edn, Washington DC.

10. See IMF (1985), *Guide to the International Banking Statistics*.

11. See Bank for International Settlements (1988), *Guide to the BIS Statistics on International Lending*, Basle.

12. Organization for Economic Co-operation and Development (1988), *External debt: definition, statistical coverage and methodology*, published on behalf of the International Working Group on External Debt Statistics, Paris.

3 The bargaining position of debtor nations [1]

Stephany Griffith-Jones*

In attempting to analyse the management of debt crises in Latin America from 1982 to the present, several difficulties present themselves. In the first place, we are analysing an extremely complex process, whose final outcome is not yet known. In some ways, it is like analysing a play at a time when only two or perhaps three of the acts have actually taken place, and in circumstances when nobody — including the actors — know the full script. Second, analysis is made more difficult due to the differences between rhetoric and reality. For example, since mid-1985 in the analysis made in industrial and developing countries alike, there seemed on the whole to emerge a consensus that debt crisis management, as practised till then, was both unsustainable and undesirable, given future likely trends in the world economy. It was therefore concluded that new ways had to be found and rapidly implemented to handle the problem, which would allow for growth in debtor economies. In spite of this consensus, at the level of rhetoric, two years later, effective multilateral action had not been taken, except for specific countries (e.g. the Mexican 1986/87 deal) or for limited and insufficient measures (e.g. the structural adjustment facility for low-income Sub-Saharan African countries).

THE KEY QUESTIONS

Four main questions will be addressed in this chapter. First,

*The author is with the Institute of Development Studies, University of Sussex.

why were the deals on debt and adjustment, agreed and implemented since 1982, so much closer to the interests and aims of creditor institutions than of debtor countries? The question seems even more relevant after mid-1985, when the above described broad consensus emerged — in developed and developing countries — that debt crisis management was unsatisfactory, particularly for debtor nations' growth and development prospects. However, the new actions taken multilaterally, within the broad umbrella of US Treasury Secretary Baker's initiative — though positive in themselves — did not, at least till 1987, amount to a new way of handling the problem, and did not overcome the basic limitations of the approach developed since 1982.

Given this evaluation, supplementary questions arise: why have debtor governments been so patient during such a long period of large negative net transfers, and why have most of them (except for the Peruvian government) not followed unilateral actions earlier and in a more consistent way? Furthermore, given that debtor governments have been so patient in servicing debts at levels which have in several cases contributed to cause significant declines in investment, employment, real wages, and social welfare expenditure, why have the societies in those nations been so patient?

It should however be emphasized that since mid-1985, a number of Latin American and African governments have either taken or seriously threatened to take unilateral action. In early 1987, the picture changed significantly, especially as the Brazilian government suspended interest payment on its bank debt, and as Ecuador, as well as a number of other small Latin American governments, took similar action.

The second question is: to what extent were there differences in the debt/adjustment deals reached by different countries? What reasons could contribute to explain such differences?

Third, how have the debt rescheduling/new money/adjustment deals varied from year to year, after 1982? Have qualitative changes been introduced?

A fourth and perhaps crucial question relates to the future search for an alternative more 'positive sum' framework of debt management. This clearly consists of two elements, when viewed from the point of view of debtor countries and governments: what are more appropriate technical solutions than the ones adopted till now, such that debtors' growth and development can be safeguarded without threatening the stability of the international banking system?; and what tactics and strategies should debtor governments pursue to make the adoption of such measures feasible?

ATTEMPTING TO EXPLAIN THE NATURE OF THE DEALS REACHED

Looking at the first set of issues, the fact that major debtor governments (except for Peru) have not consistently pursued a line of unilateral action is itself one of the main reasons why debt rescheduling/new money deals continue to be closer to the interests of creditors than that of debtors.

Among the reasons why such unilateral actions were not taken by major debtor governments was the *uncertainty* of the impact of such actions on the international banking system, and more importantly, on the funding of world economic activity and trade. More than the fear of retaliation against their own trade flows, which experiences like that of Peru seem to show is not very serious, debtor governments legitimately feared in the past the risk of declining volumes of world trade that could accompany a possible disruption of the international banking system.

The threat to the private banks' solvency of unilateral action by major debtors has diminished since 1982, as private banks strengthened their capital base and increased their loan-loss provisions, as well as expanded their non-LDC business far more than their LDC lending. The risks to the private banks' solvency from LDC default are seen in industrial countries to have diminished significantly, though not totally. Even before the major loan loss provisions made by US, as well as British banks, a 1987 British All Party Parliamentary Group report[2] concluded that, 'American banks are now more vulnerable to domestic energy, farming and housing loans than to LDC debt. For most of the major banks, simultaneous default (collective or coincidental) by a number of large Latin American debtors would shake them; *a single default would be absorbed*.' A similar conclusion was reported in January 1987 by Salomon Brothers,[3] when it stated that 'the 34 major US banks they track should be able to write off some US$20 billion, or nearly 40% of their total cross-border lending to Argentina, Brazil, Mexico and Venezuela by 1989, without impairing equity ratios'.

As Table 3.1 indicates, levels of loan-loss provisions vary quite significantly among countries. In late 1986, they were highest in continental European countries, such as Switzerland, Netherlands and West Germany; the lowest provision rates were till May 1987 made by banks based in the USA, the UK and Japan. For US banks, provisions were already high in 1986, however, for countries that have ceased or limited payments of interest for over 90 days; thus for Peru's loans, an initial provision of 15 per cent was required.[4] Since May 1987, a radical change has occurred in the loan-loss provisions made by the twelve main US banks, most of which had by the end of June 1987 made such large loan-loss provisions that those reached around US$10 billion, and 25 per cent of those were banks' loans to developing countries. The US banks' action was followed in mid-1987 by very large loan-loss provisions by the main UK banks.

Though a fairly important part of developing countries' debts to private banks have been written down or written off on banks' balance sheets, this has not led to corresponding debt forgiveness. Furthermore, practically all debts of most LDC debtors are traded by creditor banks at a discount on secondary markets; this seems further clear evidence that these banks do not think it likely that they will recover the full value of their outstanding loans. However, in debt-servicing and even in debt-rescheduling operations, debtor countries are still obliged to service the debt at its full original face value, which is indeed no longer its market value. Indeed, taking the debt of twelve major borrowers as an example (which underestimates the problem), US banks holding some US$77 billion in book assets could sell those assets at only $50 billion on the secondary market, that is at only two-thirds their face or book value.[5]

Far higher bank loan-loss provisions, as recently made by

Table 3.1   *Problem sovereign debt reserve levels, June 1987*

Belgium	No specified percentages but there is a requirement to provide. Reserve levels vary but probably average around 15 per cent.
Canada	10–15 per cent reserve required by end October 1986 for 32 designated countries. All the major banks will meet the requirement in 1986. Higher levels of reserves are expected to be required after October 1986.
France	No formal rules but most major banks have set up large reserves. BNP and Société Générale are running at over 30 per cent; Crédit Lyonnais has somewhat less.
Germany	No formal rules but tax authorities generally helpful. Most major banks have reserved between 30 and 50 per cent.
Japan	Amount per country varies but Ministry of Finance 'guidance' stipulates an average maximum 5 per cent against exposure to 36 problem countries. Virtually all banks have reached this level and, with the fall in the value of the dollar, banks have been required to write back their reserve to the 5 per cent limit. Early 1987 offshore company established to take over part of Japanese banks' loans to countries that may not be able to repay their debts.
Netherlands	From 5 to 100 per cent on countries specified by the central bank. Most banks now have a reserve of around 20 per cent of problem sovereign debt.
Spain	Bank of Spain circular requires from 1.5 to 100 per cent on country groupings defined in circular. Most major banks have around 10 per cent, and some more.
Sweden	From 35 to 80 per cent on countries selected by Bank Inspection Board. Most banks' reserve levels now average around 50 per cent.
Switzerland	General guideline that banks should maintain reserves of at least 20 per cent against problem country exposure. Banks left to decide which of their exposure falls into this category. Most major banks have reserved between 30 and 50 per cent.
UK	Reserves vary from 100 per cent to very little. Large banks running at around 5 to 10 per cent at end 1986; in mid-1987 made provisions of 25 to 30 per cent on loans to countries in payments difficulties or rescheduling their debt.
USA	Varying percentages on Poland, Nicaragua, Zaire, Bolivia, Sudan and Peru. No rules on others. Most large US banks had 5 per cent or less for all problem sovereign debt at end 1986. In May–June 1987, most of the major 12 US banks made large provisions, such that their total loan-loss reserves reached around 25 per cent of 'doubtful' LDC loans.

Source: IBCA Banking Analysis Ltd, *Real Banking Profitability*, November 1986. Newspaper clippings (*Financial Times*), June 1987.

large US and UK banks — and previously by other banks — clearly have advantages in the long term for debtor developing countries. It reduces uncertainty about the risk to banks' solvency and stability should debtor governments take (or be forced by circumstances to take) unilateral action. Furthermore, it strengthens the possibility for intermediate solutions, that have been amply discussed in a variety of circles, which would imply LDC governments would service the debt, but with some element of forgiveness, either attached to the level of the debt and/or of the interest payments.[6]

Paradoxically, however, the strengthening of banks' loan-loss provisions — and even more the requirements by bank regulators to make provisions against new loans to those sovereign debtors for which provisions were made — has possibly reduced the willingness of banks to increase their lending to LDC debtors. Differences between levels of provisions and regulations on provisions (and their tax treatment) in different creditor countries also make it increasingly difficult to make collective arrangements, for negotiating and distributing (amongst banks) new money, as the difficulties for arranging the 1986/87 Mexican deal clearly illustrates. In the short term and within the framework of traditional packages of debt rescheduling/new money, the strengthening of the banks' balance sheets by increased loan-loss provisions may have some problematic effects for debtor countries; however, these problematic effects should not be exaggerated, as there was already very little new net bank lending to Latin America in recent years.

In the medium term, and within the context of a new framework or a new phase of handling the debt problem, the existence of large loan-loss provisions in many of the large banks provides an important range of manoeuvre for solutions which recognize that the real market value of the debt is no longer its face value, and that reductions should either be made in the level of the debt itself, or in debt servicing it. It is likely that pressure from debtor governments, as well as from enlightened private actors and/or governments within industrial countries, will necessarily play a significant role in the transition to the next step. Thus in a medium-term perspective, banks' greater ability to absorb LDC losses should strengthen the confidence with which debtor governments can use threats of (or even in extreme cases take) unilateral action, without fearing as much as in the past that such threats or actions would endanger the stability of the international financial (and even trading) system.

Furthermore, the availability of significant loan-loss provision in banks' balance sheets makes more feasible the adoption of a framework for managing debt, which implies that banks acknowledge some losses and that debtor governments reduce their level of debt servicing (without this implying an increase in the total level of debt). Such a package would clearly also further increase the role of industrial governments in the deals, either by increased lending, subsidizing banks' losses, or takeover of discounted bad debts (the latter measures already being pursued by the Japanese government).

It is interesting that bankers and bank economists are not only expecting something like this to happen, but are saying so publicly. For example, Holley, op. cit, concludes his study arguing that a debt consolidation on concessional terms 'would certainly be preferable to a seemingly endless series of negotiations, that would inhibit long-term policy-making on both sides and would not excessively affect banks' standing in the market'. There also seems to be a gradual, but consistent, trend in public opinion and in political circles within industrial countries towards a view that new ways of handling the debt problem need to be found, which will imply some element of discounting such debt or its servicing; amongst the reasons for this shift is not only a wish to improve development prospects in debtor nations, but also trade and investment prospects for industrial nations.[7]

Perhaps the clearest recognition that a chapter of debt crisis management was closing in May 1987 came from Mr John Reed, the chairman of Citicorp, the bank with the highest exposure in Latin America, when he explicitly recognized that 'the debt problem will be with us into the

1990s and we see nothing in the global economy that would enable these countries to get out of this situation . . . The global economy is less solvent today than when the present approach was devised in 1982' (*Financial Times*, 21 May 1987).

An important element may have been a more long-term perception of costs and benefits obtained by debtor countries from their links with the international financial system, than is obtained by looking only at the massive negative net transfers from the debtor economies since 1982.

Indeed, debtor governments may have compared the large positive net transfers which they had received, particularly during the 1970s, with large negative resource transfers since 1982, and felt especially initially, that the net impact on their economies of the total period was still positive or at least zero. The incentive to take unilateral action would be reduced, particularly if and while a reversal of the sign of net resource transfers was seen as likely to occur in the near future. Around 1986, that perception began to change; this was reflected, for example, in the analysis made by the Inter-American Development Bank, which estimated in its 1986 Annual Report that in nominal terms, the negative net transfers from Latin America as a whole since 1982 had roughly wiped out the entire net inflow of capital generated in the massive petrodollar recycling of the 1970s.

As the evaluation of costs and benefits of the link with the international financial system takes place basically at a national level, it seems useful to calculate the total net resource transfer to and from the countries we are studying over the 1973–85 period.

A technical, but clearly relevant, issue to determine the correct measure is the choice of deflator. The most precise deflator seems to be an index which reflects countries' terms of trade, given that we are trying to compare the real value in domestic resources of the additional foreign exchange obtained by a country when net transfers were positive with the real resources used by the country to make negative net transfer of foreign exchange. Though the use of terms of trade index as a deflator may not incorporate all the effects of world inflation on the real value of total net resource transfers, it does appreciably reduce the margin of error involved in other calculations. [8]

As can be seen in Table 3.2, by the end of 1985, the real net resource transfer, taking the whole of the 1973–85 period, was negative for Venezuela (and Argentina), and around zero for Brazil, Mexico and Peru; indeed if the 1986 figures are added, the net resource transfer for Brazil, Mexico and Peru would also be negative. For all these countries, by late 1986, there had been no net contribution in net resource transfers from the international financial system, since 1973, even though their stock of debt had grown significantly. The situation is slightly better for Chile and Costa Rica (particularly the latter if grants and aid are included), but even in those two cases a continuation of negative net transfers at the levels of recent years would imply that the net contribution from external capital flows since 1973 will become zero or negative, while their external debt has

Table 3.2 *Real net resource transfer, deflated by the barter terms of trade, as a percentage of GDP, expressed in 1984 US$, 1973–85*

	1973–81	1982–85	1973–85	Ranking of case studies, best to worst
Brazil	1.5	−2.9	0.2	2
Chile	4.8	−3.0	2.4	1
Costa Rica	4.4	−2.3	2.4	1
Mexico	2.8	−5.4	0.2	2
Peru	0.6	−0.7	0.2	2
Venezuela	2.4	−10.5	−1.6	3
Memorandum				
Argentina	0.2	−6.0	−1.7	
Colombia	0.7	2.4	1.2	

Sources: Net resource transfers in nominal values, from Table 4, J. Elac, 'Latin American Debt: Resource Transfers, Investment and Growth'. *Mimeo*, Inter-American Development Bank, October 1986. The figures differ somewhat from ECLAC figures given above, because they do not include grants and aid, which is particularly significant in the case of Costa Rica.

Terms of trade figures, by country, from UNCTAD *Handbook of International Trade Statistics, 1986 Supplement*.

GDP figures, also from Table 4, J. Elac, op. cit.

increased very significantly during that period. If this perception is combined with the prospect of continued negative net transfers for future years (as projected by most international institutions and independent observers) the net contribution of international capital flows will increasingly be seen as negative by the major debtors.

Our assessment is too aggregate, as it does not examine the use made by the borrowers of the positive net transfer of funds in the initial period. In this aspect, the welfare effects of borrowing on the national economy are more positive, the larger the proportion of those additional resources which were used in expenditure that increased growth capacity of the economy and/or their ability to generate additional future foreign exchange flows.

This leads us to a third element in the exploration of why debtor governments may not have taken more consistent unilateral action or even tougher bargaining positions. Most analysis centres on 'the national interest', that is the interest of the debtor country as a whole, assumed to be represented by its government. This concept is too aggregate, given the complex social and political realities of debtor countries, which are reflected in the actions of governments.[9]

In terms of the special interest of those wealthy citizens who benefited from the huge inflows of the 1970s by increasing their consumption levels domestically or exported their wealth abroad and who have been more sheltered from the cost of adjustment to negative net transfers and deteriorating terms of trade in the 1980s, the net impact of those external flows may still be seen as positive. For poorer and more vulnerable groups, who benefited somewhat from improved living standards as a result of positive net transfers of financial resources, but have been severely affected by negative net transfers — bearing a disproportionate share of the cost of the adjustment — the net balance may be very negative.

To the extent that wealthier groups had a larger influence on debtor governments than poorer groups, this may have discouraged unilateral action or tougher bargaining. However, to the extent that broader strata of the population are affected by slow growth or recession, to the extent that democratization in several of the larger debtors implies a far greater influence for the interests of the poor and the vulnerable, and that even wealthier groups perceive as potentially unsustainable the huge 'social and human' cost of adjustment, without improvement in the near future, the balance within debtor governments can be expected to shift (and has broadly been shifting), either to far tougher bargaining positions and/or to unilateral action. This shift broadly corresponds to that indicated by bargaining theory. Significant changes in negotiating posture are likely to occur when — in assessing the concessions made by both sides — it is found that there was 'unfair advantage' to one of the sides, in this case the debtor countries, and particularly to the poorer and more vulnerable groups within them.

To the shift of power and perceptions within debtor nations should be added the shift of perception within industrial countries, where concern has been growing, within government, representatives in international financial institutions, and more broadly in the media and public opinion, of the excessive human cost of adjustment of developing economies to the debt problem and to the deteriorating international environment.[10]

Some of the reasons why governments, and peoples, have been so patient in servicing their debt, even at the cost of large domestic sacrifices of adjustment, are country-specific and related at least partly to non-economic variables. For example, several countries faced the initial stages of the debt crisis at a time when their countries were beginning a return to democratic rule after years of military dictatorship. Such processes, in countries like Argentina, Uruguay and Brazil, imply a number of delicate domestic negotiations for the creation of new institutions, for the establishment of political coalitions, for mutually acceptable relationships between civil society and the armed forces. The difficult and complex nature of the tasks already facing governments may have inclined them, particularly initially, to avoid an additional potential source of tension or conflict with international creditors and financial institutions. However, when popular pressure has mounted for higher real wages and employment (or a recovery of previous levels), these new democratic governments have hardened their stance towards the international creditors and have increasingly placed minimum economic growth on the agenda of negotiations with them.

On the other hand, the lack of patience of the Garcia Peruvian government and its unilateral and somewhat defiant actions can also to an important extent be explained by political variables. The Garcia government faced since mid-1985 not only a difficult economic climate, but also a very tense political situation, with an extremely serious challenge to the government's stability (and that of democracy in Peru) coming from the extremist Sendero Luminoso guerrillas, and with a country that lacked both a sense of future and of national unity. President Garcia's unilateral action on debt, and particularly the uncompromising harshness of his language towards foreign creditors and international financial institutions, can thus to an important extent be explained by the 'need' to find an 'external enemy' that provides a catalyst for national unity; naturally, the particularly severe trade-off between growth in Peru and servicing the debt fully provided an additional incentive for unilateral action, especially given strong democratic pressures for growth and increased living standards of the very poor.

The priority given by a country's government and society to economic growth, in relation to other objectives, also has a large impact on the government's attitude towards debt servicing. For example the Brazilian government and entrepreneurs give very high priority to economic growth; recession is seen as extremely undesirable, both by the government and the private sector. While full debt servicing was consistent with high economic growth, the Brazilian government continued to service debt in a timely way; however, when a conflict arose between growth and debt servicing in early 1987 (exacerbated by excessively expansionary macroeconomic policies, as discussed below), the Brazilian government suspended temporarily servicing of the debt to private banks. In Mexico, the priorities of objectives seem somewhat different to those in Brazil. Mexican entrepreneurs and the Mexican government seem to give far higher priority to objectives different from growth, than their Brazilian counterparts. Thus, stable and friendly relations between the Mexican government with foreign creditors, as part of a harmonious relationship with industrial countries, and particularly with the USA, are seen by Mexican entrepreneurs and government as an important policy objective; it is within such a harmonious context that the private sector will be more willing to invest domestically. If relations between Mexico and the outside world are not seen to be clear and harmonious, and/or domestic confidence of private capital diminishes for other reasons (e.g. high inflation, overvalued exchange rate), then an important part of domestic savings leaves the country as capital flight. Thus, in an economy such as the Mexican one, with practically no capital controls, with such an 'internationalized' entrepreneurial class and with such close proximity and growing integration to the US economy, the government seems to objectively be (and feel) constrained in its bargaining on debt and in the design of its macroeconomic and development strategy by the need to avoid massive capital flight and to avoid disrupting friendly relations with its important neighbour.

Similarly, in Venezuela, the government and the entrepreneurs seem to attach higher priority to objectives other than growth. For example, a stated policy objective of the Venezuelan government has been to be able to return to 'voluntary' market borrowing. In such a context, any radical or even unorthodox option of limiting debt service payments would be very counter-productive to its main policy objective. Furthermore, the Venezuelan government has even made fairly large amortization payments, partly with a view to increasing the country's 'creditworthiness'. However, at the time of writing, it would seem very unlikely for Venezuela to be able to seize important new sources of finance on the private capital markets.

COMPARISONS BETWEEN COUNTRIES

Net transfers and policy conditionality

In analysing the deals on debt rescheduling/new money/

adjustment that different Latin American countries have agreed with their creditors, it becomes clear that there are certain important trade-offs between the quality of the financial package and the conditionality of the adjustment. It should however be stressed that the trade-offs are basically within a fairly narrow range, as since 1982 for almost all the Latin American countries analysed here and for almost every year examined, net resource transfers have been negative and conditionality on their economic policies has in several cases been fairly heavy.

A very relevant variable for the type of financial deals obtained seems to be size, as small countries, particularly if they have geopolitical importance to industrial governments or can make a special case on humanitarian grounds, can more easily obtain positive net transfers. A clear illustration of this is Costa Rica, which still obtained positive (though very low) net resource transfers since 1982 and is also one of the two countries doing best, if the whole 1973–85 period is evaluated (see Table 3.2). The reasons are clear: large (in proportion to the country's economy) official flows are feasible financially, because these flows are small in relation to the US budget; they are actually made, to an important extent (though not only) because of Costa Rica's geopolitical importance to the USA and particularly because it borders with Nicaragua. (The magnitude of aid flows to Costa Rica has risen dramatically since 1983;[11] while total aid (ODA) flows from industrial countries to Costa Rica averaged less than US$30 million between 1979–82, they rose to an average of above US$200 million between 1983 and 1985, almost a tenfold growth!) Undoubtedly, other reasons also contribute to explain the relatively favourable deals obtained by the Costa Rican government, such as the design and implementation (since 1982) of viable macroeconomic packages.

The cost of positive net transfers for small countries is usually very heavy conditionality, often exercised simultaneously by different international financial institutions. Such heavy cross-conditionality not only generates an extreme form of dependency of national economic policy on foreign decision makers, but is also extremely inefficient, due to its heavy administrative cost, both in terms of time of senior decision makers and actually in financial terms. Cross-conditionality is a very common feature in Sub-Saharan Africa. For example, structural adjustment loans from the World Bank (which include a significant amount of policy conditionality) are far more common in Africa than in Latin America.

The only fairly large Latin American economy that has had World Bank structural adjustment loans (SALs) is Chile. Furthermore, since 1983, Chile has almost continuously had IMF upper credit tranche agreements, and has on the whole complied with its performance criteria better than any other Latin American country. More broadly, the orthodoxy of Chilean economic policies — which often exceeds that of the IMF or World Bank — has made it easier for Chile to obtain slightly better deals in terms of net resource transfers than other Latin American debtors, mainly due to a fairly large increase in public flows.

There seems in this case to have been a 'trade-off' between obtaining a slightly better net resource transfer deal (see Table 3.2) than for other countries, related to an important extent to the fact that the Chilean government has been willing to adopt both very drastic and very orthodox adjustment packages, and implement them successfully, particularly since 1985. Indeed, it could be argued that the Chilean government only bargains genuinely on debt re-scheduling and new flows, but *not* really on the type of adjustments, as its views on the subject are as orthodox, if not more, as those of international financial institutions. Two caveats seem useful here: first, Chile has obtained such slightly preferential treatment, in spite of concern among several of its creditor governments about the country's extremely slow transition to democracy, and poor human rights record, reflecting perhaps the overriding importance attached by international financial institutions till now to Chile's commitment to orthodox adjustment and to financial objectives, such as inflation control, and its punctuality in servicing its debts. Another caveat is that although Chile's NRT outcome is less bad for the 1982–85 period than other Latin American countries, it is still strongly negative.

A somewhat different trade-off seemed to emerge in the deal signed in 1986 for Mexico. The Mexican government was able to negotiate in 1986 both a fairly gradual and unorthodox adjustment package, as well as a fairly favourable financial deal, in terms of net resource transfers, changes in maturity of the debt, spreads; furthermore, new ground was broken by the innovative elements in the package, such as the contingency clauses for minimum growth and protection against oil price fluctuations.

This favourable deal cannot merely be attributed to the clear geopolitical importance of Mexico to the USA and to the size of the Mexican debt to the banks. The importance of these elements was enhanced by the fact that after very tough bargaining — in which the possibility of unilateral action was a clear option — the Mexican government accepted a multilaterally agreed deal, which though very favourable, had no purely concessional elements in it.

The Mexican bargaining experience of the 1986/87 package shows that better financial deals seem to be struck within the multilateral framework of negotiations, by governments that have clear objectives in their bargaining stance, that are willing to threaten unilateral action (with a clearly studied and broadly supported — within the government — option for such action), but that permanently continue a conciliatory dialogue with creditor governments and international institutions. Because international financial markets are so influenced by perceptions, respect for formalities (such as keeping key actors informed of changing developments, using friendly and conciliatory language, expressing the wish to reach agreement, as well as willingness to service the debt in the long term even when short-term unilateral action is being presented as an option) is of great importance. In that sense, the radical rhetoric used by the Garcia Peruvian government in criticizing its bank creditors and the IMF (though explained by domestic political reasons and pressures) was in some ways more damaging to Peru's relations with some of its creditors and lenders (such as the Inter-American Development Bank and the World Bank) than the unilateral action itself taken by the Garcia government. This is so particularly because the previous Peruvian government (under President Belaunde) had in fact been during its last year servicing less of its foreign debt than the Garcia government has!

The Garcia government in Peru has tackled the trade-off between financial deal and policy conditionality in a different way from that of other Latin American debtors. Since 1985, it has both taken unilateral action on debt and has embarked on its own adjustment programme, openly rejecting IMF conditionality and even suspending repayments on previous IMF loans. At least at the time of writing (mid-1987), the results of these actions have been positive both in terms of the financial deal on net transfer (see Table 3.2), in its effect on the country's growth record in 1986 and early 1987, as well as in the extent to which economic policy has favoured or protected more the poor and the vulnerable.[12] Indeed, partly as a result of Peru's unilateral action of limiting payments on debt which released some foreign exchange, the Peruvian economy in 1986 was the fastest growing in Latin America. However, the fact that debt payments were limited has by no means eliminated the constraints for economic growth. Thus, in mid-1987, very rapid growth plus weak prices of Peru's exports, and policy mistakes, such as overvaluation of the exchange rate, are leading to accelerating inflation, and — even more problematically — to rapidly declining foreign exchange reserves. Unless growing macroeconomic imbalances are reversed in time, there is a risk that in Peru, the heterodox or alternative (to the IMF) economic policy package will run into severe problems.

From the point of view of international financial flows, the Peruvian experience has shown that after two years of unilateral action no legal response has come from the creditor banks to confiscate assets or other drastic measures. The only 'cost' of the unilateral action, as regards creditor banks, has been their curtailment of short-term credit lines. It should also be stressed that the creditor banks' response to the Brazilian unilateral action in 1987 of suspending interest payments, has been equally — if not more — low-key. As a consequence, there seems to be growing, though obviously not conclusive, evidence that creditor banks will tend to respond to unilateral action defensively, by curtailing

short-term credit lines, but not aggressively, e.g. by legal
actions. On the other hand, the Peruvian government's
suspension of payments to the IMF (and its failed attempts
to reschedule payments to that institution) has had negative
effects. Suspension of payments to the IMF, as well as
Garcia's harsh critique of the Fund, seems to have seriously
inhibited new credits from the World Bank and the Inter-
American Development Bank.

The fact that the Brazilian government refused to sign an
agreement with the IMF in 1985 and 1986 implied costs,
such as the fact that its financial deals with the banks were
less attractive, e.g. as relates to level of 'spreads', than say
those of Mexico, and more importantly implied a lack of new
credits from private banks. However, the freedom to define
its own macroeconomic policy allowed the Brazilian government to pursue growth-oriented policies. During the 1985–86
period, per capita GDP growth in Brazil (at 5.8 per cent) was
by far the highest in Latin America, and well exceeded the
Latin American average (at only 0.8 per cent during the two
years). Two very important caveats should however be made.
First, sustained growth in Brazil in the mid-1980s was made
more feasible than in other Latin American countries, due
to the structural adjustment investment in tradeables and
capital goods so effectively carried out by the Brazilian
government in the 1970s. Second, even though the Brazilian
government launched an innovative and unorthodox macroeconomic stabilization programme to curtail inflation (the
Plan Cruzado), policy mistakes in the Plan's implementation implied that severe financial disequilibria emerged,
leading both to extremely high levels of inflation and to a
dramatic reduction in the balance of payments trade
surplus.

The subordination of economic policy to short-term
political objectives, so frequent in Latin America, led inevitably in Brazil to unsustainable financial disequilibria, and
to the failure of the unorthodox package. The failure of an
unorthodox package clearly reinforces the attractiveness of
more conventional packages, and the perceived desirability
(within and outside the country) of reaching an agreement
on stabilization with the IMF, which implies exactly the

opposite result to that desired by the authors of unorthodox macroeconomic packages.

As a result of declining trade surpluses and foreign exchange reserves in February 1987, the Brazilian government declared a unilateral moratorium on all interest payments of its debt to private banks. The unilateral moratorium implied an important step, which clearly marked the beginning of a new stage in debt crisis management. The largest LDC bank debtor of all, Brazil, when confronted with a choice of restricting growth or unilaterally limited debt servicing, chose the latter path. Even though Brazil's unilateral action may well prove to be temporary, it posed a far deeper challenge to the multilaterally agreed package framework prevalent since 1982 than, for example, Peru's unilateral action since 1985.

There were several problems with the Brazilian moratorium. The declaration of unilateral cessation of interest payments was not part of a clear strategy, but a response to the rapid deterioration in the trade surplus and foreign exchange reserves. Also, the Brazilian government did not for several months make explicit its objectives in negotiations with the banks on key aspects such as interest capping, amount of new money required, debt relief, etc. Thus, the Brazilian government did not present a concrete alternative proposal on how the debt problem should be managed, which could serve as a base for negotiation of a new type of deal.

In any case, the Brazilian moratorium has had two beneficial effects on Latin American economies, by mid-1987. First, it provided Brazil with some breathing space in the first half of 1987, allowing for higher growth than otherwise possible. Second, other Latin American governments, such as those of Mexico, Argentina, and Chile, found it easier to finalize their rescheduling/new money deals, due to the bankers' wish to avoid any risk that Brazil's precedent should spread to other debtors.

The hidden agenda

Evidence has emerged that in the multilateral negotiations on

debt, new lending and adjustment, there were some hidden
agendas, often not made explicit in official documents. As
could be expected, political matters and bilateral economic
issues, particularly those of interest to the US government,
were high on those agendas in negotiations with Latin
American countries. For example, several Central American
countries have benefited from more lenient economic conditionality, but have had to accept political and even military
conditions.

At an economic level, issues such as countries' position on
the new GATT round have been made part of the negotiation
on debt rescheduling and new money. It is, however,
interesting to point out that pressures can be successfully
resisted by debtors. For example, in one case, the reduction
of tariffs posed as a condition of a structural adjustment
package was not only negative for the particular country's
industry, but also threatened to undermine an existing
regional common market agreement. The maximum political
authority of that country resisted this condition, and the
potential danger to the regional common market agreement
was lifted.

Another area insufficiently studied till the present, where,
to some extent there has been a hidden agenda, has been the
rescheduling of private non-guaranteed external debt, carried
out in a fundamentally different way in different countries.

The most extreme case has been that of Chile, where
initially most (around 65 per cent) of the external debt was
originally private, without government guarantee. In this
context, it was paradoxical that, when the debt crisis came,
the Chilean government *ex post* acted as borrower of last
resort. This is in sharp contrast to the attitude of industrial
creditor governments, who have consistently refused to
grant *ex post* lender of last resort facilities to the credits
held in LDCs by their private banks. The Chilean government
gave an *ex post* guarantee to an important part of the
private debt, that of the private financial sector. This can
be partly explained by the fact that it was the private
financial sector whose debts were being bailed out; bankruptcy or serious financial distress in an important part of the
banking sector would have had potentially very disruptive

macroeconomic effects. In those cases where it did not grant *ex post* guarantees, the Chilean government gave different types of subsidies (including a preferential exchange rate) to the private sector, so as to enable it to service its debt.

Interestingly, in the Venezuelan case, creditor banks did not even demand *ex post* government guarantee for private debt. However, the creditor banks did exert pressure on the Venezuelan government to grant a preferential exchange rate for private debt servicing, and linked explicitly the granting of this concession on the private debt to their willingness to reschedule the public debt. The amount of the subsidy granted by the Venezuelan government has been fairly substantial.

Other countries gave less favourable treatment to the servicing of its private debt. Perhaps the most complete and interesting scheme was that developed by the Mexican government, which established a system that neither granted official *ex post* commercial government guarantee on the private debt, nor gave an explicit exchange rate subsidy.

Within the framework of multilateral negotiations, the Mexican government seems to have negotiated relatively best on better financial terms (first country to get multi-year arrangement, relatively low spreads, long grace and maturity period and abundant new money in the 1986/87 package) and important degrees of flexibility and heterodoxy in its adjustment package (e.g. growth clause, acceptance of the operational deficit concept). Similarly, the mechanism it has agreed for the private debt has been the least burdensome for the national Treasury. The Venezuelan financial package has clearly been less favourable than that obtained by Mexico, particularly as it has implied no new money. Similarly the Venezuelan government granted large subsidies to the private sector for its servicing of the foreign debt. The most damaging treatment of the private debt (from the point of view of the national interest) has been that accepted by the Chilean government, which both granted *ex post* guarantee for an important part of the debt and gave large subsidies for its servicing in the rest of it. The Chilean government's weak bargaining in this aspect coincides with its very weak bargaining on the nature and timing of adjustment.

CONCLUSIONS

An important conclusion from recent experience is that
debtor governments have achieved better results when they
have taken the initiative and put forward clear, specific
proposals to the creditors. Though all their suggestions have
not always been accepted, a clear initial position by the
debtor governments can serve as a basis for the package
to be adopted. The Mexican deal signed in 1986/7 seems to
illustrate this rather well. On the other hand, the Argentine
position in 1984, in which a tough stance *vis-à-vis* creditors
was hinted at, but no clear proposals emerged, did not contribute to obtaining an improved deal.

A limitation of the Mexican negotiation in 1986 may have
been the complexity of the financial package proposed, even
though net financial flows required for the next two or
three years were clearly put forward. The package put
forward by the Mexican negotiators had many interesting
and innovative elements (e.g. use of exit bonds, linking
payments to the relationship between the price of oil and
interest rates, etc.). However, in a sense the package contained too many innovative elements at the same time to be
easily implemented and, above all, to be acceptable to the
banks. The package adopted implied a great improvement in
the financial deal and incorporated some but not the main
new concepts supported by the Mexican authorities.

It would seem best to make proposals, or at least monitor
developments, in terms of the variable that affects most
of the indebted developing countries, that is net transfer of
resources. A drastic reduction or elimination of negative
net transfers for middle-income debtors, at least till the
end of the 1980s, may seem radical in the present context,
but in terms of economic development theory or international justice, it is a fairly modest target. An elimination
of negative net transfers would free an important amount of
resources to allow for restructuring of middle-income debtor
economies, to make feasible their development in the 1990s,
as well as to start servicing their domestic 'social debt'. An
additional secondary objective would be that the level
of total foreign debt in relation to the value of exports

should not continue to rise, as this only postpones the problem.

Of importance in the case of middle-income heavily indebted countries is the proposal of reduction in interest rate payments to a certain level (e.g. 5 or 6 per cent), the excess of which would only be repaid if and when interest payments fell below that level during the period of the loan. The difference between the 'market rate' and the fixed rate would be financed by an interest compensatory fund. In November 1986, a concrete proposal along these lines was made by Mr A. Herrhausen, Speaker of the Management Board of the largest German bank, Deutsche Bank. The idea has received an important amount of support in European circles. One of the proposal's interesting features (increasingly relevant after May 1987) is that part of the 'subsidy' would be funded by private banks, drawing on loan-loss provisions they have accumulated.

Another area where specific proposals are important is that of principal payments. Till now the main way of reducing amortization payments has been through rescheduling, which postpones the problem (in the case of the 1986/7 Mexican deal, the postponement has been significant). However, the market value of the debt is increasingly recognized to be below its face value, as is reflected in the rapidly growing (though rather thin) secondary market and in widespread loan-loss provisions. It seems absurd that if the market and most of the creditor banks have recognized explicitly that the book value is unrealistic, debtor governments and economies are still obliged to service the debt as if it was worth 100 per cent of this value. To allow the value of the debt being serviced to reflect closer market realities, a number of options can be pursued. Amongst these, debt equity swaps are already being implemented in a number of countries; the 1987 Argentine package also includes exit bonds used by banks wanting to withdraw from the process of rescheduling/new money, albeit at a loss. A third option, partially implemented in early 1988 by the Mexican government, is for the debtor government to purchase its own debt at a discount. This requires that the government either has a high level of foreign

exchange reserves (Mexico, 1988) or receives loans or aid to
be used for debt repurchase (Bolivia, 1987). A fourth variety
has been suggested, but not yet implemented; these would
be so-called 'debt development' swaps. In that case, part of
the debt or debt service would be converted into investment/
expenditure in the domestic economy for high priority
activities, such as exports, import substitution or social
expenditure, under the monitoring of an international organization, such as the World Bank, the corresponding regional
development bank, or another specialized agency.[13]

In the Latin American context, the Inter-American
Development Bank President, Sr Ortiz Mena has launched
an interesting proposal which implies a debt/development
swap. Part of the interest on foreign debt incurred would be
deposited in local currency by the debtor government in an
escrow account, administered by the IDB. The funds would
be used for productive expenditure within the country,
monitored by the IDB. In the context of low-income
countries, mostly but not only in Sub-Saharan Africa,
UNICEF is launching a somewhat similar proposal, which
would imply that part of debt or interest relief would be
placed in a national child survival fund. This fund would
be used for additional expenditure, in nutrition, health and
education for poor children. The programme would be
jointly designed, implemented and monitored by the government and UNICEF, as well as another multilateral
organization, such as the World Bank.

Such innovations may require changes in banking and
taxation regulations in some or all creditor countries, that
would smooth (over the years) and make less costly to
creditor banks the partial writing down and writing off of
debt, and/or some sort of interest relief. Existing regulations
have become too much of an obstacle to innovative solutions
to the debt crisis; it has often been almost forgotten that
regulations are only man-made and can be modified if they
do not suit current needs!

As regards new credits, it seems important for debtor
governments to focus more on negotiations with governments, institutions and private agents, both willing and able
to provide significant new flows. Far less time perhaps should

be spent than at present in negotiations with the US government and banks. The US economy is itself in a large current account deficit, and US financial intermediaries are far less able as well as less willing to provide significant new flows to most developing countries than they were in the 1970s. Greater emphasis, both nationally and collectively, needs to be made by debtor governments to attract flows from the Japanese and West German governments, as well as private institutions.[14]

Another area for concrete proposals is that of contingency arrangements for financial flows, in case of fluctuations in international economic variables, such as the price of countries' main export products.

THE BARGAINING PROCESS

A precondition for successful negotiation on debt/new money deals is the existence of clearly defined and appropriate development strategies as well as a consistent short-term macroeconomic programme. The existence of such plans clearly strengthens the case for extracting concessions/new flows from creditors, as these concessions/new flows can be more easily justified in the industrial country. The existence of development plans and targets also changes the focus of discussion from a purely financial one to the 'real economy'; if a particular growth rate and income distribution is targeted, as well as levels of investment required to achieve such targets, then the external financial flows required are dependent to a far more important extent on those national objectives.

Particularly in cases of governments not wishing to accept upper credit tranche conditionality from the IMF, it is essential that foreign creditors and lenders, as well as the citizens of the debtor country, see that the government has its own effective and consistent macroeconomic programme, that will avoid major financial disequilibria. The lack of such a clear 'alternative adjustment' package seems to have weakened the position of the Argentine government *vis-à-vis* its creditors in 1984, and may also weaken the pursuit by the

Brazilian government in mid-1987 of a far more favourable deal with its creditors. In the case of unilateral action, prudent and careful macroeconomic management, as well as a clear development strategy, becomes even more crucial than for multilaterally agreed deals.

A second element relates to the bargaining itself. Even though unilateral action by debtor governments is undesirable in itself for all actors involved (as it implies the risk of unquantifiable negative effects), either such unilateral action or the threat of it, may be necessary for debtor governments to achieve financial deals that are consistent with growth and development in their economies. It would seem that such tough bargaining positions, or even unilateral action is more effective if it has unified support of all branches and levels of the government and the active support of a large part of the countries' population, political parties, trade unions, etc. It is also very important to establish at all times that the position is not confrontational, and wishes to avoid harming the creditor institutions. There seems a clear need for debtor government negotiators to show 'good will' in negotiations with creditor banks and governments, to maintain 'channels of communication' open, to maintain formalities and use conciliatory language, not only when taking a very tough negotiating stance, but even when unilateral action is raised as a possibility or carried out. The successful effect of tough positions or actions and diplomatic behaviour is well illustrated, for example, by the Mexican experience in 1986/87.

If some element of concessionality is being negotiated, it seems essential for the debtor government to show not only that the resources freed are used in a developmental context, leading both to sustained economic growth and increased welfare of the population; but also that a significant contribution is made by wealthy citizens of debtor countries toward funding development. The containment of capital flight, as well as an attempt to return capital already fled is a very crucial example, as would be increased taxation on high-income groups, restrictions on luxury goods imports, etc.

A third important tactical element is to recognize that

important differences exist in the interests, aims and regulatory environment of different creditors, particularly but not only private banks. These differences have tended till now to work against debtors in multilateral negotiations, as the relief or new money granted has tended to be 'the lowest common denominator' acceptable to all creditor banks. For example, banks with large loan-loss provisions, e.g. some European ones, may be willing to write off or postpone some interest payments, but are not keen to lend new money, as this will imply they have immediately to increase their loan-loss provisions. On the other hand, the big US banks are more willing to lend new money, but are unwilling to give any concession or even postponement of interest payments, as this lowers the rating of the debt in their books. As a result, it is extremely difficult either to get new money or to get interest rate postponements or concessions.

If debtor governments were to fix a target acceptable to them in net transfers, they could then negotiate separately with different types of creditors, on the concrete mechanisms through which this target of net transfers would be achieved. The deals would in this case be equitable amongst creditors, but different.

The final issue relates to the appropriate forum for negotiation of new flows and rescheduling. Clearly the steering committees and the IMF provide too narrow an outlook on the problem. The greater involvement of the World Bank, though adding an extra fairly heavy element of conditionality, has the positive element that its perspective is more on the long-term and on development issues. It is necessary that financial matters are not left only to financial interests, but that broader interests representing, for example, productive and trading sectors in industrial countries and the poorer groups in developing countries (e.g. through their Industry and Labour Ministries or international institutions, such as UNICEF or ILO) are represented. It is crucial that these latter interests and concerns are represented at the time the major financial decisions are being made, and not as now, left to 'pick up the pieces' of the productive or social cost of the adjustment, after the adjustment was designed by those with fundamentally financial criteria in mind.

NOTES AND REFERENCES

1. This chapter draws on the Conclusions Chapter of a forthcoming book (ed.) S. Griffith-Jones, *Managing World Debt*, Wheatsheaf (UK) and Fondo de Cultura Economica (Mexico). The book and this chapter are the result of an ESRC/IDRC funded international research project. I am very grateful to my project colleagues for very valuable comments on an earlier draft, and for the valuable insights provided by their papers.

2. *Managing Third World Debt*, Report by the Second Working Party established by the All Party Parliamentary Group on Overseas Development, ODI, London 1987.

3. Salomon Brothers, 'Less Developed Countries' Indebtedness: Secular Developments in US Banking are Defusing the Problem', *Bank Weekly*, 20 January 1987.

4. Holley, *Developing Country Debt, the Role of the Commercial Banks*, Chatham House, Paper 35, 1987.

5. Source: *International Financing Review*, FFIEC Statistical Release, E. 16 (126), 13 February 1987.

6. For a recent review of different options for solution, see P. Wertman, 'The International Debt Problem: Options for Solution' in Hearings before the Sub-Committee on International Finance, Trade and Monetary Policy of the Committee on Banking, Finance and Urban Affairs, House of Representatives, *Banking Committee Provisions of the Trade Bill*, Washington, 1987.

7. These concerns are clearly reflected in the US Banking Committee Provisions of the Trade Bill quoted in (6) in the proposals of US Senator Bradley, Congressman Schumer and other US Congressmen, as well as in the Report by the British All Party Parliamentary Working Party quoted in (2).

8. The proper use of deflator for debtor countries for similar variables is discussed in detail and with rigour in C. Massad and R. Zahler, 'World inflation and foreign debt: the case of the improper deflator' and C. Massad, 'The real cost of the external debt for the creditor and the debtor' in *Latin America: International Monetary System and External Financing*, UNDP/ECLAC, Santiago de Chile, 1986.

9. For an interesting discussion, see A. McEwan, 'Es posible la

moratoria en America Latina?', *Comercio Exterior*, January 1987, vol. 37, no. 1, pp. 60–64.

10. For a very articulate statement of this problem and an empirical review of the evidence, see G.A. Cornia, R. Jolly, and F. Stewart (eds), *Adjustment with a Human Face: Protecting the Vulnerable and Promoting Growth*, Oxford University Press, 1987. Increased concern has also been expressed by the World Bank and by the IMF, in their declarations and in their studies.

11. OECD, *Geographical Distribution of Financial Flows to Developing Countries, 1982/5* (Paris, 1987).

12. For the latter, crucial point, see chapter on Peru by L. Figueroa, in A. Cornia, R. Jolly, F. Stewart (eds), *Adjustment with a Human Face*, vol. II, Oxford University Press, 1987.

13. This idea was developed first in Latin America: see, for example, O. Sunkel, *America Latina y la Crisis Economica Internacional*, Grupo Editorial Latinomericano, Buenos Aires 1985, and R. Prebisch, 'Statement to the US House of Representatives in July 1985' reproduced in *CEPAL Review* no. 27, Santiago de Chile, December 1985. The idea has increasingly received support in industrial countries, particularly by the UK All Party Parliamentary Report in (2). Recently, the Bolivian government has swapped some of its debt for increased expenditure on the environment.

14. See *Financial Times*, 11 July 1987; for details, see WIDER, 'Mobilising International Surpluses for World Development: a WIDER Plan for a Japanese Initiative', Study Group Series, May 1987, WIDER, Helsinki.

4 The Latin American debt crisis: the debtor's view

Miguel A. Olea

. . . He did not care to put off any longer the execution of his design . . . seeing what wrongs he intended to right, grievances to redress, injustices to repair, abuses to remove, and debts to be honored . . . .

Don Quixote de la Mancha

Not everyone concerned in one way or another with the analysis of the Third World debt problem, or more narrowly Latin American debt, would view it as, first and foremost, a problem with wide political implications for all the parties involved. Perhaps it is they who are right; but perhaps not. Let me, then, rehearse a few of the arguments with which I intend to support my main thesis. I take it that a problem is a *political* problem if it brings in its wake a significant impact on the economic and political relations between states, or else, if it affects the relationship that exists between a government of a given country and its citizens. The debt crisis qualifies as a political problem on both counts: it has generated unexpected costs for some and great net benefits for others; it has thereby altered the relations between states. Internally, the debt crisis has caused an amazing strain in the relationship of government and citizens in all Latin American countries — a natural consequence of the decrease in their income, per capita income, and welfare in general. The questions, then, that seem to me to be worth pursuing are these:

- Has the external debt incurred by the Latin American countries altered the equilibrium that existed in the

transactions and transfers of international resources?
- Are there any solutions to the problem of the Latin American debt which entail a symmetrical effort on the part of both, debtors and creditors, in the process of adjustment?
- What are the limits of the political responsibility of the debtor countries *vis-à-vis* their creditors? And, what is the political responsibility of the Latin American governments *vis-à-vis* their citizens? Where, exactly, does the former end, and the latter begin?

All these questions cry out for an answer — and no easy answer seems to be forthcoming. The problem is aggravated because there really is not an objective description of what the problem is and, therefore, a consensus is far from attainable at this stage. There are many interpretations of what the nature of the problem is, different criteria by which to judge whether or not there has been an advance in the process of adjustment, and various putative explanations released to the press, all of which implicitly assume a political stand towards the issue at stake. Before telling you what I consider to be the most plausible political perspective, let me briefly review some of the most relevant data revolving around the Latin American external debt:

- The Latin American debt has increased by more than 400 per cent in the last ten years. From 1975 onwards the accumulated debt increased by an average growth rate of more than 20 per cent annually.
- During the same period, the ratio of service payments to export income increased from 26.6 per cent to more than 65 per cent. What this means is that the debtor countries run the risk of going back several decades in their development and welfare, which in some cases is already in the lowest brackets in international terms.
- The growth of debt service has accelerated more rapidly than the growth of the debt itself. This is due to the change in the debt profile, the hardening of financial terms as well as the significant increases in interest rates.

It is common knowledge that the constraint imposed by the foreign exchange gap in the Latin American economies, has resulted in severe decreases in their income, per capita income and their welfare and development. It would be redundant to expand in great detail on the explanation of the origin of the problem. Somehow, we all recognize internal as well as external factors which contributed to trigger the crisis: overexpenditure in the public sector, disequilibrium in the public finances, inadequate handling of macroeconomic policies, overvaluation of exchange rates and speculative capital movements surely played an important role in the process. But there were also exogenous causes: significant increases in interest rates, drastic decreases in the prices of primary products, including oil, and a severe contraction of financial flows to developing countries.

Not so well known are the political issues and arguments of the Latin American debt problem. Here, we can mention the internal political adjustments generated by the 'zero-sum' effects in the core of our societies; the disentangling of some of the elements that bind our social systems together; the perverse impact in the democratization processes of our societies; the pressures exercised on our social contracts, given the deterioration in the quality of life of the average citizen, and the rather meagre expectations for the future development of our countries.

One can find, at the very heart of the whole issue, the problem of transfers. During the 1960s and 1970s Latin America received positive net transferences of resources from the international community. Thus the development of our countries was fostered by international economic cooperation, which made possible a huge transfer of capital that helped to relax constraints that hampered the political progress. The close link between internal and foreign policy made it imperative to satisfy the basic needs of our societies, while simultaneously opening the possibilities of political participation, and to play a constructive role in the design of the international system.

Notice that the billions of dollars of accumulated Latin American debt not only mean industrial infrastructure, steel and petrochemical complexes, roads and better agriculture;

but also, and no less important, the access of the population to better nourishment, health services, education and welfare in general. They also represent a slow process of enriching our political culture and democratic institutions. Latin American debt can thus be seen from two different perspectives. First, there is the liberal conception embodied in the Western tradition, in which the debt stock is nothing but a transitory contribution of societies that have satisfied their most pressing economic demands to others which are in the process of consolidating their political and economic systems. Second, there is the view that the debt is a surplus of rich economies, which can be conceived as a political investment and used as a suitable instrument to foster oppression and economic dependence.

Keynes himself, at the time when he wrote *The Economic Consequences of the Peace*, refused to see the Versailles Treaty as a retributive instrument which would entail enormous negative transfers for Germany. He was well aware that what was needed at the time was a vast credit programme that would help to revitalize European industry, just after the First World War had come to an end. The importance of achieving social and political stability and, at the same time, a reasonable rate of economic development, did not escape his notice.

It would be utterly unrealistic to think that the net transfer of resources which industrial societies made to Latin America was purely humanitarian, or altruistic. Those societies faced severe limitations in their internal markets, that is to say, their capacity to absorb whatever goods they produced was limited, and, hence, they had to go in search of other markets that would offer them better marginal rates of return, and would allow them to capitalize monopoly profits. The benefits were thus not only for the recipient countries, but for the investors as well.

As things now stand, the international scene cannot be seen optimistically from a Latin American standpoint. The thesis that the economic recovery of industrialized countries will help the Latin American countries to transcend the economic crisis in which they find themselves cannot stand any close scrutiny. Interest rates in international markets are expected to rise; there are pressures for oil prices to go down and for substantive decreases in the prices of primary products. These elements, combined with an ever growing protectionist trend, cannot be said to compose a favourable scheme for Latin American countries. There is, to be sure, one healthy effect that the recovery of the industrial societies will bring in its wake, namely, an increase in their demand of industrial products; but it is here that the protectionist barriers are felt more strongly.

With respect to the internal problems that the Latin American countries have to face, it must be stressed that the whole process of adjusting our economies has really left no more room for manoeuvre. There are some cases in which one could truly say that the government has reached the bottom line. These are cases in which the political cost of abandoning altogether the international financial system is less than carrying on trying to abide by the present rules of the game. After severe adjustment processes, one becomes aware that what has been achieved is really minimal; one is thrown back to square one and gains a new awareness of the deterioration in the social and political systems which no government can stand for very long. To reduce inflation or unemployment; to pay higher interest rates is, day to day, more and more costly for the whole of society. In short, the crisis has now become notoriously insensitive to any of the policy instruments that a government can deploy to attack it.

It cannot be forgotten that the new democratic currents in Latin America have come into being as a result of more than two decades of stable and sustained development. These societies have experienced a general level of welfare which is not so easily abandoned. The debt crisis is beginning to undermine the very basis on which every democratic government may stand: the sovereignty of the people, universal suffrage and the principle of representative democracy are possible, only if certain economic prerequisites are met. How could it be otherwise? Can it possibly be the case that men, and the countries to which they belong, are able to exercise their political freedom in conditions of extreme economic dependence and, through it, by being subjected to the will of other people? Eighteenth-century republicans thought, correctly, that this situation is simply not possible. As Hamilton put it, 'A power over a man's subsistence amounts to a power over his will'.

It was on the basis of assertions like Hamilton's that other participants to the Philadelphia Convention gave their entire support to linking universal suffrage and the distribution of property. It was then the task of the social reformers of the nineteenth century to define and give full content to the idea of democracy in social, economic and political terms. There simply is no other way to understand such an idea; for, they thought, if the idea of democracy is severed from these other concepts, it would condone social and economic injustice which, in the long run, cannot but undermine the political liberties. Can we honestly renounce this conception, deeply embedded as it certainly is, in our political lore?

To hamper in any way the democratic process, whether in the countries of Latin America or in any other region of the world, is to demolish the prevailing social contract at an international level. The continuous search for formulas and schemes of negotiations based on multilateral agreements, as well as all the steps taken in favour of the open and participatory action of developing countries in the international economic order, are all neutralized the very moment that the links offered by political dialogue and communication are severed.

The debt crisis is not only a problem of balancing assets and liabilities. It might well be that, before analysing several recipes which recommend economic contraction and the reestablishment of the financial balances, we should begin by asking ourselves which is the residual variable. If we take it to be the worker's or the peasant's salary; or the welfare which less privileged classes enjoy, and, if this is achieved through transfers of welfare to the entrepreneur and the foreign investor, it is evident that we have entered not only into the political arena, but into the grounds of ethics and morals as well.

The problem of Latin American debt must also be viewed in the context of a given set of priorities in international relations. Does a dollar spent on development contribute more to social and political stability than one spent on nuclear

weapons? A thesis like that of deterrence, based on terror
and inventories of nuclear weapons, cannot be sustained on
any scheme of moral and political responsibility whatsoever.
There are opportunity costs and, if the general goal is peace-
ful coexistence amongst nations, the relevant question is
whether the $800 billion spent on nuclear armament are a
better alternative than education, health, and development
in general. Can a transfer of welfare from a South American
peasant to finance the so-called Star Wars programme be
justified? Given the inherent irrationality of such a scheme
of priorities, it is amazing to find that in a country such as
the USA, even the Middle West farmers and college students
are now involved in this absurd circuit of welfare transfers.

Latin America has certainly played a serious and mature
role in facing the crisis. The answer to such a complicated
problem must comprise different actions at different levels.
With respect to the multilateral level, 'Quito's Declaration'
and 'Cartagena's Consensus' are clear signs that point to the
deep transformation which has taken place in intraregional
politics. Quito and Cartagena represent a substantive contribution in the integration process of Latin America, and
have helped to define the new parameters that will govern
regional relations in the years to come. They also represent
an all-encompassing view of the problem, for not only do
they envisage alternative courses of action that may be taken
at the regional level, but also they have come forward with a
proposal of a set of general principles and terms in which the
debt problem can be solved through political dialogue and
understanding.

As far as external debt is concerned, the approach acknow-
ledges the political implications which may accrue. Its
purpose is not to try to find solutions that would only offer
immediate relief, i.e. multiyear restructuring, or the elimination of commissions and brokerage fees, or to cap interest
rates, which would only mean transferring the problem to
our future generations. The goal is to look for a genuine
political solution to the problem, which begins by
recognizing principles like that of co-responsibility between
debtors, creditors and international financial institutions on
the one hand, and a symmetrical distribution of adjustment

costs between debtors and creditors. The consultation mechanism of the Cartagena Group is perhaps the most valuable political outcome that has emerged from the process. It certainly opens channels for a more fluent political communication between the Latin American debtors, creditors, and international financial institutions.

The great challenge in our search for a solution to the debt crisis is to provide a realistic timetable that would allow us to substantially reduce and defer the costs in a temporary framework so that our political and historical heritage will not be destroyed. What this presupposes is a very close link between short-term policies and the required structural changes considered in a long-run horizon. This is, in effect, the main contention of this chapter: the Latin American countries can only travel a certain distance in their adjustment processes; and no farther. The limit is the point where our social and political institutions begin to bear more than their legitimate share of the burden. The costs must be distributed in accordance with the principles of co-responsibility and it is the international financial system that must guarantee a fair distribution. It is of necessity that one has to work at two different levels: one that refers to the sharing of the burden between the parties involved; and the other that concerns the distribution of costs in an adequate time horizon. So far, there is only one fixed point of reference any effort towards a solution must take into account: any option for a permanent solution must be bound by the principles of fairness, equality and a link between debt, trade and the re-establishment of financial flows to developing countries.

5 Issues arising from the spread of obligatory adjustment

Tony Killick*

Part of the response of the creditor countries and the Bretton Woods institutions to the 'debt problem' that surfaced in 1982 has been to insist, on a country-by-country basis, that debt reschedulings and additional finance will only be approved in support of agreed programmes of adjustment measures by debtor governments. A large number of heavily indebted and African countries have subsequently adopted such programmes.

Especially in the last few years, such programmes are seen as going well beyond conventional stabilization measures of the type associated with the IMF, to address a wide range of policies directed to the 'real' economy, so the spread of such 'structural adjustment' programmes, particularly in Africa and Latin America, has been directly related to the problem of external indebtedness. Since 1985, in addition, there has been from the USA and the Bretton Woods institutions some public stress on the importance of creating the conditions for resumed growth, especially within the heavily indebted countries of Latin America, and there has been much talk of achieving 'adjustment with growth'.

The purpose of this chapter is to explore some of the issues arising from the spread of adjustment programmes, and

*The author is Senior Research Fellow, Overseas Development Institute, London. This chapter borrows extensively from two papers on 'Adjustment with growth' commissioned for the Group of 24 by UNCTAD but responsibility for views expressed here rests entirely with the author. It was originally presented at an ESRC Study Group on Debt and Development at the University of Essex. I should like to acknowledge the valuable assistance provided by Matthew Martin and Lucy Nichols in preparing the original papers.

he associated policy conditionality of creditor agencies. The
irst section traces the spread of obligatory adjustment.
he second section takes up various issues regarding the
esign of adjustment. Various institutional issues, mainly
oncerning the Bretton Woods institutions, are explored in
he third section; and a few concluding observations are
ffered.

A notable exclusion from the chapter is a discussion of the
dequacy of external finance being made available in support
f adjustment programmes. This is omitted to keep the
hapter to a manageable length and on the assumption that
ther contributions to this volume will deal with this aspect.

HE SPREAD OF OBLIGATORY ADJUSTMENT

he spread of adjustment-related lending by the Bretton
Voods institutions is well illustrated by the African case.
Vhile the IMF has had a substantial number of stabilization
rogrammes in operation in African countries for many
ears, the entry of the World Bank into 'policy-related
:nding' is a more recent innovation, largely stemming from
ie introduction of its structural adjustments loans (SALs),
ie first of which was made in 1980. Considerable additional
iomentum was added to this trend by the introduction by
ie Bank of sectoral adjustment loans (hereafter SEALs),
hich began to assume importance in 1983. With few, if any,
xceptions a country must have an agreed standby or other
rogramme with the Fund before a SAL or SEAL can be
pproved (although they can continue in force after a Fund
rogramme has ended) so the activities of the two
istitutions should be viewed together. In addition and even
iore recently, the African Development Bank has been
rged to move in the direction of adjustment-related lending
nd has recently been voted an increase in its capital to
icilitate this. Following the same trend, a number of
ilateral aid donors, most notably USAID, have increased
ie proportions of their bilateral aid programme which are
i support of adjustment programmes.

An idea of the extent to which such programmes have

spread within Sub-Saharan Africa (SSA) is conveyed by
the fact that as at early December 1986 no fewer than 2
SSA countries had adjustment-related programmes with the
Fund and/or the Bank. The Bank alone counted 24 such
programmes, of which 13 were attributable to 1986. Within
the Bank, the number of SEALs considerably outnumbered
the SALs and it appears to be Bank policy to encourage this
trend. The IMF had standby programmes with 18 SSA
countries at end 1986. Now only few countries in the
region have no programmes with either of the Bretton
Woods institutions and we shall consider the position of
these countries later. While the coverage is less complete
in Asia and Latin America, in these regions too there are
Fund- and/or Bank-assisted adjustment programmes in
considerable number of countries, including Argentina
Bangladesh, Mexico and the Philippines.

Another way of illustrating the movement toward
adjustment-related lending is to point out that while until
recently the Bank was supposed to keep its policy-related
lending to within 10 per cent of its total lending that ceiling
has now been raised to 25 per cent. Fund and Bank credit
for stabilization and structural adjustment programmes are
of course, subject to various policy conditions so the trend
towards such programmes has greatly extended the influence
of these agencies on national economic policies.

There are other factors also increasing the extent of this
influence. One is that SALs and (perhaps to a lesser extent
SEALs commonly require an extensive number of policy
commitments by the borrowing governments. Indeed, an
internal Bank review of its early SALs concluded that this
proliferation of policy conditions was a source of weakness
in the SAL programme and the Bank's 1986 Annual Report
(p. 54) identified the need to concentrate on a limited
number of reforms as the main lesson it had learned about
SAL effectiveness. But although the Bank now says it is being
more selective it is not clear from the long lists of conditions
written into more recent SALs and SEALs that this is
actually the case.[1]

With its structural adjustment lending the normal intention
is that there will be a sequence of up to five one-year SAL

nd this is proving to be another means by which the
overage of conditionality is being progressively extended.
'or as the policy actions called for in one SAL are implemen-
ed so the next SAL will call for additional policy changes.
he Bank describes this process as a 'deepening' of adjust-
1ent; to borrowers it must seem that it has an insatiable
ppetite for 'reform'.

Yet another factor is a greater tendency in recent years to
1sist upon preconditions ('prior actions' in the parlance of
he Fund) before a credit will be approved. Such provisions
ave been common in the Fund for many years but their use
vas intensified in the early 1980s[2] and there has apparently
een a move in the same direction on the part of the Bank.
'et another twist is added by the Fund's practice in some
ases to make the release of the final tranche of one stand-
y credit conditional upon commitment to a new programme
hereafter.[3]

As the previous sharp division of labour between the Fund
nd Bank has become blurred in recent years, another potent
1eans of extending international pressures for policy reform
as been the increased incidence of cross-conditionality
etween them, whereby the conditionality of one (usually
1e Fund) becomes a precondition for the credits of the
ther.[4] We have already mentioned that the existence of a
:andby or other agreement with the Fund is virtually a *sine
ua non* for the approval of an SAL or SEAL by the board
f the Bank.

The modalities adopted with respect to the structural
djustment facility (SAF), created in the Fund in 1986 and
1uch enlarged in 1988, provide yet another aspect of the
xtending net of conditionality. The rules under which this
perates are that the policies to be supported by an SAF
:edit are to be described in a 'policy framework paper'
:tting out a three-year programme, to be developed jointly
y the government in question and the staffs of the Fund
1d Bank. In addition, the actions to be taken in the first
f the three years are to be spelled out in greater detail
1 a document from the government directly comparable
) the 'letter of intent' used in connection with IMF stand-
ys. There have been six-monthly 'benchmarks' for the

monitoring of progress but there have not been any per
formance criteria as such and there has not been any
tranching of the release of the credit within the year. There
have, however, been some preconditions and countries have
been told that past progress will be taken into account by the
staffs during negotiations for subsequent years.

It being still a relatively recent innovation, there is as yet
little published evidence on how the SAF has been working
in practice, although the Group of 24 complained at an early
stage that it was being operated in an inflexible manner. A
high proportion of SAF credits have been to countries where
there was already a Fund standby credit in place, although
this is not a fixed requirement. This practice does, however
make it difficult to disentangle those aspects of government
actions which could be attributed specifically to con
ditionality attached to SAF credits *per se*.

Dominica provides an example of a country which received
an SAF credit without a prior standby programme where some
thing is known of the conditions attached. These included

- Provisions concerning the levels of government capital
  expenditures and domestic borrowings.
- Provisions relating to tax reform.
- Measures to strengthen incomes policies.
- Measures to reduce the size of the civil service.
- Restrictions on non-concessional external borrowing
- A commitment not to accumulate external payment
  arrears.
- State divestment out of electricity services and
  variety of measures to reorganize and strengthen the
  para-statal sector.

What this makes abundantly clear is that the conditionalit
of both the original SAF and its successor, the Enhance
SAF, is appreciably more rigorous than that associated wit
the original Trust Fund credits, the reflows from which pro
vided the original resources for the SAF. In this sense, it to
marks a clear further intensification of conditionality

In the context of the spread of conditionality, mentio
should also be made of developments in the Fund

:ompensatory financing facility (CFF). For most of its life he CFF offered quick-disbursing, non-conditional and nainly automatic access to financial support when countries net certain criteria for unexpected shortfalls in export :arnings. These qualities differentiated the facility from :tandbys and other upper-tranche credits but they have now)een largely eroded.[5] First the requirement for recipient :ountries to 'cooperate' with the Fund was redefined in a way which meant that by 1987 the CFF was being used :hiefly as a way of providing supplementary financing for tlready-negotiated standbys. As such, it mostly ceased to rave the quality of automaticity and was associated with .he full rigour of upper-tranche conditionality. Then in 1988 t was merged into a new 'external contingency mechanism' within the Fund 'to help the momentum of adjustment in .he face of a wider range of adverse external shocks'. Here tgain it is expected that all or most such credits will be in :upport of already existing high-conditionality programmes.

Taking all these developments together, it is apparent that .he 1980s have seen a veritable explosion of conditionality. [t is for this reason that the title of this chapter refers to obligatory' adjustment. Note, though, that 'obligatory' is lot synonymous with 'involuntary'. By no means all the neasures should be thought of as imposed by the creditor tgencies, for there is often genuine agreement between them tnd governments about the policy changes that ought to be tdopted.

Nevertheless, there is a new orthodoxy about the desirable :ontent of adjustment programmes which clearly emanates :rom certain creditor governments, as well as the Fund and Bank. A recent aspect of that orthodoxy, at least as far as)ublic pronouncements about the position of the main lebtor countries are concerned, is an emphasis on the need :or renewed economic growth in those countries, a position which originates from the speech in Seoul in 1985 unveiling :he 'Baker plan'. Against a background of severe recessions tmong Latin American debtors and significant payments and lebt problems in African countries, pressures had been)uilding up for a resumption of growth (or in the case)f the African region, a halt in the decline) for a variety of

reasons: to restore income levels and living standards; to
facilitate the very process of structural adjustment itself
to make that process politically sustainable; and to permi
the expansion of output and exports necessary to eventuall
bring debt burdens down to manageable proportions. Re
sumed growth and enlarged import capacity has also been
viewed by some as a means of creating incomes and employ
ment in the export industries of the OECD, particularly in
the USA. It also came to be realized that while the post-1982
responses to the 'debt crisis' had brought a breathing space
they had provided no lasting solution, with debt-servicing
ratios even higher in 1985 and 1986 than they had been in
1982.[6] There was an appreciation that the net outflow o
financial resources from debtor countries would have to be
reversed if there was indeed to be some resumption o
growth. And there was a growing concern about the con
tinuing economic deterioration in SSA.

The rapid spread of obligatory adjustment, and the
associated conditionality explosion articulated around a rather
clearly defined and generally applied new orthodoxy about
the measures necessary for successful adjustment, throw up
a number of issues about the design of adjustment, to which
we now turn.

THE DESIGN OF ADJUSTMENT WITH GROWTH

The new orthodoxy

'Sustainable growth with adjustment must . . . be the central
objective of our debt strategy' according to Secretary Baker
But what actually is meant by programmes of adjustment
with growth? Representatives of the USA have, in fact, been
quite willing to articulate their understanding of this, as have
the IMF and World Bank. Moreover, donors increasingly see
the effectiveness of aid as determined by the quality of the
policy environment within recipient countries and hence have
been increasing the extent to which their support is tied to
what they see as policy reforms. It may, therefore, be useful
to begin this section with a summary statement of how

adjustment with growth is viewed in these quarters.[7] This is encapsulated in an article published by the World Bank.[8]

> Four years after the onset of the world debt crisis, the issue is how to restore growth. The answer is structural adjustment, both macro and micro. At the macro level, adjustments have to be made to the structure of aggregate demand and supply to restore growth while generating the needed trade surpluses. This means primarily real exchange rates that are maintained at appropriate levels and an emphasis on investment. At the micro level, it is argued that most developing countries need to liberalize trade, allow the price system to operate, develop financial systems, reform taxes, and improve the efficiency of public enterprises, perhaps by selling them.

Within the US administration, adjustment with growth is seen as a package of measures which will:

- increase the role of the private sector;
- include supply-side measures to mobilize domestic savings;
- include 'market-related' measures to encourage foreign direct investment and liberalize trade.

Considerable emphasis is placed on the need for measures (including fiscal actions) that will raise domestic saving but there is stress too on the need to ensure that savings remain at home, i.e. on the avoidance, or reversal, of capital flight. Indeed, the direction of movement of flight capital is seen as a 'litmus test' of whether progress is being made and confidence is being restored.

The need is also articulated for structural reforms within developing countries to lay the foundations for stronger growth. These include, in a passage included in at least two main speeches:

> the privatization of public enterprises, the development of more efficient domestic capital and equity markets, growth-oriented tax reform, improvement of the environment for both domestic and foreign investment, trade liberalization and the rationalization of import regimes.

Mention is also made of the necessity to persist with stances
on fiscal and monetary policies similar to those associated
with the IMF. While the general stance is a pro-market one
it is recognized that there will remain areas where the state
is the chief supplier of services and in these cases the
emphasis is on improving cost-effectiveness.

Statements by the IMF cleave fairly closely to the American
position. For example, the April 1986 issue of *World
Economic Outlook* (p.102) advocates such measures as:

- the improved mobilization of domestic saving through
  higher interest rates and capital market development
- measures to discourage capital flight, such as improved
  interest rate, exchange rate, investment incentive and
  demand management policies;
- privatization or reform of public enterprises, including
  better pricing policies;
- the elimination of trade and exchange controls, and
  reduction of 'excessive' tariffs.

The Fund lays particular emphasis on fiscal and monetary
measures that are intended to lead to higher investment
levels, including relative reductions in government recurrent
expenditures.

There is also little that deviates from the above in the
recent publications of the World Bank. Comparing successive
issues of its *World Development Reports*, what stands out is
that those of the earlier 1980s were more system-neutral than
those of the mid-1980s, placing less emphasis on expanding
the role of the private sector, and that the stress was rather
on the shift of resources from non-tradeables to tradeables –
language that appears less often nowadays, although it seems
to be no less relevant. Perhaps the best evidence on Bank
attitudes to adjustment with growth, however, can be derived
from the policy content of its own structural adjustment
programmes. In addition to the stress on export-led growth
already recorded, these have commonly included such com-
ponents as:

- trade policy reforms;

- reductions in public sector deficits and mobilization of public revenues;
- mobilization of private saving;
- improving efficiency of revenue use through better public sector investment programmes;
- correction of price distortions affecting the productive system;
- the strengthening and development of key public institutions, such as public enterprises and ministries.

Some nuances are noticeable, however. The fourth and last items above, for example, are not prominent in US statements. Nor is the Bank's stress on the large differences between countries and the need to tailor programmes to country circumstances; and on the crucial role of supporting external finance.

A rather large number of questions can be raised about donor attitudes to the design of adjustment with growth. These are grouped below as questions about the conceptualization of the strategy; on its consistency with long-run development; and on other issues concerning the policy content of the strategy.

Conceptualizing the strategy

First, there should be concern about the loose way in which the word 'adjustment' is used. In some writings it appears to mean little more than the adoption of 'policy reforms' of which the agency or government in question happens to approve. More commonly, it is used to refer to any measure which will have a positive effect on the balance of payments current account. There is almost never any discussion of what it is that is to be adjusted nor what the adjustment is intended to be a response to. While there is some acceptance that adjustment differs from stabilization (in the traditional IMF sense of the word) and that it is narrower in meaning than economic development, these differences are rarely subjected to much scrutiny or articulation.[9] And where adjustment is used to refer to the need to reduce balance of payments imbalances it is almost always confined in its application to policies within deficit countries, as if it were possible to reduce deficits without corresponding reduction in counterpart surpluses.

It is not possible to go into this matter in any detail here This writer has done so elsewhere, reaching the following conclusions:[10]

- adjustment is a concept that is most appropriately applied to the international economy, including surplus countries, although it is nowadays largely applied to the national economies of deficit countries
- adjustment in a deficit country is the response of an economy to an unviable balance of payments defici and an attempt to reach some equilibrium;
- adjustment should be distinguished from the tem porary suppression of the symptoms of the problem
- it is a gradual process involving changes in the allo cation of resources among sectors, factors and categories of expenditure, as well as among key in stitutions;
- it can occur automatically, in response, for example, to monetary stringency or a depreciating currency, but will generally also require government intervention

It is perhaps worth drawing attention to a few of the point which emerge from this. One is that adjustment should be viewed as a symmetrical matter, involving surplus as well a deficit countries. Another is the rejection of the suppression of symptoms, e.g. through import compression, as adjust ment. A third — of particular importance in the context of adjustment with growth — is the insistence that adjustmen is a gradual process, taking a considerable time. This is a feature which the World Bank has learned through ex perience, with a recent review of its record with structura adjustment programmes referring to the Bank's chronic tendency to underestimate how long it will take to bring about significant changes.

Another long-standing issue which appears to have rather slipped out of current debates is the circumstances in which adjustment is, and is not, economically desirable. It was par f the attempt at Bretton Woods to safeguard against global leflation that countries were only expected in the IMF rubric o take corrective actions in the face of fundamental disquilibria. Implicit in this view was the assumption that on-fundamental disequilibria could be financed and that it vas not desirable to contract absorption or reallocate esources in the face of temporary imbalances. This position as now become eroded, if it has not been altogether abanloned. The stress now is on the need to introduce adjustment neasures whenever deficits cannot be financed — an ncreasingly common occurrence in the face of diminishing apital inflows and weakening terms of trade. The changes hat have been introduced to increase the policy conlitionality associated with the compensatory financing acility are both symptomatic of this shift in the intellectual :limate and a further aggravation of the problem.[11] Adjustnent has come to the short end of the market. The industrial :ountries need to be constantly reminded of the rationale f the Bretton Woods arrangements and of the deflationary ias implicit in their present-day policies. This relates not nly to policies towards the CFF but to issues such as the lesirability of a new allocation of SDRs and more generally o the question of resource flows to deficit countries.

The discussion above has concentrated on adjustment *per e*, but another question is what puts the 'growth' into djustment with growth? There seem to be three new :lements in the Baker approaches to adjustment favourable o more rapid growth. One is the greater stress, noticeable n the description of the 'new orthodoxy' above, on measures o raise domestic saving and investment. Another is the ;reater attention to measures addressed to the productive ystem. Third and above all, is the apparent prospect of a arger volume of supporting international capital. We will eturn to discuss various of these later but a number of ssues can be signalled here.

First, how are increments of foreign exchange to be used? As is well known, import volumes have been severely compressed, both in Latin America and Africa. Taking all leveloping countries together, the volume growth in imports n 1980–87 averaged under 1.2 per cent p.a., against 6.7 per

cent in 1970–79.[12] The imports of low-income Africa
countries actually declined at 2.5 per cent in 1980–87. Th
same period also saw large reductions by Latin America
countries. The relevance of this is the strong connection tha
exists between the ability to import and economic growth.[1]
The connection is strong because of developing countr
dependence on imports of investment and intermediat
goods. In some circumstances, even improved access t
imported consumables can have production-raising effect
by acting as incentive goods. The new emphasis on restorin
sustainable growth therefore implies a continuing access t
greater amounts of foreign exchange that can be used t
purchase imports. But in conditions of scarcity this us
of foreign exchange can compete with its employment t
service external debt. Thus, the question can be asked of th
creditor countries: are they willing, if necessary, to reduce
or at least postpone, debt service claims in order to permi
the imports necessary for adjustment with growth?

Another issue is thrown up by the stress on raising invest
ment levels. It has been the experience of both the IMF an
the World Bank — to say nothing of the governments i
question — that when the necessity arises to restrict goverr
ment spending it is far easier to cut capital expenditure
than the recurrent budget. In their 1980 review of the fisca
content of IMF programmes, for example, Beveridge an
Kelly drew attention to this feature, with government capita
spending below target in 49 per cent of the programme
studied but with its current spending in excess of target i
73 per cent of the cases.[14] They also reported that attempt
to protect capital expenditure by concentrating on cut
in current spending and increases in current surpluses wer
generally unsuccessful. An internal Fund evaluation of it
1977 programmes similarly drew attention to this problem
with its probable detrimental effect on growth, and aske
whether programmes should not safeguard against it b
setting minimum targets for budgetary savings on recurren
account. A recent World Bank review of structural adjust
ment loans found the same result. The Fund did, in fact
take up the suggestion in the review of its 1977 programm
but decided against further action. It would be consisten

with the thrust of adjustment with growth that both agencies, and other donors in comparable positions, should henceforth introduce such safeguards. But, however desirable this may be in principle, it raises difficult issues for developing country governments, for the resulting requirement to act more on the current budget would further raise the political sensitivity of adjustment programmes, because of possible job or income losses within the civil service, and reductions in welfare and other services. Nevertheless, it is an issue which will surely surface with greater frequency in the future.

Another set of questions relates to the differential ability of developing country economies to achieve adjustment. There are good reasons for expecting the capacity to adjust to be roughly correlated with the level of economic development. In a mixed economy this capacity will be governed by the efficacy of the market system, by the structure and technical characteristics of production, and by the quality of decision making and implementation in the organs of the state. The extent of industrialization, particularly the export of manufactures, is likely to be a crucial variable. So are the extent of the diversification of output and exports; the general standard of education; and the extent of access to external capital markets, to augment domestic saving. A large share of primary production in GDP and exports is probably a strongly negative influence. By and large, all these considerations suggest that the capacity to adjust is likely to be a rising function of the level of economic development.

One of the obstacles to the widespread resumption of growth in Third World countries, particularly in Sub-Saharan Africa, is that the agencies involved in the design of programmes of stabilization and adjustment appear to pay limited heed to differential abilities to adjust. Thus, the Fund does not interpret its principle of uniformity of treatment among members to mean uniformity relative to this ability. The position of the Bank is less clear. A further question that could be asked of these agencies and those who determine their policies, therefore, is whether they are willing to recognize that adjustment among low-income primary producing developing countries will be more difficult

than among more advanced developing countries, requiring
more time and therefore greater financial support.

Yet another question is who gets left out in present
approaches to adjustment with growth? This aspect concerns
the polarization that is implicit in present approaches to the
distribution of aid and other forms of financial support, with
almost exclusive attention being paid to Latin America (plus
a few other heavily indebted countries) and Africa. The
question arises, what of Asia — a region that encompasses
the most populous and some of the poorest countries in the
world — the Pacific and other developing countries which do
not belong to the favoured regions? It arises acutely in regard
to China and India — countries which take no advantage of
the IMF structural adjustment facility and which will experience real reductions in loans from IDA under the eighth
replenishment (the second successive cut in the case of
India). But it is also a question of considerable importance
for other countries such as Burma and Sri Lanka. The UN
Committee for Development Planning (April, 1986, p. 30)
commented aptly on pressures to induce the large Asian
countries to meet their capital needs from private sources

> To assume that the gap will be filled by private finance may be to
> entice these countries onto a path that has already proven dangerous
> to others that have preceded them. It is to ignore the potential costs
> of variable interest rates which assume that borrowers, rather than
> lenders, must bear the entire macroeconomic risk. It is to disregard
> the vulnerability of medium-term finance for development projects
> with a long-term pay-off period. And it is to forget the lesson of the
> unreliability of private capital supply.

While it is generally agreed that Africa stands in particularly
acute need of assistance and it is inevitable that much attention will continue to be paid to the positions of the main
debtors, the legitimate requirements of the rest of the Third
World must not be forgotten. This again raises the question
of the overall volume of resources going to developing
countries, as well as the maintenance of a reasonable balance
in its distribution.

Lastly, under the heading of conceptual problems, there is

he broad question of what 'policy-related lending' can realisically be expected to achieve. There is general agreement hat the success of a donor-assisted adjustment programme is ikely to hinge critically on the extent to which its policy :ontent is based on a genuine meeting of minds between the lonor agency and the executing government. The experiences of the IMF appear to bear this out: a study by the present author of IMF programmes reached the conclusion that conlitionality is unlikely to have much effect if it is perceived is having been imposed from the outside and if there is less :han wholehearted commitment to the programme.[15] A iimilar conclusion has been reached by the World Bank in he light of its experiences with structural adjustment loans ind it is paying increasing attention to the establishment of nechanisms in the negotiation of its programmes for securing :onsensus. While it is probably true that there exists today a wider degree of agreement on the desirable content of nacroeconomic policies than has been held in earlier periods, here are limits to this and the consensus tends to break lown when it comes to choice of development strategy and :ransition paths.[16] There is no single agreed model of levelopment policy, nor is it sensible to strive for one given he great variety of country circumstances and competing /alue systems.

There is also the problem of the second best: the absence of rigorous theoretical grounds upon which to make policy :ecommendations in the face of a large number of allo:ational inefficiencies.[17] With what confidence, for example, :an the Bank in its 1986 *World Development Report* urge upon developing countries a liberalization of production and :rade in agricultural goods in the face of continuing gross .evels of protection of agriculture in many industrial :ountries which will certainly not be abolished in the near future? The further question can be raised of how much economists — wherever they are based — know and with what legree of confidence they can offer advice that depends for .ts validity on an ability to forecast future world economic levelopments? For example, there was understandably much attention by donors in the later 1970s and early 1980s to :he promotion of energy-creating projects in oil-importing developing countries. One wonders how many of these have today been rendered economically unviable by the subsequent fall in world oil prices.

A further aspect of this set of doubts concerns the staffing of the main multilateral agencies and bilateral donors, both as to quantity, quality and orientation. While they contain many excellent professionals, the ability of these agencies to offer sound policy advice — to know better than national governments — is often severely constrained by this factor. The increasing shift to policy-related lending can only stretch more thinly resources that are already inadequate. This, as well as the limited capacity in all public administrations to simultaneously implement a wide range of policy changes, helps to explain why the World Bank believes that the main lesson it has learned from its SAL programme is that 'it is more important and more effective to design a program that addresses essential and feasible reforms than to seek overly broad coverage'.[18] In an earlier evaluation of its own experiences the IMF arrived at a similar conclusion.[19]

Notwithstanding all these doubts, however, current donor stances on policy reform can be characterized as both ambitious and self-confident.[20] More modesty and pragmatism would be appropriate in approaches to the design of adjustment with growth, and a greater willingness by donors (including the IMF) to experiment with alternative designs.

Related to this is the question: what is it reasonable to expect of domestic adjustment measures in the face of adverse changes in the external environment? This affects the desirable degree of flexibility in IMF and World Bank programmes in the face of unforeseen changes, and the extent to which additional financing should be made available in the face of such occurrences, rather than requiring further retrenchment with its deflationary consequences. The experiences of countries such as Mexico are pertinent here, countries which embarked upon a stringent and politically risky set of adjustment measures only to find them undone by unforeseeable 'external shocks'.

The questions raised in the last two paragraphs and by the greater uncertainty which has affected world trade and payments during the last 15 years provide *prima facie* reasons for developing countries to pursue risk-minimizing strategies. The issue raised is the extent to which the industrial countries recognize this, with the greater emphasis that would result on self-sufficiency measures, and whether they agree to such approaches being built into adjustment programmes.

Consistency with long-run development

The next set of concerns to be taken up relates to the consistency of 'adjustment' with long-run development. There are a number of aspects to this. These include the relationship of adjustment, as discussed above, to development; the implications for long-run economic growth of present approaches; the consistency of the pattern of structural change that is envisaged in adjustment programmes with longer-term models of structural change; and the implications of present approaches to adjustment for poverty alleviation and the quality of life. These will be discussed in that order.

The relationship between adjustment and the concerns of longer-term development has been well described by Please:[21]

> Adjustment programs can be differentiated from development programs in terms of their time horizon. Development programs embody measures — improved provision of infrastructure, technological change, education, health, population and so on — that are required to ease the basic constraints on growth and development and, therefore, have a long-term focus. Adjustment programs, on the other hand, embody measures which aim at achieving viability in the medium-term balance of payments while maintaining the level and rate of growth of economic activity at as high a rate as possible. Thus, adjustment programs take the basic constraints as given, and ask the question 'How, through changing policies and institutional arrangements in a country, can existing productive capacity be more efficiently used?'

One qualification of the above, presumably, is where the balance of payments itself constitutes the binding constraint on long-run growth, in which case successful adjustment

would be making a significant and lasting contribution to the
development of the country in question. This has always
been the argument of the IMF: that by helping to strengthen
the balance of payments it is helping to build the foundations
for sustainable development. This is a highly pertinent consideration for the large number of developing countries which
have experienced chronic shortages of foreign exchange,
shortages which appear likely to retard development well
into the future.

Another question which arises from this discussion is
whether there is not a danger, with all the present-day
emphasis on adjustment, that the longer-term concerns
and constraints mentioned by Please will be lost sight of,
or at least be downgraded. The risk here is one of attention
bias, that preoccupation with adjustment will divert policy
makers (and resources) away from needed improvements in
the basic infrastructure or in the provision of educational and
other human development services. A particular source of
concern is for the future of support for social projects and
programmes, which have received a substantial share of
World Bank loans in the past.[22] With reduced donor priority
for such programmes, as revealed in the summary statement
of the new orthodoxy above, there is a real danger of a
damaging reduction in governments' abilities to sustain social
programmes. One possible remedy would be to secure agreement that adjustment programmes should always be set in
the context, and contribute to the goals, of a longer-term
plan for economic and social development.

This brings us to the implications of present approaches
for long-run growth. One of the features of present-day
thinking about policy choices in developing countries is
that it marks a return to the primary concern with maximizing economic growth which marked the 1950s and much
of the 1960s. We have already noted that there are elements
in the design of adjustment with growth which are indeed
conducive to growth, particularly the emphasis on measures
to raise domestic investment, the prospect of additional
capital inflows from the rest of the world and the attention
to supply-side measures. In this respect it does appear to
offer a more encouraging framework than one which

emphasizes the reduction of domestic absorption. Consistent with this, the World Bank claims that in countries which have undertaken structural adjustment programmes, growth has been significantly raised, roughly in proportion to the degree to which the programmes have been implemented, citing Turkey, Thailand and the Ivory Coast as cases in point.

Against this, the awkward question has already been raised of whether under present conditions increments to foreign exchange would be available to purchase imports needed for accelerated growth or whether they would have to be devoted to servicing debt. Looking at the absorption side of the equation, the same question could be asked about increments to domestic saving and whether they would be available for financing higher levels of capital formation.

This issue relates to the volume of capital inflow that can be expected, a question to be taken up later. However, there is evidence that present plans are based on rather modest growth targets. The clearest example relates to Africa. The latest World Bank report on Africa[23] undertakes estimates of the foreign exchange requirements of the poorer (i.e IDA-eligible) African countries and in doing so is clearly at pains to guard against possible criticisms that they have overstated the case. They therefore define the objective underlying their estimates as 'to halt the trend of decline in per capita consumption by 1990 and to achieve some growth thereafter'. This implies achieving a GDP growth rate of 3–4 per cent by 1990.

By any standards, the goal just described is modest, with per capita consumption in 1990 well below the levels achieved in the 1960s. The resulting estimates of capital requirements are consequently kept to a minimum. Nevertheless, even these modest requirements are unlikely to be satisfied under present donor policies, with the inference that GDP growth will be even slower and that per capita consumption standards must be expected to continue to fall beyond 1990.

It is not possible to be so categorical about targets for the Latin American countries, not the least because of the large changes in country requirements resulting from the 1986 falls in oil prices. In its 1987 *World Development Report*[24] the World Bank produces high and low growth scenarios for 1986–95, giving per capita GDP growth rates for middle-income oil importing countries of 3.2 and 1.4 per cent respectively, and of 1.9 and 1.1 per cent for middle-income oil exporters. (The forecasts for low-income Africa are 0.7 and 0.0 per cent!)

Space does not permit detailed analysis of the assumptions upon which these forecasts are based; suffice it to say here that in the past the actuality for capital inflows and for other variables has more nearly approximated the Bank's low case than its high. Even here, therefore, there are grounds for questioning whether present approaches are consistent with satisfactory long-run rates of expansion.

Those who have studied the long-run histories of the now well advanced economies agree that an accelerated rate of structural change is one of the key features of modern economic development.[25] In facilitating change, structural adjustment can, in this sense, be described as conducive to long-run development. But is the type of change now being urged by the donors of the kind that is conducive to the structural shifts that have occurred in earlier cases of development? A number of doubts may be expressed here. One concerns the role of industrialization in present approaches, for a long-run rise in the share of manufacturing in GDP is one of the most firmly established historical patterns, together with an even more steeply declining share of primary production. In the Latin American case there may be no particular problems in this area. Indeed, in urging the merits of export-led industrialization − whatever other problems may be associated with it − modern approaches to structural adjustment are fully consistent with what appear to be the lessons of history.[26]

There are, however, doubts about the tendency for the World Bank and some bilateral donors to emphasize export promotion in the design of adjustment programmes. Given expectations about world market conditions and present levels of protection, the obvious question is whether the aggregate effect of single-country export expansions will not result in self-defeating price declines or run up against quota barriers. That this is a real problem is illustrated by an unpublished World Bank study of experiences with structural adjustment loans. All those studied were designed to achieve export-led growth. In all except two cases there were resulting increases in export volumes but only two of the countries were able substantially to raise their export earnings because of declining world prices. As a result, there may have been some retreat by the Bank from emphasis on export promotion but we may ask whether this has gone far enough and extended to enough donors.

In the African case the position of the donors on indus- trialization is less clear. For well-known reasons, much attention has instead been paid to improving the performance of the agricultural sector, both in foodstuffs and export com- modities. None of the series of World Bank reports on Sub-Saharan Africa contains any substantial discussion of industrialization policy and, although the first of them does mention the limitations of an agriculture-based strategy,[27] there is little donor activity in the promotion of industriali- zation in Africa and little discussion of its desirability.[28] Exclusive emphasis on agriculture does not, however, offer a promising long-term approach to development in Africa. Agricultural development itself, as well as the need to diversify away from primary product exports and increase the capacities of African economies to adjust, requires the complementary development of manufacturing, although one which is more soundly based on efficiency considerations than much of the industrialization of earlier years.

Another area of concern under this heading relates to the role of productivity-raising changes in the process of growth and development. As is well known, investigations of the sources of long-term economic growth have found such factors as improved education, training, health and communications as very important determinants, along with technological progress.[29] Our concern here is one that has already been raised above: that the shorter time horizons of the present day will result in a neglect of policies relating to such productivity-raising factors. Indeed, the present pressures to shift resources from the public to the private sector and to cut back on govern- ment spending may well threaten the maintenance of precisely those services which are of such long-term benefit.

One of the outcomes of the upsurge in interest in questions of income distribution in the late 1960s and much of the 1970s was to dispense, it was hoped for ever, with the mistake of equating economic growth with development and of neglecting the ways in which the benefits of growth were distributed within society. Nevertheless, it was the resumption of growth that dominated discussion after the launch of the 'Baker plan' in 1985. For a time the idea of 'adjustment with equity' seemed largely off the agenda, which was all the more troubling because there is both some *a priori* expectation that adjustment may have adverse distributional consequences and evidence that it has done so in some cases.

A shift in the functional distribution of income towards the owners of capital is a likely consequence of measures to improve incentives to save and invest, and falls in urban real wages have been widespread in Latin America and other adjusting economies. Moreover, as already mentioned, budgetary pressures make it more difficult to maintain programmes for the delivery of basic needs and social services.[30] One of the difficulties here is that measures to reduce income inequalities and/or protect the position of the poor require a conscious political decision on the part of governments but that the necessary political will may be undermined by the frequent unpopularity of adjustment programmes, where the temptation will often be to try to safeguard the programme by offering concessions to urban populations while the bulk of the poorest live in the countryside.

The danger of a neglect of such concerns underlay a campaign by UNICEF to ensure that the interests of the poor were safeguarded in the design of adjustment programmes.[31] They argued that there is no fundamental incompatibility between adjustment and the protection of the poor and this conclusion was supported by work at the Overseas Development Institute and in the World Bank.[32] Depending on the structures of production and asset ownership in a country, adjustment strategies which, for example, include better producer prices for farmers or the development of labour-intensive manufactured exports can be highly supportive of such protection.[33] Similarly, social sector programmes targeted on poor groups can generate large productivity gains by raising the rate of return on human capital.[34] By raising the output of tradeable goods, such productivity gains can also contribute to balance of payments adjustment. In rural economies where poor smallholder farmers operate at low levels of technology, raising the productivity of their land and capital will both increase their contribution to adjustment with growth and raise their welfare.

Moreover, the need in adjustment to re-evaluate government spending and other programmes can provide an opportunity to refine these so that they more effectively reach the poor groups for which they are intended. Greater selectivity of this kind is, in fact, crucial to the adequate retention of equity concerns in adjustment programmes. Through its structural adjustment programmes the World Bank has already supported specific actions along such lines, for example in Brazil, Chile, Indonesia, Jamaica and Thailand.

'Adjustment with growth and equity' would require measures that:

- enhance the access of the poor to productive assets;
- increase the rates of return to assets held by the poor;
- improve access of the poor to productive employment;
- increase the rate of human capital formation among the poor through education and health services;
- compensate poverty groups for adverse changes in living standards, e.g. because of reduced subsidies, by selective income and consumption transfers.

In large part the design and implementation of such programmes are matters for developing country governments. Not all of them are much interested in such measures but the scope for action among those that would wish to act is also limited by the international environment. The less time they have to achieve adjustment the harder it will be for them to protect the poor in their programmes and that, in turn, will be highly sensitive to the amount of supporting

finance they can expect from abroad. Under its President
Barber Conable the World Bank has demonstrated a con
tinuing concern with the effects of its programmes on the
poor and even the IMF has begun to be somewhat more
responsive on this subject,[35] but the prevailing climate of
opinion among their main shareholders is not always sup
portive of approaches which give priority to protecting the
poor.

Much the same type of argument can be made about the
increased concern in recent years with the problem of environ
ment degradation — in developing as well as developed
countries — and the importance of building ecological safe
guards into government policies. Although this writer is not
aware of any study of this matter, it can probably also be
said in this connection that there is no necessary incom
patibility between adjustment with growth and ecological
protection — but that most discussions of adjustment have
paid scant regard to this set of concerns, that the need to
adjust quickly has made the environmental task more difficult
and that governments' ability to act in this area is not in
dependent of the amount of outside support they can expect

To a considerable extent the issues raised in the last few
paragraphs are matters for consideration and action by
developing country governments. But there is also an issue
for the donor countries and international agencies: do they
recognize the distributional and ecological concerns as central
ones and would they support the inclusion of poverty
alleviation and environmental protection measures in
adjustment-with-growth programmes — even though these
might slow down the adjustment somewhat and/or require
more financial support? At least in principle, the World Bank
has responded to these questions, although it is unclear how
much influence its concerns at the most senior levels has had
on actual programme designs, and the position of other
agencies and donors is even less clear.

Other issues in the policy design
of adjustment with growth

The design of adjustment with growth leaves us with a

number of additional issues to discuss. Those to be treated below relate respectively to the relative roles of the private and public sectors; and measures to raise saving and investment, and the related issue of capital flight.

As regards the first of these topics, the context is one where spokesmen of the USA, other donor governments and, to a lesser extent, the IMF and World Bank emphasize almost exclusively the benefits of increasing the relative influence of private enterprise and have little that is positive to say about the role of the state in the economy. There is no doubt that many mistakes were made in expanding the relative role of the state in the past, that planning has often been ineffectual, that many public enterprises are a drag on development and that government pricing policies have often created a gravely distorted set of relativities and incentives. In that sense, the present intellectual mood can be a useful corrective.

However, this reaction is in danger of going too far and of obscuring what is surely the case, that development is best promoted by a judicious and mutually reinforcing blend of public and private sector activities. It is often overlooked that the period from the 1950s through much of the 1970s was, historically speaking, one of remarkable progress, yet it was also the period of the most rapid relative expansion of the state.[36] It has, moreover, never been shown convincingly that the big adjustment problems of the 1980s were directly related to the expanding role of the state, even though policy mistakes did undoubtedly aggravate the difficulties. It can also be argued that proponents of the pro-private enterprise thrust have been unable to provide convincing reasons for believing that their path would not replicate the socially unacceptable inequalities in income, wealth and opportunity that were one of the reasons for the expansion of the state in the first place.

Certain Asian countries, chiefly Hong Kong, Singapore, South Korea and Taiwan, have been widely cited as exemplars of the pro-market approach but this overlooks that the state was, in fact, a very active agent in all except perhaps Hong Kong. As Bradford has pointed out, in these countries 'government intervention has played a decisive role in export promotion. Credit allocations and interest rate subsidies in Korea, fiscal subsidies in Taiwan and tax and regulatory incentives . . . in Singapore have been integral parts of development policy'.[37] Bhagwati[38] is another who cites the important role of the state in Korean export performance, and in Japan as well, but stresses the importance of the 'key assurance that governments will not behave erratically'.

In such areas as agriculture it is difficult to believe that in the circumstances of most developing countries the development of that sector could proceed at a satisfactory pace without the active participation of the state and there are good reasons for believing so even within the terms of neo-classical price theory.[39] In some countries land reform is an essential prerequisite both for poverty alleviation and agricultural progress but this form of intervention fits uneasily with the present climate of opinion among donors. So too does the suggestion that in some countries the best way of achieving the higher levels of domestic saving and investment desired for adjustment with growth is by way of higher tax ratios. The 'tax burden' varies greatly across crountries. In many, tax evasion could be greatly reduced, and in some tax rates could be raised or new taxes levied without counter-productive effects on incentives, but suggestions along these lines nowadays appear to receive a scant hearing.[40]

A related point can be made about the present-day emphasis on 'getting prices right'. Controversies about the efficacy of price measures centre on such issues as the speed and magnitude of likely responses to altered price signals, the mobility of resources, and the efficiency and costs of information flows. But well-chosen government actions – say in improving the transportation network or in the provision of extension services – can themselves much increase the efficacy of price incentives, which incentives may themselves be ineffectual without such supporting action. Finally – and this is a point which perhaps has particular relevance to Africa – it should not merely be assumed that private businesses will necessarily step in to fill entrepreneurial gaps left by any withdrawal of the state.[41] It was often because the gaps were there in the first place that the state moved in.

The thrust of the above remarks is not to reassert the

superiority of a dirigiste model but rather to urge the desirability of a more balanced and pragmatic approach to the respective roles of the public and private sectors, of prices and non-market interventions. The key, it is suggested, is not to see these as in ineluctable opposition to each other but rather as partners, each with their own important contributions to make. This was the conclusion reached in Bradford's study of the four countries already cited, that the key characteristic of these economies was the highly interactive relationship which existed between government and the private sector, so that to see a dichotomy between the two 'misconceives the fundamental dynamic at work'.

The second set of issues to be raised here concerns saving, investment and capital flight. The points to be made can be put briefly. That there is a general need for actions to raise domestic saving and investment is without question. Recent years have seen serious declines in both variables, particularly grave in Sub-Saharan Africa. The only point of concern in the design of adjustment programmes is that too exclusive an emphasis may be placed on measures to raise saving and investment ratios, for the present stress on these aggregates reminds the present writer of a similar emphasis in models of economic growth in the 1960s.

There are two observations worth making. The first is the at least equal importance of the quality, or productivity, of the investment that takes place. This is demonstrated by the considerable number of countries which have failed to achieve satisfactory growth even though they have maintained high investment levels, and of others which have managed to achieve growth on the basis of rather small volumes of investment.[42]

The second observation is that in many countries, both in Africa and Latin America, raising the utilization of existing capital is at least as important — and probably promises quicker, more certain results — as creating new capital. The World Bank, for example, has urged for Africa that public expenditure programmes should give priority to measures to rehabilitate and maintain existing infrastructure, rather than the creation of new facilities.[43] This has quite important implications for short-term import management policies in adjustment with growth programmes, emphasizing the value of intermediate goods and items for maintenance and re-habilitation over imports of new capital equipment and the like. In the longer term, however, the balance would have to shift to new investment with high economic rates of return.

This brings us to the question of capital flight. As was mentioned earlier, measures to stem or reverse capital flight have been given much importance by the USA and others as a 'litmus test' of whether progress is being made towards adjustment.[44] Although this is an obviously difficult variable to measure and there is at present a tendency to treat all investments in foreign assets as capital flight, there seems no doubt that capital flight did assume large proportions in a number of developing countries, partly, or in a few cases wholly, cancelling out the benefits from capital inflows.[45] There is also some attraction to the idea of using this as an indicator of progress towards adjustment, because of its sensitivity to changes in domestic confidence in the future of the economy.

Its value for this purpose should not be overstated, however. Capital flight is particularly sensitive to the appro-priateness of exchange rate policies and, to a lesser extent, to the level and variability of inflation, domestic interest rates and industrial protection policies.[46] Progress in these areas can hence only be a very partial indicator of success, for adjustment with growth is likely to require policy action on a considerably wider front. It may also be subject to lengthy time lags. Moreover, capital flight, and the expec-tations which underlie it, are not exclusively determined by domestic policy actions. They are also influenced by the state of world demand for a country's exports, and its access to external markets, the perceived adequacy of international capital which becomes available in support of the adjustment process, and changes in world interest rates. To the extent that these determinants are unfavourable, capital flight will be as much an indicator of international as of national failure.[47]

INSTITUTIONAL ISSUES

We turn next to discuss a number of unsettled questions relating to adjustment with growth which can be grouped under the heading of 'institutional' issues. These include the roles and resources of the IMF and World Bank; the design of IMF programmes; and the coordination of G10 support for adjustment with growth.

Roles and resources of IMF and World Bank

The issues to be taken up under this heading can be stated briefly. The first relates to the contributions that these two agencies can make to a shift towards adjustment with growth. While emphasis has been placed by creditor governments on the importance of additional financial support, there was actually a substantial net return flow to the IMF from developing countries in 1986 and 1987.[48] Including its IDA soft aid window, the World Bank has at least been able to continue positive net flows, albeit on a reduced scale. There was a net flow from it to developing countries of $2.6 billion in 1987, compared with an annual average of $4.3 billion in the previous four years.

In the case of both institutions, these results are at least partly the consequence of a long-term denial by the main shareholder countries of the resources that would be necessary to maintain the abilities of both institutions to carry out their responsibilities successfully. In consequence, the value of the quotas of the Fund has diminished greatly relative to world trade; and there is continuing uncertainty about a general capital increase for the Bank.

The outcome of negotiations for the eighth replenishment of IDA meant that the real value of new IDA lending was far below that achieved in the IDA5 period. IDA8 also incorporated some toughening in lending terms; it necessitates another large real reduction in lending to India; and a cut in lending to China as well. By any objective standards, the scale of IDA8 will be entirely inadequate relative to the needs of the countries it serves. The size of the original structural adjustment facility was also small in relation to

estimates of need. The reconstitution in 1988 of the SAF on
a greatly enlarged scale, on the other hand, was a welcome
recognition of the special needs of the poorest countries but
the resources of the Bretton Woods institutions are still small
enough to pose the question, how can donor policies with
respect to these agencies be consistent with a move to adjustment with growth?

The criticisms of developing countries and others of IMF
conditionality are too well known to need elaboration here:
that it depends too much on demand repression, thus tending
to have a deflationary effect and to neglect the supply side
of the economy; that it is too short term; that it applies a
too uniform package to a wide range of differing country
circumstances; that it is linked too mechanistically and
rigidly to quantified performance criteria whose values are
hard to predict and control; and so on. Suffice it to note
here that, although of long standing, these criticisms persist
and the Fund is not perceived as having responded
adequately to them, although we have noted earlier that its
programmes now include more supply-side provisions than
was formerly the case. What should also be noted, however,
is that certain of these criticisms, particularly that regarding
the deflationary bias of the Fund, were in the mid-1980s
given greater weight by public complaints along these lines
by its largest shareholder, with US Secretary of the Treasury
James Baker urging that Fund programmes should become
more 'growth-oriented'. Senior officials within the World
Bank have been similarly critical of what they see as the
Fund's failure to provide deficit countries with realistic
prospects of resumed growth at the end of the stabilization
period.

In the face of such complaints, however, the Fund has
shown a limited willingness to undertake an adjustment of
its own. Notwithstanding American support for the criticism
that it has a deflationary bias, for example, it has not given
the concept of 'growth orientation' any operational meaning
in its programmes. It has remained essentially business as
before and growth has not been accepted by the Fund as a
constraint upon the design of its balance of payments programmes. A review of Fund conditionality that was due for

completion in 1988 appears unlikely to differ from earlier examples in proposing only minor, incremental changes.

A further question that could be raised in connection with growth-oriented programmes concerns the role of demand management. If more emphasis were to be placed on measures to raise productivity and output these could be frustrated by inadequate domestic demand if too restrictive a view were to be taken of demand management. It could similarly be asked whether the Fund would be willing to take a less negative view of the role of domestic credit in its programmes. Within the monetarist framework this is viewed negatively, as tending to weaken the balance of payments and increase aggregate demand, but it can also be viewed as contributing to capacity utilization and capital formation, and the possibility of structural adjustment.[49] In addition, we have already raised the question of whether the Fund would be willing to institute safeguards against too much of the burden of restraints on government spending falling on capital expenditures.

But while it is true that the Fund's management and staff have in the past revealed little eagerness for any radical redesign of Fund conditionality, there has seemed a greater willingness since Michel Camdessus became Managing Director in 1987. The essential problem is on the councils of that institution. Were the Interim Committee and the Executive Board to agree on the desirability of such a redesign the staff would be obliged to implement that decision, but there is no political will on these committees to initiate such a change. For example, the Fund did display flexibility in its November 1986 standby agreement with Mexico. This contained a number of innovative provisions intended both to make the programme more flexible and to safeguard against low growth. There was much speculation at the time about whether these innovations might be treated as setting precedents for future standbys but it was not allowed to do so and the special features of the Mexican programme have remained just that. Similarly, the main shareholders have scaled down the enlarged access policy of the Fund, apparently to reduce the Fund's exposure in African countries, which had been among the principal beneficiaries of the earlier relaxation of access policies.

A shift in favour of a growth orientation in its programmes would pose the Fund some awkward questions. But it would pose questions also to the countries who supply most of its resources, which can be summed up in the question, how would it be possible to build more growth into these programmes unless the Fund was provided with more resources so that it could support programmes over the longer time span necessary for growth-oriented programmes? The freedom of action of the Fund management in achieving such a reorientation is slight in the face of its present limited resources. Shifting more to policies directed at the real economy would mean shifting to slower-acting measures than the customary compression of demand and imports. That means it would take longer before payments viability could be restored and the need, therefore, for more financial support over a longer period. Since they are apparently willing a modified set of ends will the creditor countries also consent to will the means?

Coordination of creditor country responses

Secretary Baker's proposals envisaged a package of financing from various sources in support of adjustment programmes. But such a package could not come about spontaneously. There is need not only for leadership and commitment but also for some institutional means by which the decisions of the various actors among the creditors can be coordinated and made consistent. It is implicit in the US proposals that such a machinery already exists or will be forged but so far that condition has not been satisfied. Indeed, the actions of the aid agencies, Paris Club negotiators, bank supervising authorities, export credit agencies, the IMF Executive Board and others sometimes seem at variance with each other. We can here do no better than to cite a Vice President of the World Bank on this problem:

The Consultative Groups discuss the economic situation of the debtor country in a comprehensive manner and consider medium-term scenarios, with an operational focus on the balance of payments for the next year or two. Representatives of the donor and creditor governments generally come from aid ministries and decisions by the Consultative Groups are more or less confined to official concessional assistance. Export credit agencies and private banks meanwhile make their own independent decisions on new loans. Action on debt restructuring is taken by the Paris Club for official debt and by the London Club for private debt. Responsibility is consequently very fragmented and diffused, and the cumbersome and uncertain nature of the process imposes additional costs on debtors. It is therefore imperative to improve existing organisations, strengthen the international machinery and generally become more business-like in tackling the debt problem. In particular, it is essential to have an authoritative donor–creditor forum for decision making. To this forum must come representatives of donor and creditor governments that have the authority, after taking account of actions by private donors and creditors, to contribute sufficient resources on appropriate terms in support of debtor governments engaged in serious reform. This role must be enacted with clarity and coherence at the authoritative forum proposed here.[50]

CONCLUDING OBSERVATIONS

No attempt will be made here to summarize the foregoing. Instead, it may be useful to conclude with a few observations which have so far been implicit rather than explicit in the text.

First, we should consider for a moment the position of countries which, by choice or force of circumstances, have not joined those undertaking adjustment programmes supported by the Fund or Bank (although they may be pursuing their own adjustment programmes). Confining ourselves to Africa, by way of illustration, on the basis of Bank 1986 classifications, the 'non-compliers' included:

Angola	Benin	Botswana
Burkina Faso	Cameroon	Ethiopia
Lesotho	Liberia	Mozambique
Sudan	Uganda	Zimbabwe

Between them, these countries contain a third of the total SSA population. This is obviously not an homogeneous grouping. Some (e.g. Botswana, Cameroon) were there because they had no need for that type of support. In others (e.g. Angola, Liberia, Mozambique, Sudan, Uganda the political situation was either too chaotic for meaningful adjustment programmes to be feasible (in some cases because of destabilization from South Africa) or the government was still working out its economic policies. In yet others (e.g. Ethiopia, Benin, perhaps Zimbabwe) there was an ideological resistance to the policies of the new orthodoxy.

Most of them, however, are at risk. The risk is threefold In some, at least, there is a failure to tackle effectively grave economic problems, with all the high costs which are usually attendant on any persistent neglect of the need for adjustment. There is a risk, second, that these countries will suffer particularly from inadequate export earnings. It is not merely that some of them are pursuing policies which may discourage export production — part of the neglect of adjustment already mentioned — but also that they stand to be squeezed by the downward pressures on world prices that may result from attempts by the 'complying' countries which are attempting through conventional adjustment measures to expand their own export volumes. The third risk is that the 'non-compliers' will receive diminishing proportions of such limited external assistance as is available with more and more of this being allocated in support of the compliers.

What advice might be offered to such countries? Most obviously, they should by all means not neglect their adjustment needs. And notwithstanding the questions raised earlier about the conventional design of adjustment, if at all possible they should adjust in ways that are likely to command external approval: 'if you can't beat 'em, join 'em'. But this group of countries offers some lessons for the donor community as well. One is for them to be more responsive to the political sensitivities created by what we earlier called the 'conditionality explosion', and to be pragmatic (as distinct from ideological) and experimental in deciding whether or not to support a given programme. A second

esson is not to overlook the humanitarian claims of those
iapless countries whose political institutions have deteriorated
o such a degree that they cannot design or implement
meaningful programmes, or are still in the process of trying
o do so.

A second observation which can be derived from the fore-
oing is that there is a considerable danger that too many
xpectations are being built upon a design of adjustment
vhich may fail to deliver the goods. This is partly to return
o the point that our knowledge of the linkages and dynamics
s very limited and that there is as yet no firm theoretical
inderpinning for the programmes of the new orthodoxy.
Sut it is also to return to the sheer force of the negative
xternal influences to which LDCs have been subjected in the
ast. Many Fund and Bank programmes have broken down
ecause of large 'exogenous shocks' and the world environ-
nent continues to be unfavourable. The policy instruments
hat are deployed in any programme have a certain finite
ower to influence target variables. In many cases, the power
f the instruments available to the government is severely
mited and it is more than likely that they will fail in the
resence of adverse exogenous shocks. It seems to this writer
hat a rather uncritical faith may be being placed in the
istruments of adjustment and that, if the programmes fail,
his may spark a severe, but unjustified, reaction against
irther support for the countries in question.

Finally, mention should be made of the dangers inherent
i recent preoccupation with the problems of developing
ountries with large debt-servicing problems. In many cases
iese problems are, of course, severe. But there are other
.DCs, also with very large economic problems, which, by
ood management or good luck, have avoided running into
irge debt difficulties. It would be particularly unfortunate
′ their need for international support were pushed aside by
ie large financing requirements of a small number of heavily
idebted but actually rather advanced 'developing' countries.
'o some extent, this repeats the earlier plea that the position
f still very poor Asian countries should not be overlooked.
ut even within Africa and Latin America there are a good
iany countries whose external debts are not especially large

but which need to adjust to a world economic environmen
turned more hostile and require international capital i
support of their efforts.

NOTES AND REFERENCES

1. Mosley, Paul, 'Conditionality as bargaining process: a study c
    World Bank structural adjustment lending, 1980–86', Universit
    of Manchester, October 1986 (mimeo.).
2. See Killick, Tony (ed.), *The Quest for Economic Stabilisation
    the IMF and the Third World*, London, Overseas Developmer
    Institute and Gower, 1984, p. 212.
3. Bhatia, Rattan J., 'Adjustment efforts in sub-Saharan Africa, 1980
    84', *Finance and Development*, vol. 22, no. 3, September 198!
4. See Commonwealth Secretariat, *Co-operation Without Cros.
    Conditionality: an Issue in International Lending*, Londo
    Commonwealth Secretariat, Economic Affairs Division, Septembe
    1986 for a valuable discussion of this topic.
5. Dell, Sidney, 'The fifth credit tranche', *World Developmen
    vol. 13, no. 2, February 1985.
6. World Bank, *World Debt Tables, 1988*, Washington, 1988, vol.
    p. 5.
7. The sources used in the following summary include:
    — For the US: speeches by Secretary Baker on 9 October 198
      and 10 April 1986; speech by Assistant Secretary Mulfor
      4 February 1986; speech by Federal Reserve Chairman, Pa
      Volcker, 9 May 1986; cable to USAID Missions by Secretar
      of State Schultz, February 1985.
    — For IMF: interview of Deputy Managing Director Erb in *Finan
      and Development*, March 1986, *World Economic Outlook*, Apr
      1986.
    — For World Bank: various issues of *World Development R
      port*; the four successive Bank reports on Sub-Saharan Afric
      various supplementary sources.
    — For the United Kingdom: article by J. Roberts in the Overse
      Development Administration's *British Overseas Aid in 198.
      London, Summer 1986.
8. Fischer, Stanley, 'Issues in medium-term macroeconomics adjus
    ment', *World Bank Research Observer*, vol. 1, no. 2, July 198
9. For an exception, by a former senior officer of the World Ban
    see Please, Stanley, *The Hobbled Giant: Essays on the Wor
    Bank*, Boulder and London, Westview, 1984, chaps 3 and

10. The following discussion is based on this author's essay in Posner, Michael (ed.), *Problems of International Money, 1972–85*, Washington and London, International Monetary Fund and Overseas Development Institute, 1986.

11. This matter is discussed in Dell (note 5).

12. International Monetary Fund, *World Economic Outlook*, Washington, April 1986 and April 1988, Table A25.

13. See Helleiner, Gerald K., 'Outward orientation, import instability and economic growth: an empirical investigation', in Lall, Sanjaya and Stewart, Frances (eds), *Theory and Reality in Development*, London, Macmillan, 1986; and UNCTAD, *Trade and Development Report 1985*, New York, United Nations, 1985 for evidence on the existence and strength of this correlation.

14. Beveridge, W.A. and Kelly, Margaret R., 'Fiscal content of financial programs supported by stand-by arrangements in the upper-credit tranches, 1969–78', *IMF Staff Papers*, vol. 27, no. 2, June 1980.

15. Killick, Tony (ed.), *The Quest for Economic Stabilisation: the IMF and the Third World*, London, Overseas Development Institute and Gower Publishing Co., 1984, p. 262.

16. Helleiner argues this in respect of Africa. See Helleiner, Gerald K., 'The question of conditionality', in Lancaster, Carol and Williamson, John (eds), *African Debt and Financing*, Washington, Institute for International Economics, May 1986. See also Bacha, Edmar L. and Feinberg, Richard E., 'The World Bank and structural adjustment in Latin America', *World Development*, vol. 14, no. 3, March 1986.

17. The classical statement of the problem of the second best is in Lipsey, R.G. and Lancaster, Kelvin, 'The general theory of the second best', *Review of Economic Studies*, no. 1, 1957.

18. World Bank, *Annual Report 1986*, Washington, 1986, p. 54.

19. For example, see Beveridge and Kelly (note 14), p. 241.

20. See John P. Lewis's characterization along these lines in Lewis, John P. and Kallab, Valeriana (eds), *Development Strategies Reconsidered*, Washington, Overseas Development Council, 1986.

21. See Please (note 9), p. 18.

22. Bacha and Feinberg (note 16), Table 5, record that in 1980–84 15.7 per cent of total World Bank lending to Western Hemisphere LDCs was for social projects.

23. World Bank, *Financing Adjustment with Growth in Sub-Saharan Africa, 1986–90*, Washington, 1986, chap. 4.

24. World Bank, *World Development Report 1987*, Washington, 1987, Table 2.6.

25. The following discussion refers particularly to findings in

Kuznets, Simon, *Modern Economic Growth: Rate, Structure and Spread*, New Haven, Yale University Press, 1966; and Chenery, Hollis, *Structural Change and Development Policy* New York, Oxford University Press, 1979.

26. Chenery (note 25) finds the expansion of manufactured export a particularly important aspect of historical patterns of development.

27. The World Bank, *Towards Sustained Development in Sub-Saharan Africa*, Washington, 1984, p. 6, argues that its policy recommendations are 'an essential beginning to a process of long-term transformation, a prelude to industrialisation' and accepts that an agriculture-based strategy 'is not a permanent course for any country'.

28. In response to this recent neglect Roger Riddell and associates of the Overseas Development Institute have commenced a research project on industrialization strategies for Africa.

29. See Maddison, Angus, 'Growth and slowdown in advanced capitalist economies', *Journal of Economic Literature*, XXXV(2) June 1987 for a useful recent survey of this literature.

30. For evidence on these matters see Cornia, Giovanni; Jolly Richard; and Stewart, Frances (eds), *Adjustment with a Human Face*, Oxford University Press, 1987; and Inter-American Development Bank, *Economic and Social Progress in Latin America: External Debt — Crisis and Adjustment*, Washington 1985.

31. Cornia et al. (note 30).

32. The discussion in these paragraphs borrows heavily from the results of research conducted at ODI by Demery, Lionel and Addison, Tony, *The Alleviation of Poverty under Structural Adjustment*, Washington, World Bank, 1987. See also Cornia et al. (note 30).

33. See Adelman, Irma, 'A poverty-focused approach to development policy', in Lewis and Kallab (note 20), who argues this conclusion.

34. Thus, in Indonesia a project to provide iron supplements to anaemic workers achieved productivity increases of 15–25 per cent within two months, worth $260 for each $1 spent in supplying the supplements (Basta, S.S. and Churchill, A., 'Iron deficiency anaemia and the productivity of adult males in Indonesia', World Bank, *Staff Working Paper No. 175*, April 1974).

35. See, for example, Heller, Peter S.; Bovenberg, A. Lans, Catsambas, Thanos; Chu, Ke-Young; and Shome, Parthasarathi;

The Implications of Fund-Supported Adjustment Programs for Poverty: Experiences in Selected Countries, Washington, IMF, May 1988.

36. This line of argument is developed more fully in Killick, Tony, 'Twenty-five years in development: the rise and impending decline of market solutions', *Development Policy Review*, vol. 4, no. 2, June 1986.

37. Bradford, Colin, I. Jr., 'East Asian "models": myths and lessons', in Lewis and Kallab (note 20), pp. 41–42.

38. Bhagwati, Jagdish N., 'Rethinking trade strategy', in Lewis and Kallab (note 20), p. 94.

39. See Mellor, John W., 'Agriculture on the road to industrialisation', in Lewis and Kallab (note 20) for example, on the crucial importance of government support measures in the process of agricultural development.

40. An illustration of this may be provided by the 1983 IMF programme in Ghana, which sought to reduce the budget deficit primarily through expenditure cuts even though the tax ratio in Ghana had fallen to extremely low levels.

41. See Lancaster, Carol, 'Multilateral Development Banks and Africa', in Lancaster and Williamson (note 16) for an argument along these lines.

42. See World Bank, *World Development Report 1986*, Washington, 1986, Table 2.9 and accompanying text.

43. World Bank, *Towards Sustained Development in Sub-Saharan Africa*, Washington, 1984, p. 5.

44. The expression is from the Volcker speech cited in note 7.

45. See World Bank, *World Development Report 1985*, Washington, 1985, Table 4.4, for estimates for selected LDCs.

46. See ibid., pp. 63–64, for a discussion of the causes of capital flight.

47. This point is argued in an interesting article by Devlin, Robert, 'External debt and crisis: the decline of the orthodox strategy', *CEPAL Review No. 27*, December 1985.

48. IMF (note 12), Table A45.

49. See Keller, Peter M., 'Implications of credit policies for output and the balance of payments', *IMF Staff Papers*, vol. 27, no. 3, September 1980 for an argument along these lines from within the Fund.

50. Jaycox, Edward V.K., 'What is to be done?', in Lancaster and Williamson (note 16), p. 183.

6 The debt problem and the IMF's perspective

Bahram Nowzad

In the 1980s external debt difficulties have emerged as one of the biggest problems facing the international monetary system. By now the reasons why debt problems have moved to centre stage need little elaboration. These difficulties, which have affected several borrowing countries, notably the large borrowers in Latin America, have had two aspects. On the one hand they have put a great deal of pressure on the balance of payments, and indeed the economic viability, of the debtor countries concerned; on the other, the very scale and magnitude of the debt problems have posed a serious threat to the soundness and stability of the international financial system, raising questions about the portfolio of a number of so-called money centre banks in large financial markets and, in turn, posing a threat to financial stability in those countries.

The factors responsible for the emergence of the debt crisis suggest an interesting topic, but one that is beyond my terms of reference. I should, however, like to caution that, in my view, it would be a mistake to seek to identify a single factor on which to pin all the blame, or even the main part of it, for the debt difficulties that we have seen in the last four years.

Several quite disparate factors were at work and it is the interplay of these factors and, in many instances, the concurrence of several of them, that have brought to a head what we have come to know as the debt crisis. There are three main factors.

First, inadequate economic policies (such as inappropriate

exchange rates or expansionary budgetary policies) in many borrowing countries put pressure on the balance of payments and hence helped weaken their debt-servicing capacity.

Secondly, the rapid rise in the rate of international borrowing — and of lending, especially by commercial banks — put further pressure on the capacity of debtor countries to service debt.[1] Semanticists may argue whether there was excessive lending or excessive borrowing; the answer, of course, is that it takes two to tango. Following the oil crisis of 1973–74, and the huge surpluses of OPEC countries, commercial banks were often applauded for helping recycle some of these funds. However, it is now apparent that a great deal of international lending during the 1970s and early 1980s took place without adequate scrutiny and attention to how it would be used by the borrowers. Thus, borrowers acquired financial resources on market terms (i.e. less favourable terms than official sources), but in many cases did not channel them to investments that would, in time, allow the debt to be serviced; the resources were used to finance consumption, or investments with a low rate of return; or they simply fuelled capital flight.

Thirdly, and this must not be underestimated, the debt-servicing capacity of many countries was affected by factors entirely beyond their control. Apart from the massive shock of the two oil price increases, the 1970s and early 1980s were characterized by two large-scale recessions, which affected the debtors' ability to export and hence to service their debt, and by the very sharp rise in international interest rates, which made it much more costly for debtor countries to service their loans to commercial banks, many of which were at floating rates linked to interest rates in the large financial markets.

ROLE OF THE IMF

Before discussion in any detail of the role of the IMF in helping its members with their external debt problems, it is important to bear in mind a number of general points.

First, the role of the Fund in assisting countries with their debt problems is not a new one: for almost 30 years the

Fund has been involved in this endeavour. It is true that the recent activities of the Fund in this area have attracted considerable interest and publicity; but the Fund has had an interest in debt problems ever since the Argentina rescheduling way back in 1956. Another indication of the Fund's long-standing involvement in this area was the establishment, in the early 1970s, of an external finance division, a unit specifically designated to keep abreast of debt problems.

Second, the Fund is concerned about the debt problems of its members because, as I have already indicated, these problems are intertwined with and reflect balance of payments difficulties, and coping with such difficulties is, after all, at the heart of the Fund's purposes and responsibility. Balance of payments pressures and debt problems affect the economic well-being of individual Fund members; on the other hand if several large debtors experience severe difficulties, this could create disturbances for the international monetary system as a whole and threaten international financial flows. Thus the Fund is doubly concerned about debt problems: they affect its individual members, and they influence the international financial system. The Fund is not (as some have suggested) involved for any particular partisan reason, such as bailing out the banks, or enforcing the policies of creditor countries, or acting as a special advocate for debtor countries.

Third, it is important to remember that the role of the Fund is not merely that of a fire fighter: in other words, it is not limited to the resolution of crises after they have arisen. The Fund's role is much broader and the Fund has expended considerable effort in encouraging policies that would prevent debt problems from arising in the first place.

Fourth, as we shall see later, the Fund in recent years has played an unprecedented, active role especially in regard to commercial bank debt. This is a manifestation of the Fund's ability to adapt and change according to changing circumstances.

ADVICE, CAUTION, PREVENTION

One of the main objectives of the Fund is to promote international monetary cooperation and a principal vehicle for this is the annual consultations that take place between the Fund and its members once every 12 to 18 months. These consultations take place with every member country, whether or not that country is experiencing payments difficulties and needs to borrow resources from the Fund, and irrespective of the economic size and importance of the country (consultations are held with the USA, the Fund's largest member, as well as with the Republic of the Maldives, the Fund's smallest member in terms of quota). The consultations involve first, a visit by a Fund staff team to the country for a review with the authorities of the economic situation, policies, and prospects in their broad setting. In these discussions, particular attention is focused on the balance of payments and external policies and, more specifically, the review includes an analysis of financial policies, and external debt management. Since the emergence of significant debt difficulties in 1982, the Fund has attached even greater importance to the external debt aspects of the consultation process. Increased emphasis has been placed on analysis of debt positions over the medium term, and a forward-looking quantitative external debt analysis has been incorporated in the consultation process.

In discussing debt matters the staff team may, where appropriate, alert the authorities to aspects of their external debt situation that may be of concern. For instance, the staff team may draw the attention of the authorities to the composition or total size of the country's external debt and may recommend vigilance in any future borrowing, including amounts and terms. Or, to take another example, if the review so warrants, the staff team will alert the authorities to potential or incipient external debt-servicing problems. In all cases debt matters will be considered within the context of the country's balance of payments situation and prospects. In specific cases, the staff team may recommend that the authorities establish better debt monitoring and control procedures so as to be able to exercise a more direct and

effective control over the country's external debt situation
For this purpose, if a country so requests, the Fund will con
sider and, if appropriate, provide the services of a specia
team or resident expert to help the country set up such :
control mechanism.

Once the staff team has returned from the country in
question, its review of that country's economy, including
the external debt situation, is presented in a report prepare
for the Fund's Executive Board. In due course the Executiv
Board discusses the staff's assessment and, in this way, th
economic situation of each country, including its externa
debt situation, becomes the focus of international discussion

As already mentioned, these procedures take plac
whether or not a particular country needs to borrow from
the Fund, and whether or not that country is experiencing
debt difficulties. When a country needs to borrow from the
Fund, the staff team works out with the authorities an appro
priate mix of adjustment policies and financing. In thi
process, an important aspect is the monitoring of externa
debt developments, including the use of borrowing limits

However, as recent history amply demonstrates, in spit
of all the caution and precaution and analysis, countries d
encounter external debt difficulties. The remainder of thi
chapter concerns the Fund's role in cases where a membe
country encounters debt problems.

BACKGROUND ANALYSIS AND PREPARATION

When a country finds it difficult to service its external debt
what is it to do? Broadly speaking (and simplifying con
siderably) it has three choices: first, it can simply refuse to
honour its debt or, in other words, default. This option
however, is most unacceptable for everyone concerned. Were
this to happen the debtor country would find it very dif
ficult, if not impossible, to borrow again on internationa
capital and credit markets, at least not for a very long time
Moreover, there would be all sorts of legal complications
its assets overseas, such as buildings, airlines, and ships could
be attached by creditors. It would probably find it difficult

o obtain trade credit. In short, life would become very difficult for that country and, in the longer run, its development prospects would suffer. Internationally, large-scale defaults could create chaos in financial markets and harm the interests of other countries.

The second option would be for the country to go to the other extreme, that is to try to service its debt obligations irrespective of the sacrifice required. This, too, may be very difficult, if not impossible. In many developing countries imports have already been compressed to the basic minimum and to reduce them further to generate resources to service the external debt might simply be out of the question on social and political, as well as economic, grounds.

A third possibility, and the one most countries opt for, is to reschedule the debt. A rescheduling is nothing more than rearranging of the original payments schedule or time-table of an obligation or a series of obligations. Rescheduling the obligations falling due in a particular year amounts, therefore, to stretching out those payments over a longer period than originally envisaged in the loan agreement. For instance, to reschedule over five years the obligations falling due in 1988 with a three-year grace period means that no debt payments are made in 1989–91 (the grace period), but that the debt is paid off in 1992–95. In essence what a re-scheduling does is to lighten the burden of payments in a particular year and allow the country time for the impact of adjustment measures to be felt. Of course, because repayments are delayed beyond their original date, interest payments increase.

Thus a country facing debt-servicing difficulties may at its own initiative, or at the urging of creditors, or at the suggestion of the Fund, consider rescheduling as an alternative. Once it has decided to follow this option, considerable preparations must be made and, if requested, the Fund can provide assistance at this stage. A rescheduling, like the original debt itself, essentially involves an agreement between two parties, the debtor and creditor (although, because of guarantee provisions, these may not be the original parties). Before the rescheduling process can begin, the debtor who, after all, is 'petitioning' for a revision of the loan terms, must prepare its case, its 'brief' if you will, for presentation to the creditors. This consists of an analysis of its debt situation in the context of its balance of payments and prospects. Apart from the collection and collation of a considerable amount of statistical and factual information, the debtor's presentation must also describe the policies that have been adopted or that are envisaged to improve the balance of payments. In the preparation of this background documentation many countries have sought the technical assistance of the Fund, either as part of the consultation discussions mentioned above or through the visit of a special Fund staff team for that specific purpose.

PARTICIPATION IN THE RESCHEDULING PROCESS

Once the documentation has been prepared, the next stage is the debt rescheduling itself and here the Fund has played a very important role. As a general point it is important to bear in mind that the Fund participates in debt rescheduling meetings at the invitation of both parties, the creditor and the debtor. The Fund, in other words, has traditionally played a low-profile, 'honest broker' role. It is not and has not been an advocate for either the debtor country or for the creditor's position, although this has not prevented it from providing considerable technical assistance to the debtor country, which has generally been a developing country. The Fund's main interest is to ensure that the rescheduling process results in a successful outcome, and that due account is taken by all parties of the economic situation and prospects of the debtor country as well as the efforts it is making, or must make, to correct its position. Only in these ways has the Fund been able to retain the trust and confidence of all parties.

Debts that are owed to official entities (such as government agencies), or to private parties that are officially guaranteed in the creditor country, are renegotiated multilaterally under the aegis of the 'Paris Club'. This is an informal grouping (or framework) of official creditors which, over the years, has evolved certain norms and rules of procedure. In such reschedulings the Fund has been an active participant. Following the debtor country's presentation of its case at the opening of the rescheduling meeting, the Fund representative is requested to make its own presentation of the country's economic position and prospects, generally a statement specifically prepared for the purpose and approved by the Fund management. Thereafter the Fund representative has to be ready to assist both the creditor and the debtor by providing information and views and, in some cases, to act as a sort of go-between.

A crucial feature of Paris Club renegotiations has been that traditionally the official creditors have not been prepared to consider a rescheduling of official debt unless the debtor country had in effect an adjustment programme with the Fund in the upper credit tranches. This link, which is not something that was sought by the IMF, has been very important: it is in reality the only way in which the creditors can have some assurance that adequate adjustment measures will be adopted by the debtor country, and that economic policies are conducive to an improvement of the economic situation. The rationale for this is clear: since a rescheduling is a postponement of payments, creditors wish to have some guarantee that the postponement will, in fact, contribute to improved economic conditions in the debtor country and enable it to service its external debt. And the only convenient way this can be done is to insist that the debtor country has in place an adjustment programme supported by the Fund.

The situation as regards the rescheduling of commercial bank debt in the past has been less well defined and less formalized. The role of the Fund has been more *ad hoc*, but in many respects it has been similar to that in the Paris Club. While banks generally encouraged the authorities to seek a Fund-supported programme, there was, in some cases, no direct link between a commercial bank rescheduling and the entry into force of an adjustment programme supported by the Fund.

CHANGED ROLE SINCE 1982

Since the onset of the debt crisis in 1982 the Fund has come
to play a more active role in helping resolve debt problems.
The situation, as already intimated, had changed considerably
by the early 1980s: the magnitude of the debt had risen
sharply; the composition of the debt had changed, with more
and more debt at floating rate interest rates and shorter
maturities, due to commercial banks; and once debt-servicing
difficulties surfaced there was a need to keep order, to keep
credit lines open as much as possible, to maintain market
discipline, and, broadly speaking, to preserve the international financial system.

Faced with this situation, the Fund has become more
deeply involved in the debt problems of its members in two
ways: it has in selected cases openly adopted a coordinating
role, designed to bring together all parties to a debt problem,
and it has acted as a catalyst to attract the financing that
would be necessary to support adjustment efforts in
particular debtor countries. At the same time virtually all
commercial bank debt restructurings have been made conditional upon the debtor country having a Fund-supported
programme in place, and in many instances banks have linked
their disbursements of new lending to purchases under Fund
arrangements, with non-observance of conditions under
Fund arrangements leading to delays in disbursements. Also,
at the request of debtor countries, the Fund has engaged in
a greater exchange of information and discussion with banks
on the implications of alternative levels of financing, including policy measures that were undertaken and followed
under Fund-supported programmes.

In the process outlined above, the banks and the debtor
countries have perceived the benefit of a greater role by the
Fund. The Fund, for its part, has modified its approach. In
some cases, the magnitude of the financing required to
support an adjustment effort and the uncertainty of its
availability has led the Fund to seek formal assurances from
commercial banks that the external financing assumptions of
a particular programme would be met. In such cases the Fund
management has been prepared to submit a programme for

approval of the Executive Board only when sufficient progress had been made in assembling the financial 'package', and reasonable assurances received that the package would be forthcoming. The size of the necessary package is based on the Fund's analysis and judgement regarding the mix of finance-cum-adjustment that is necessary, taking into account the accumulation of interest arrears and the banks' traditional reluctance to reschedule interest. The importance of the share of the banks in the total financing package has made it imperative to make Fund support conditional upon the banks' participation.

All this is rather an interesting twist; it is a considerable change from the previous situation: whereas in the past, under the Paris Club reschedulings, creditors would not be prepared to agree to a rescheduling until a Fund-supported programme were in place, in the new situation the Fund management has been prepared to present a programme for Executive Board approval only if sufficient progress has been made in assembling an adequate financial package.

A recent development has been the advent of the so-called MYRA — that is, the multi-year rescheduling arrangement. MYRAs are intended for debtor countries that have made progress in restoring their creditworthiness and where banks are interested in a viable, medium-term, restructuring schedule. A key objective of such arrangements is to remove the 'hump' in the repayment schedule that would be an obstacle to normalizing debtor–creditor relations. MYRAs are, therefore, particularly appropriate in cases where, in addition to significant progress in correcting the imbalances in its economy, a country is perceived as being committed to appropriate policies on a lasting basis, and where it has shown the ability to forgo the need for concerted lending, thereby setting the stage for the restoration of normal creditor–debtor relationships. In the case of a MYRA, the debtor country may no longer have a programme with the Fund in effect but there will be a continuing link between the banks' participation and the Fund's evaluation of the economic situation of that country. In these circumstances arrangements are made for the Fund, with the concurrence of the debtor country, to provide periodic reports to the banks —

enhanced surveillance. It is for the banks, however, using these reports, together with their own information, to review and appraise the situation in the country concerned.

Briefly, these are some of the ways in which the Fund has sought to assist its members. It is a flexible approach, based on a case-by-case examination and assessment of debtor countries. There has, of course, been a whole range of proposals in which the Fund would play a more extended role.

CURRENT PERSPECTIVE ON DEBT ISSUES

What of the perspective regarding the debt situation at present? To recapitulate, the Fund's objective is to help normalize creditor–debtor relations and to promote a restoration of country access to sustainable flows and more spontaneous lending.

How are these objectives to be achieved? The first requirement is a vigorous and sustained adjustment effort by the debtor countries themselves. Without such an effort, all other arrangements and assistance would be to no avail. The second requirement is that efforts to improve the situation are not *only* the responsibility of debtor countries; a cooperative, concerted approach is needed. Here debtor countries have an important role to play, as mentioned above; creditors – the Paris Club creditors, the commercial banks, the export credit agencies – also have a part to play; and the Fund itself has a very important role as catalyst, coordinator, and as an institution uniquely placed to promote and support programmes of adjustment with its own resources.

What is the record to date? The answer must be in two parts. First, progress to date has been encouraging. There has been substantial adjustment by a number of major debtor countries; concerted action has been shown both by creditors and debtors; and the strength of the economic recovery in industrial countries, especially in the USA, has been of considerable help to adjustment. And the so-called case-by-case approach, which simply means that each country's situation is assumed to be different, that it must be analysed in the context of the nature of its problem, and that the programme must be tailored with a mix of adjustment and financing policies to suit its circumstances and prospects, has basically been vindicated.

But the second part of the answer is also important: it is that progress has been uneven and, even more important, the situation remains vulnerable, subject to adverse developments in the world economy. For countries that have embarked upon adjustment efforts to continue to recover from their debt difficulties, it is crucial that the international economy continue to grow, that world trade expand and remain open, and that real interest rates moderate. Most of these developments depend on policies and events in the industrial countries, and therefore are to a large extent outside the control of the debtor countries.

From the foregoing it follows that the future course of the debt problem will depend crucially on the general economic environment, on the one hand, and continued adherence to adjustment policies by debtor countries on the other. The history of the past few years provides many lessons: the importance of vigilance (by both debtors and creditors) regarding the rise in external indebtedness, the importance of a cooperative approach when debt problems do arise, and the importance of adjustment measures by the debtor country.

NOTE

1. Aggregative data can be misleading, but to take just two broad indications of the increase in the rate of lending: in 1974 the ratio of disbursed outstanding debt to export earnings of large borrowers (12 countries each with an outstanding long-term debt of $15 billion at the end of 1983) was 97 per cent; it had risen to 128 per cent by 1982 and 167 per cent by 1983. For the same countries the ratio of debt service to export earnings was 11 per cent in 1974, 21 per cent in 1982, and 22 per cent in 1983 (World Bank data).

7 LDC debt: Is activism required?

Benjamin J. Cohen*

More than five years after Mexico's dramatic financial collapse in the summer of 1982, the LDC debt problem remains seemingly as intractable as ever. The good news is that the threat of a global banking crisis appears to have been successfully contained, at least until now. The bad news is that most Third World countries continue to stagnate under the burden of their external debt-service obligations. It is now widely acknowledged, by scholars and practitioners alike, that the LDC debt dilemma will not be truly resolved until the severe cash flow strains on debtors can be durably eased in a context of renewed economic development. And this, everyone agrees, will require the cooperation of all the actors currently involved in the problem, including transnational actors such as commercial banks and the multilateral credit agencies (the International Monetary Fund and World Bank) as well as state actors in both debtor and capital-market countries.[1] The core questions are: Why has genuine cooperation on the issue of debt proved so elusive until now? And what, if anything, might be done to reduce or eliminate obstacles to cooperation on debt in the future?

For analytical purposes, cooperation may be defined in terms of mutually beneficial adjustments of behaviour. Using the language of game theory, cooperation is a function of a particular class of pay-off structures where joint gain is possible but will not be achieved automatically. In a previous paper,[2] the first of a series of three papers on the political economy of LDC debt, I suggested that two key conditions

*The author is with the Fletcher School of Law and Diplomacy, Tufts University, Medford, MA 02155.

are essential to the attainment of cooperation in a given issue area of international economic relations. First, there must be a consensus among all the principal players in the game that despite elements of competition, a potential for joint gain does exist. And second, there must be some mechanism or incentive structure sufficient to ensure that despite unenforceability of contracts, players will undertake the requisite mutual adjustments of behaviour. Lacking the first condition, actors will proceed as if the game is zero-sum even if it is not: they will not *perceive* any interest in cooperation. Lacking the second condition, actors will proceed as if the joint gain is unrealizable even if it is not: they will not be willing to take any *risk* for cooperation. Both conditions are necessary for cooperation to emerge on an issue such as debt: together, they are sufficient.

The first of these two conditions was taken up in my previous paper, with discussion focusing on the issue of potential mutual benefit. My conclusion there was that an opportunity for joint gain does exist in creditor–debtor relations but is not currently being exploited. The second condition now remains to be considered: how to ensure that the opportunity for joint gain will be *realized*. That is the problem we take up in the present chapter as well as in the third paper of this series.[3]

The central issue for the present is: can we expect the second condition to be satisfied *spontaneously*, or must cooperation be actively *promoted*? The answer is critical. Active promotion of cooperation obviously would be unnecessary if actor incentives could realistically be counted upon in the near term to change *endogenously*, that is, as a function of the dynamics of the game itself, in a manner sufficient to induce all concerned to undertake the requisite mutual adjustments of behaviour. But it is equally obvious that this could be a vain, indeed even naive, hope. If such a spontaneous reordering of preferences cannot be counted upon, then activism is the only alternative: some mechanism would have to be deliberately *designed* to persuade all players to take the necessary risks for cooperation. The purpose of this chapter is to evaluate just how likely it is that an endogenous shift of actor preferences — in particular, creditor preferences — might soon occur to support a genuinely co-operative solution of the debt problem. Briefly put: is it realistic to expect that the game itself may reduce or eliminate existing obstacles to cooperation? Or is activism indeed required?

The organization of the chapter is as follows. The first section summarizes the argument of my previous paper, highlighting the key factors that appear to account for under-exploitation of the potential for joint gain in current creditor–debtor relations. The story is then picked up in the second section, which focuses on cognitive influences on the effective ordering of creditor preferences. Potential changes in the broad distribution of power between the creditor and debtor sides of the game are considered in the third section; and the internal dynamics of preference formation on the creditor side in the fourth section. The argument of these sections is that it is not realistic to expect that the game itself will reduce or eliminate existing obstacles to cooperation. The implications of this conclusion are spelled out briefly in the final section.

JOINT GAIN AND
CREDITOR–DEBTOR RELATIONS

The argument of my previous paper focused on three issues essential to any effort to understand the political economy of LDC debt. First, what is the nature of the debt 'game' as it is currently played by developing countries and their creditors? Second, why is the game played as it is? And third, is the game as currently played the best we can do?

Definitive proofs, of course, are impossible on any of these three issues, owing to limitations of existing methodology. Hence with respect to any one of them, the analysis in my paper could modestly aspire to no more than a demonstration of some degree of plausibility rather than absolute certainty. From the outset, therefore, it must be acknowledged that the paper's conclusions — as, indeed, this chapter's conclusions — are bound to be regarded as debatable, if not downright controversial. It could hardly be otherwise. On matters such as these, sincere people most assuredly may sincerely disagree.

In that spirit, consider the first issue: the nature of the game. The analysis of my previous paper suggests that the strategic interaction between debtors and creditors until now has most closely resembled an asymmetric non-cooperative game of Bully, with LDCs obliged to bear by far the greatest share of the burden of adjustment. The primary technical characteristic of a Bully interaction is that while one side has a preference ordering equivalent to that of a game of pure conflict (Deadlock), the other orders its preferences more as in the game of Chicken.[4] Hence the former side is able to exploit the latter's fears of the consequences of a breakdown of relations to gain a better outcome for itself — just as the creditor side seems to have been able to do in its negotiations with debtors ever since Mexico's rescue in 1982. Rudiger Dornbusch likens the outcome to a mugging.[5] If so, debtors have collaborated fully with their muggers, in effect consenting to play the game on creditors' terms. LDCs, with few exceptions, have not chosen to 'defect', as they might by (say) repudiating their debts or otherwise refusing to acknowledge their full contractual obligations. Instead, most have been careful, no matter how hard-pressed, to preserve their lines of communication with other major actors and as much as possible to abide by the results of creditor–debtor negotiations, however unfavourable. Technically, they have settled for a policy of acquiescence in an outcome of 'unrequited cooperation'.

This in turn leads to the second issue: why do debtors acquiesce in the Chicken role, in effect accepting a Bully pay-off structure as the most accurate representation of their interests? Explanations of the effective ordering of debtor preferences could in principle be sought at all three of the levels of analysis that have been developed in the emerging scholarly field of International Political Economy. *System-level* analysis focuses on constraints and incentives for state behaviour that derive from the broader structure of international and transnational relations. *Unit-level* analysis emphasizes the role of domestic politics in the formulation and implementation of foreign economic policy. *Cognitive* analysis encompasses the base of consensual knowledge, or 'economic culture', that legitimates policy making at both the unit and system levels. In practice, however, only the first two levels appear to provide much insight into the actual performance of debtors, despite the evident importance of market-based norms, such as sanctity of contract and the non-politicization of commercial relations, in shaping the value systems of LDC policy makers. The dissonance between debtor words and deeds is simply too great to lend much credence to the view that they have been motivated by any sort of sincerely held belief in the essential rightness of creditor demands for full satisfaction of contractual obligations.

Far more influential in determining LDC behaviour, it would appear, have been underlying configurations of power, both in the political game at home and in relations with creditors abroad. Domestic politics, until now, has not made it unduly difficult for most debtors to eschew the option of defection; while realistic fears of the consequences of defection have been greatly reinforced by the international influence of creditors. Power relationships, in short, have intersected at the two levels, unit and system, to make the Chicken role appear by far the least-cost choice for policy makers.

At home, the acquiescent acceptance of a Bully outcome by most debtors can be traced directly to the ability of politically dominant elites to shift the lion's share of the burden of adjustment on to groups less well positioned to influence the course of official policy. The more successful local elites have been in these domestic distributional struggles, the less pressure there has been on LDC governments internally to seek a change in the terms of the game. Meanwhile, in relations abroad, acquiescence has been reinforced through the power of creditors, despite intra-industry differences and coordination problems, to shape pay-off structures to their advantage through side-payments or sanctions, carrots, such as multi-year reschedulings or liberalized terms, being dangled before debtors as promised rewards for good behaviour; the stick of tough bargaining (or, in the background, damaging retaliatory penalties) being held as threats over the heads of stubborn recalcitrants. This approach has been variously described as a strategy of 'divide and rule'[6] or, quite simply, 'containment'.[7] The more effective creditors have been at the tactics of either bribery or coercion, the more pressure there has been on LDCs externally *not* to seek a change in the terms of the game. No wonder, then, that debtors have collaborated so fully with their muggers. As refracted through the lens of power relationships — the combination of weak internal pressures for change plus strong external pressures for the *status quo* — a Bully pay-off structure really has seemed to most accurately represent their interests. Frustrated though LDCs may be with the outcome, they have ample reason to believe that this truly is the best we can do.

As indicated, however, my conclusion is quite different: this is *not* the best we can do. Debtors, along with creditors, may believe that the situation is already Pareto-optimal, in the sense that no one (e.g. LDCs) can be made better off in absolute terms without someone else (e.g. creditors) being made worse off. But my contention is that this perception is myopic — that opportunities for Pareto-improvement do exist but are *underappreciated* by the key actors involved. The myopia manifests itself in a tendency by all concerned to behave as if the distribution of the burden of adjustment is the only question that matters, effectively discounting or ignoring the benefit side of the calculus in their comparisons of policy alternatives. The reason for the myopia, I argue, lies in the players' failure to recognize or acknowledge the dynamic instability that is inherent in the game as it is currently played.

Until now, the stability of the game has depended on the acquiescence of debtors, which in turn has been ensured only because of the effectiveness of relevant power relationships both at home and abroad. But these relationships are by no means independent of the course of the game itself. On the contrary, the durability of key underlying configurations of power must be seen as endogenous rather than exogenous, which means that LDC preference orderings too are unlikely to remain invariant as the game continues to be played. A more plausible prospect is for a gradual decline of debtor acquiescence as frustrations over the current Bully outcome continue to mount in many countries. The danger is that, ultimately, the interaction could degenerate into a purely conflictual game of Deadlock, with a correspondingly high risk of losses for all concerned.

The crux of the issue lies in the old distinction between solvency and liquidity. Until now, most debtors have been treated as if their cash-flow strains were merely a matter of some temporary illiquidity. More than five years after the crisis first broke, however, their problems clearly are beginning to look much more like something approximating real insolvency. Most LDCs continue to find themselves mired in what has been described as a 'low-growth, high-debt-service trap'[8] in which creditor demands for full satisfaction of contractual obligations — by depressing domestic capital formation — actually have the effect of retarding rather than promoting restoration of their ability to service debt. This is crucial because the longer a recovery of healthy LDC growth is delayed in this way, the more likely it is that underlying configurations of power will soon be seriously eroded. This could occur at the unit level by a heating up of conflicts of interest among societal forces; and at the system level, by a loss of credibility in the creditors' containment strategy. And this in turn is crucial because it means that the Chicken role is likely to appear less and less the least-cost choice for LDC policy makers, propelled on the one hand by an intensification of domestic distributional struggles; decreasingly constrained, on the other, by the putative power of foreign creditors. In time, given the rising prospect of *de facto* insolvency for many countries, growing numbers of debtors could well be either tempted or driven to defect from the game, whatever the consequences for themselves or others.

As compared with such an obviously unattractive outcome, creditors as well as debtors arguably would be significantly better off with a cooperative strategy of debt relief in appropriate cases; that is, in the cases of those LDCs that do actually appear to face a rising prospect of *de facto* insolvency. Commercial banks and capital-market countries would gain in so far as the capacity of such debtors to satisfactorily service their obligations could be effectively enhanced and any threat of world financial disruption substantially reduced. Debtors would gain in so far as their economic development could be speedily resumed and perhaps also some voluntary new financing encouraged. Herein lies the potential for joint gain that, I infer, is not now being exploited — a direct function of the degree of risk of large-scale defections (intentional or 'involuntary') by debtor countries from the current game. To casually discount or ignore such a risk would surely appear to qualify as myopic. To proceed on the premise that the debt game is not zero-sum, therefore, would certainly not seem an unwarranted conclusion.

An opportunity for Pareto-improvement, however, is only the first of the two conditions necessary for cooperation. As indicated, an appropriate mechanism or incentive structure is also required to ensure that the joint gain will be realized — the second of the two necessary conditions. It is to this condition that we now turn.

EFFECTIVE ORDERING OF
CREDITOR PREFERENCES

Assuming the argument of my previous paper is plausible, the implication clearly follows that realization of the potential for joint gain must involve some degree of debt relief in appropriate cases. (By debt relief, I mean any measure to reduce the present value of future contractual obligations; by appropriate cases, I mean any country that, by objective analysis, does appear to face a rising prospect of *de facto* insolvency.) This therefore means focusing our attention on the motivations of creditors, since it is they who would seemingly risk the most by agreeing to any departure from the *status quo*. Debtors hardly need any encouragement to consider some lowering of interest and/or amortization payments, which would effectively release a larger fraction of their foreign exchange earnings to promote accelerated economic development at home. Creditors, on the other hand, quite understandably demonstrate rather more caution, not to say outright hostility, when the subject of debt relief comes up. Can anything be anticipated in the likely evolution of the game itself that might spontaneously diminish or over- come their natural hesitations? In formal analytical terms: can any endogenous change be realistically expected in the effective ordering of creditor preferences?

Following the line of discussion in my previous paper, possible answers could in principle be sought at any of the three levels of analysis developed in the formal international political economy literature.

First, at the system level, a decisive change might occur in the broad distribution of power between the two sides in the game. *Pari passu* with losses of credibility in the creditors' containment strategy, debtors could perhaps be expected to respond with more effective carrots or sticks of their own to persuade creditors to agree to some reduction of con- tractual payments obligations.

Secondly, at the unit level, new alignments might develop within the creditor side, in response to increasing intra- industry strains and coordination problems. In effect, growing distributional struggles among banks, and between them and other interested parties in the capital-market countries, could possibly weaken creditor resistance to the idea of some kind of debt relief.

Finally, at the cognitive level, new values and belief systems might emerge from a growing understanding of debtor difficulties to reshape creditor perceptions of their interests. A kind of learning process could occur, as a result of the accumulation of experience, to effectively alter the dominant economic culture and legitimate some compromise of traditional market-based norms.

As in my previous paper, however, only the first two levels appear to be of much direct relevance in practice, despite the evident potential at the cognitive level for a learning process of some kind. To argue that players in the debt game are myopic, after all, is not necessarily to suggest that they are irrational (in the sense of consciously failing to exploit opportunities to increase their own net benefits). Far more likely is that their rationality is *bounded* to some significant extent by limits on their information-processing capacity, in particular, by the high level of *uncertainty* surrounding every aspect of the debt problem, which manifestly constrains actors in their ability to make appropriate calculations when comparing policy alternatives. Clearly, there is room here for a growth of understanding of the game's unrealized potential for joint gain.

The concept of bounded rationality was first developed by Herbert Simon.[9] A key implication of the concept is that if uncertainty can be reduced by one means or another, constraints on rational benefit–cost calculations will be reduced as well, thereby raising the chances for genuine cooperation in the mutual interest. Creditor–debtor relations, as we know, are very much in the nature of an infinitely iterated game, where potential gains are both more remote and less assured than prospective losses. On the other hand, this explains why players tend to behave as if the distribution of the burden of adjustment is the only question that matters, effectively valuing future benefits at a considerable discount when comparing them with more immediate costs. (In technical terms, they implicitly have a positive rate of time preference or high discount rate.) On the other hand, it suggests why opportunities may well exist for increasing incentives for cooperation – even apart from any changes in the actors' objective environment – in so far as the subjective process of discounting could be favourably altered by decreasing ambiguity concerning the future. As Robert Axelrod and Robert Keohane have written: 'The importance of perception [keeps] asserting itself . . . including beliefs and cognition . . . . Decision making in ambiguous settings is heavily influenced by the ways in which the actors think about their problems.'[10] It follows that if thinking about the debt problem could be altered in ways that raised the value actors attach to remote future pay-offs, commitments to the requisite mutual adjustments of behaviour would appear relatively more attractive to them in the short term.

Unfortunately, as concerns the aspect of the debt problem most critical to the thinking of creditors – namely, the degree of risk of large-scale debtor defections – the level of uncertainty is unlikely to be reduced substantially no matter how much experience is accumulated. As I have already admitted, there is simply too much room here for sincere

people to sincerely disagree. Do debtors really face a rising
prospect of *de facto* insolvency? Are domestic distributional
struggles really going to intensify? Will the creditors' containment strategy really lose its credibility? Since no
definitive proofs are possible on any of these issues, no firm
basis in analysis exists to support a reshaped consensus in
creditors' subjective perceptions. In the abstract, the danger
of dynamic instability in the debt game may seem plausible.
In reality, views are apt to remain as divergent as ever regarding the appropriate probability to attach to the risk of
debtor defections. Not even a vigorous educational effort
paying particular attention to the lessons of international
financial history, as has been advocated by some observers,[11]
would suffice to overcome the ambiguity inherent in this
particularly complex setting. Little hope, then, can be
attached to the possibility that a cooperative solution to the
debt problem can somehow be achieved through an
endogenous change in the values and belief systems of
creditors. An appeal to cognitive dynamics is seductive but
unrealistic.

Much more realistic is an appeal to the same kinds of
factors that have appeared to account for the effective
ordering of preferences in the game until now, namely
underlying configurations of power at the unit and system
levels. If any endogenous basis exists for diminishing or over-
coming the hesitations of creditors toward the idea of debt
relief, it is likely to emerge from these more objective characteristics of the actors' environment rather than from
subjective culture and norms. As Peter Gourevitch recently
reminded us: 'Policy requires politics. Ideas for solving
economic problems are plentiful, but if an idea is to
prevail . . . it must obtain support from those who have
political power'.[12] In short, a new political equation must
emerge to replace previously prevailing power relationships.

DISTRIBUTION OF POWER BETWEEN
CREDITORS AND DEBTORS

Consider, first, the system level: is any substantial change ikely to occur in the broad distribution of power between he two sides in the game? Until now, creditors have been remarkably successful at 'bullying' most debtors into a policy of 'unrequited cooperation' (acquiescence). The main reason, obviously, has to do with the wide range of resources available to creditors in their ongoing relations with the developing world, which provide them with the ammunition for their tactics of bribery and coercion. With one hand, carrots can be offered to debtors that continue to acknowedge their full contractual obligations, including, as indicated, multi-year reschedulings or liberalized terms on past loans (e.g. longer grace periods, lower interest margins, relaxed policy conditions) as well as, of course, the possibility of fresh financing in the future. With the other hand, sticks can be brandished at debtors that might threaten to defect, including a cessation of new medium- or long-term lending, interruption of short-term trade credits, seizure of exports, or even attachment of a debtor's foreign assets commercial airliners, ships, bank accounts, and the like). At a minimum, countries might face considerable inconvenience in their efforts to maintain customary trade relations, particularly if they were effectively prevented from holding or transferring cash balances abroad: a cut-off from the international payments mechanism would compel them to go to something like a barter basis for imports. At the extreme, they would risk virtual ostracization and isolation from the rest of the world economy.

Debtors, however, are not without resources of their own, which can also be put to work in tactics of bribery and coercion. Creditors could be tempted into concessions by offers of possible side-payments from LDC governments, e.g. generous debt-equity conversion programmes or improved access to domestic lending markets. They can also be threatened with some manner of abrogation of full contractual obligations (reflecting one of the most fundamental characteristics of international financial markets: the inability of lenders directly to enforce repayment by borrowers). This might mean formal repudiation of all outstanding debts — *de jure* default, the ultimate weapon. Or it could mean something somewhat less dramatic, such as

perhaps a temporary postponement of amortization or ever
just a short-term moratorium on some or all interest pay
ments — intermediate actions (between full compliance anc
de jure default) variously described as 'partial', '*de facto*', or
in the phrase of the financial journalist Anatole Kaletsky,[1]
'conciliatory' default. As all concerned have long understood
both sides in the debt game are constrained to some exten
by the potential bargaining leverage of the other — mutua
hostages, as it were, to their strategic interaction.[14] As shoul
also be understood, there is no cause to assume that th
distribution of leverage between the two sides need alway
remain the same.

To some extent, it may be argued, the distribution o
leverage has already changed, in so far as the credibilit
of the creditors' containment strategy even now is beginnin
to show signs of serious erosion. Neither promises of reward
for good behaviour nor threats of reprisals for nor
cooperation seem quite as persuasive as they once did
Strenuous adjustment efforts in debtor countries, fo
instance, have yet to earn any renewal of voluntary lendin
by the markets; even Colombia, the one debtor in Lati
America that since 1982 has never requested a rescheduling
has experienced great difficulties in attempting to arrang
any fresh financing from commercial banks.[15] Meanwhile
growing numbers of involuntary, or even intentional, defec
tions by LDC governments — *de facto* or *de jure* defaults -
have failed to provoke many damaging reprisals fron
creditors.

In the first half of 1987 alone, no fewer than four debtor
(Brazil, Ecuador, Ivory Coast, and Zambia) opted to suspen
interest payments, at least 'temporarily'. This brought to ove
a dozen the list of countries in Latin America and Sub
Saharan Africa that had either ceased debt service altogethe
or else were in very serious arrears.[16] Yet not even Peru
which under its socialist president Alan Garcia has beer
perhaps the most confrontational of Third World debtors
has seen any of its exports seized or assets attached. On th
contrary, the Peruvians reportedly are still able even to rais
an adequate amount of trade financing when needed simpl
by paying slightly more than standard market rates.[17] Onl

razil, among those debtors that have deliberately resorted
ɔ 'conciliatory' default in recent years, has subsequently
eversed course owing, at least in part, to direct pressure from
reditors. The formal moratorium on interest payments that
razil initiated in March 1987 was effectively ended in
'ebruary 1988 after the country lost at least $2 billion of
:s $16 billion in short-term loans from commercial banks.[18]
ut even that pressure might not have been enough to bring
bout a resumption of debt service[19] had the banks not also
greed to offer several attractive carrots to the Brazilians,
ncluding a lower interest rate on rescheduled debt and new
ledium-term loans totalling $5.8 billion.[20] Apparently, it is
ist not as easy to 'bully' debtors as it used to be.

Two main factors appear to be responsible. One is juridical
ncertainty: the limited, not to say dubious, basis in law for
he usual list of legal sanctions threatened by creditors
gainst recalcitrant debtors. Few court precedents exist to
stablish the right of international lenders to seize exports
ɔr attach the assets of a sovereign borrower. And despite
iuch discussion in recent years, lawyers themselves are still
nable to agree on just what forms of legal redress, if any,
lay in principle be applicable under the circumstances; or
ven whether any court judgements could, in practical
erms, be enforced.[21] Awareness has grown, therefore, that
he range of resources truly available to creditors may be
ather more restricted than first thought, justifying increasing
cepticism in the minds of many debtors. As Kaletsky has
bserved:

> The law is a creditor's most obvious recourse in the event of a
> default. Various forms of legal redress, such as attachment of assets
> and seizure of exports, are generally regarded as the ultimate deter-
> rents against default. But bankers' hopes — and borrowers' fears —
> that crippling costs could be imposed on recalcitrant debtor
> countries through court action appear to be greatly exaggerated.
> Western legal systems would give private creditors only modest
> opportunities to disrupt a defaulting country's trade or to restrain
> others from doing business with it. There would be little hope of
> seizing its foreign currency reserves and other assets of its central
> bank. Even though bankers could hope to create considerable
> nuisance for a defaulting borrower through private lawsuits, the

costs of coping with all this legal trouble would scarcely be com
mensurable, particularly for a large borrower . . . .
    The practical remedies available from lawsuits against sovereig
debtors continue to be strictly limited (p. 21).[13]

The second main factor is more empirical: the sheer numbe
of debtors that have to be induced or pressured int
acquiescence to preserve creditor credibility. When only on
or two countries seem on the verge of defection — whethe
involuntary or intentional — creditors are unlikely t
encounter much difficulty in making promised rewards o
threatened reprisals believable. But neither bribery no
coercion is without cost. As the ranks of potential defaulter
grow, so too do the potential losses for creditors should push
ever come to shove. Hence creditors can be expected t
hesitate more and more to make actual use of their putativ
resources. This too justifies increasing scepticism in the mind
of many debtors.
    The trouble with bribery, for instance, is its 'demonstratio
effect'. Each LDC keeps a close watch on creditor nego
tiations with all other debtors, and any concessions made t
one soon tend to be demanded by all. Such was the case afte
Mexico's massive $44 billion rescheduling agreement signe
at the end of September 1986, including *inter alia* a new
lower interest margin of just 13/16 of a percentage poin
over the London interbank offered rate (LIBOR). This new
margin quickly became the standard for all other debtors a
well, against which to measure their own bargaining accomp
lishments. In April 1987, the Philippine finance ministe
forced commercial banks to reopen negotiations on a newl
completed restructuring accord after learning that Argentin
had just won the same interest terms as Mexico — 1/16 of
point less than the 14/16 that bankers had previously insiste
was the best they could offer the Philippines.[22] It is quit
understandable, therefore, that creditors might hesitate t
spark off the whole process by making any concessions in th
first place. According to Martin Feldstein, it is this sam
demonstration effect that explains why creditors are s
cautious about the subject of debt relief as well:

It is far better for banks to accept, for now, the de facto forgiveness entailed in the non-payment of interest by Bolivia, Peru and others with weak economies than to grant de jure forgiveness and risk the almost certain pressure for similar treatment from the major debtor countries (p. 22).[23]

The trouble with coercion, conversely, is a kind of reverse demonstration effect, namely, that to be credible, sanctions imposed on any one recalcitrant debtor must inevitably be imposed on all. Otherwise, individual LDCs could always hope to be treated as the exception rather than the rule, and incentives to defect might actually be raised rather than lowered as a result. It is quite understandable that creditors might not be eager to spark off this whole process either, given the number of potential defaulters to be kept in line by costly measures of one kind or another. The historical record is quite instructive on this point. As Peter Lindert and Peter Morton have noted,[24] a strong inverse relationship has always tended to prevail between the number of countries in trouble at any given moment and the willingness of creditors, in effect, to put their money where their mouth is. Before the First World War, the only debtors ever subjected to sanctions were those who defaulted more or less in isolation. During global crises, by contrast, in the nineteenth century as well as in the interwar period, most non-payers tended to escape significant retribution by creditors. Increasingly, history seems to be repeating itself (again)[25] in the late twentieth century. LDC policy makers might be forgiven for seeing in this past experience a lesson for their own time.

Creditors are not unaware, of course, of the signs of erosion in their own credibility, and to the extent possible have acted decisively to maintain or reinforce their effective bargaining leverage *vis-à-vis* debtors. Almost from the first moments of the crisis, banks have sought to reduce their vulnerability by gradually bolstering general capital ratios. As Table 7.1 shows for US banks, the resulting reductions in relative exposure since 1982 have been nothing less than spectacular, particularly for America's largest money centre and regional institutions. Even more dramatic was the sudden and massive build-up of loan-loss reserves in the spring of

*Table 7.1   Exposure of US banks to non-OPEC LDCs,
1982–86 (in billions of dollars and percentages)*

	All US banks	Nine money-centre banks	14 other large banks	All other
December 1982				
(a) Exposure*	107.4	66.4	21.6	19.4
(b) Capital	70.6	29.0	13.5	28.1
(a) as % of (b)	(152.1)	(229.0)	(160.0)	(69.0)
December 1984				
(a) Exposure*	107.0	66.2	22.3	18.5
(b) Capital	92.2	36.7	18.1	37.4
(a) as % of (b)	(116.1)	(180.4)	(123.2)	(49.5)
December 1986				
(a) Exposure*	92.6	59.1	17.4	16.0
(b) Capital	116.1	46.7	22.0	47.4
(a) as % of (b)	(79.8)	(126.5)	(79.1)	(33.8)

*Exposures are total amounts owed after adjustments for guarantees and extern
borrowing.

Source: Federal Financial Institutions Examination Council, *Country Exposu
Lending Survey*, various issues.

1987 by banks in the USA (as well as in Canada and th
UK) triggered by Citicorp, America's biggest bank. In Ma
1987, Citicorp announced unexpectedly that it was addin
$3 billion to its provisions against potential Third Worl
defaults. Within two months, reserve increases totallin
nearly $14 billion had been reported by some 50 other U
banks.[26] In effect, Citicorp set a new standard for America
lenders: a minimum provision of 25 per cent against overa
LDC exposure. Subsequently, even higher levels were estal
lished by a number of important US intermediaries (se
below).

Whatever Citicorp's motivations may have been in trig
gering this historic round of reserve increases,[27] and whateve
else the initiative may ultimately accomplish, the immediat
effect in the opinion of many observers was seemingly t
improve the banking community's overall strategic positio

n the debt game. The provisions did of course have to be
deducted from current earnings under US accounting conventions, thus resulting in the appearance of record losses
or many banks in their 1987 income statements. But these
were paper losses only, since most of the reserves were
created simply by setting aside a portion of already existing
shareholder equity. In reality, as David Rockefeller wrote in
he summer of 1987, 'this transfer of funds — and that is all
t is — has not cost the banks a penny'.[28] Instead, what it did
was to more effectively insulate future earnings from the
mpact of possible LDC defections, in effect signalling
debtors that banks now could, if necessary, afford to take
some hits. According to a high-level US Treasury official,
commenting off the record immediately after Citicorp's
initiative, the action would provide a 'sobering reality' for
hose LDCs 'that felt they had the banks on the hook'.[29]
A prominent business publication echoed shortly thereafter:
By preparing to recognize losses, [Citicorp] cut the value of
a strong card — the threat of default — in the hands of debtor
nations'.[30]

In the opinion of other observers, however, the effect was
rather less salutory for banks, for several reasons. In the first
place, a 25 per cent provision was still considerably smaller
than the discounts that have recently tended to prevail in the
secondary market for LDC debts (Table 7.2), suggesting that
yet more reserves would probably be required to *fully*
insulate future bank earnings against all possible losses.[31]
Furthermore, even though future *earnings* might now be
more effectively protected, bank *capital* would not be: any
charges against the banks' new reserves would automatically
reduce their capital, as currently measured, requiring them
either to market additional equity and sell off existing loans,
or else apply to the regulators for an exemption from
minimum capital requirements. And finally, there was the
possible impact on debtor incentives to consider. One consequence of the 1987 provisions, plainly, would be to
discourage future Third World financing by banks. As the
IBRD (p. xxvi) has pointed out,[16] a higher standard for
reserves acts in effect as a tax on new lending by requiring
a larger charge against current earnings for each additional

*Table 7.2   Indicative bid-offer prices for debt of
ten major debtor nations, 1986–87*

Country	Jan. 1986	July 1986	Jan. 1987	May 1987	Oct. 198
Argentina	62–66	63–67	65–67	58–60	36–39
Brazil	75–81	73–76	75–76	61–63	39–42
Chile	65–69	64–67	67–69	67–70	50–53
Ecuador	68–71	63–66	65–66	50–54	30–34
Mexico	69–73	56–59	56–57	56–57	50–52
Nigeria	n.a.	n.a.	36–42	37–40	20–25
Peru	25–30	18–23	18–20	14–16	7–8
Philippines	48–52	n.a.	72–75	68–72	50–53
Poland	50–53	42–45	42–44	45–47	40–43
Venezuela	80–82	75–78	74–75	72–74	49–53

n.a. Not available.

Source: *Swaps: The Newsletter of New Financial Instruments*, vol. 1, no.
November 1987.

credit extended; in any event, it would certainly now b
more difficult for bank managers to justify any new LD(
loans to their shareholders. But this, in turn, also remove
one of the most important of potential bribes that creditor
have traditionally dangled in front of debtors. As *Th
Economist* observed: 'If the carrot of new money is take
away, debtors have even less reason not to default'.[32] Th
result could be even more intransigence on the part of LD(
policy makers.

In reality, therefore, it is not at all clear whether creditor
have been successful in their efforts to reverse the erosion o
their bargaining leverage. Indeed, the ambiguity inherent i
this already complex setting is becoming greater, not less. *
few commentators not surprisingly continue to insist tha
banks still have the upper hand. In a book published in lat
1987,[33] for instance, investment banker Irving Friedma
dismissed any threat of default by debtors as 'nonsense'
LDCs, he wrote, 'may repudiate their debts, but the im
mediate penalties for doing so are great: seizure of asset
held abroad, loss of creditworthiness, and even virtua

oppage of foreign trade . . . . Very few countries can
olerate these consequences' (p. 40). For most other analysts,
owever, the cards remaining to debtors are beginning to
ook at least as strong as those available to creditors, if not
ronger.[34] Today, even many bankers are willing to concede
ıe extent to which the distribution of power between the
wo sides has shifted. In another book published in late
987, political scientist Jeffry Frieden quoted a prominent
ew York commercial banker, George Clark of Citicorp, on
ıe difficulty of maintaining the credibility of creditor
ınctions:

> Jack Clark notes that the banks' bargaining weapons are strong but
> not all-powerful: 'The banks try to create as many negative incen-
> tives as they can think of: they cut off trade credits, they stop
> financing government programs . . . . That might result in a more
> positive environment [sic]. Beyond that, it gets hard. We talk a lot
> about attaching assets, but that's not really a strong weapon in most
> cases. Most of these countries don't have a lot of assets to attach.'[35]

The key question, then, is: can debtors seize the oppor-
ınity afforded by the increased ambiguity of today's setting
ɔ gain the upper hand for themselves? As early as 1985,
ɑletsky likened creditor–debtor relations to a 'game of
ɔker' where 'a close look at the cards . . . suggests a deck
ʰich is stacked in favor of the borrowers, not the lenders'
ɔ. 3).[13] Citing not only the issue of juridical uncertainty but
so the prospectively growing cost of financial deterrents to
ʳeditors, Kaletsky reasoned that it was only a matter of time
efore leverage and momentum would flow to the debtor
de. Has that time finally arrived? Do LDCs now have the
ower to diminish or overcome creditor resistance to the idea
f debt relief?

Most potent, of course, would be some form of *collective
:tion* by LDC governments, to extract concessions from
ʳeditors — some variant, in other words, of the long-dreaded
ebtors' cartel. A common front would certainly improve the
ebtor side's capacity to proffer credible carrots or sticks in
ıture negotiations. Attractive new money packages, in-
uding *inter alia* generous exit options or debt conversion

schemes for banks that want 'out' or flexible 'onlending' o
'relending' arrangements for those willing to stay in,[36] coulc
be more easily agreed if the creditor side did not have tc
worry about debtors all competing among themselves fo
the most favourable treatment (the demonstration effec
again). Even more to the point, any threat of *de jure* or *de
facto* default would be far more persuasive if made jointl
rather than individually. The advantages of solidarity in con
fronting creditors have long been appreciated in the Thirc
World, most particularly in Latin America, where even head
of government openly discuss the possibility of collectiv
action on debt. At a summit meeting of eight major Latii
debtors held in Acapulco, Mexico, in late 1987, the so-callec
Group of Eight,[37] every one of the presidents in attendanc
professed support for some kind of joint initiative on th
debt issue.[38]

Potent as a debtors' cartel might be, however, the chance
of one being formed must even now be counted as rathei
remote. Not even the Group of Eight, for all the rhetoric
of its leaders at Acapulco, appeared able to bring itself ii
its final communiqué to anything more than an expressior
of 'solidarity' with those governments that 'in accordanc
with their own circumstances, may be forced to take
unilateral measures to limit their debt servicing'.[39] It is
obvious that serious obstacles exist to block effective co
ordination among debtors. For most analysts, the two mos
fundamental are: the extraordinary diversity of economic
conditions and prospects on the debtor side, which tends tc
overshadow any underlying common interest in debt relief
and the fact of national sovereignty, which maximizes the
incentive for each government individually to seek out
the best possible deal for itself.[40, 41] Additional factors
frequently cited include differences in the timing of financia
crises, in foreign strategic relationships or domestic politica
systems, or even in the personalities and values of key
decision makers.[42]

Perhaps the most important factor of all, however, is also
the least frequently cited: the fact that from the debtors
point of view, formal coordination may not even be necessary — and could well be counterproductive. Kaletsky[13] is

>ne of the few analysts to have stressed the potential *dis-*
dvantages of a formal cartel. In his words: 'The main
>bjection to a debtors' cartel is the same as the one against
lagrant repudiation: it would needlessly provoke govern-
nental and public opinion in creditor countries' (p. 63). Far
ess provocative, but not necessarily much less potent, would
>e the cumulative effect of a series of individual initiatives by
roubled debtors, just as has in fact been occurring in Latin
America and Sub-Saharan Africa in recent years. One by one,
is already indicated, more than a dozen governments have
inilaterally ceased debt service or fallen into serious arrears,
aving valuable foreign exchange; moreover, once in arrears,
lebtors have only rarely found both the will and the means
o get current on their interest payments again. Yet we know
hat precisely because of the growing number of countries
nvolved, creditors have become increasingly hesitant to
engage in any kind of costly reprisals. So who needs a
lebtors' cartel at all, when much the same impact can be
ichieved without the difficulties and risks of formal coordination? Implicitly, that would appear to be the strategic
ogic underlying the Acapulco communiqué of the Group of
Eight.

By far the most likely scenario, therefore, at least for the
near term, is a continuation of the trend already clearly
liscernible in these growing numbers of *de facto* defaults by
lebtor governments – collective *inaction* (non-payment), in
effect, rather than collective action. And of course the more
he trend tends to persist, *ceteris paribus*, the greater will be
he ultimate erosion in the effective bargaining leverage of
creditors. To that extent, the time does seem finally to have
irrived for momentum to flow to the debtor side. The
political equation is indeed changing.

But is it changing enough? That remains in considerable
doubt. An ebbing of creditor leverage is one thing; a flow of
momentum sufficient, on its own, to compel a fundamental
reform of the prevailing containment strategy is quite some-
hing else. In good part, the outcome ultimately will depend
>n which LDCs may, or may not, choose to join the ranks of
non-payers: sustained defaults by three or four of the largest
lebtor nations, plainly, would do more to concentrate minds

on the creditor side than several times that many unilateral
initiatives by smaller players. But since, by definition, it is
impossible to foresee who among the debtors might actually
in time be tempted or driven to defect, and who not, it is
also impossible to be sure that this trend alone would suffice
to alter decisively the broad distribution of power in the
game. More realistically, we must admit that the probabilities
involved are simply too low to inspire any degree of confidence in a spontaneous solution to the problem along these
lines. The odds in favour of debtors may now be shortening
somewhat — but hardly enough, it is clear, to be able to
declare categorically *les jeux sont faits*.

INTERNAL DYNAMICS OF
PREFERENCE FORMATION

The scenario of collective inaction, however, affects only
one side of the political equation: the debtor side. Much
depends as well on what endogenous changes, if any, may
be anticipated on the creditor side. Can any concurrent
changes be expected in creditor perceptions of their
interests? And if so, are these likely to complement or
counteract the accumulating tide of pressures from debtor
nations? This means taking a closer look at the *internal
dynamics* of preference formation on the creditor side.
Specifically, it means looking at *alignments* within the
creditor side — among banks and between them and public
institutions — and how these act to shape or alter creditors'
collective behaviour in their ongoing relations with debtors.
How may creditor alignments now be expected to evolve
given current and prospective developments in the overall
setting of the game?

The creditor side, clearly, is not a monolith. Quite the
contrary. Among the many actors involved as lenders to
the Third World, most notably, commercial banks and their
home governments in the capital-market countries, along
with the IMF and World Bank, the diversity of economic
conditions and prospects is at least as extraordinary as that
on the debtor side. Banks holding LDC paper number

literally in the hundreds and range in size from the largest financial intermediaries in the world, with billions of dollars of exposure, to quite small regional or local institutions, particularly in the USA, with no more than a few thousands at risk. In similar fashion, the banks' home governments in North America, Europe, and Japan vary greatly both in terms of their own LDC loan exposure and in terms of their economic and political relations in different regions of the Third World. And these variations are reflected as well in the Fund and Bank, where decision making has always been most heavily influenced by give-and-take among the main industrial and financial powers. The heterogeneity of the creditor group is obviously enormous. Yet despite intra-industry differences and coordination problems, lenders clearly have succeeded in maintaining a sufficient degree of solidarity in the debt game — at least until now — to shape pay-off structures to their advantage. What has accounted for this remarkable success?

Superficially, of course, the answer seems obvious: success has been assured because of fears of the alternative. Suppose LDC debtors had not been held to their full contractual obligations after the Mexican crisis in 1982. Widespread defaults could have triggered a wave of bank failures, possibly a repetition of the financial collapse of the 1930s, perhaps even another Great Depression. Banking, as we know, is a peculiarly influential industry, owing to the central role that banks play in providing, through their credit and deposit facilities, the means of payment for transactions of every kind — the oil, in effect, that lubricates the interlocking wheels of commerce. Indirect repercussions of any eruption in the industry (technically, any 'negative social externalities') tend to be all out of proportion to the size of the institutions directly involved; they are also difficult to confine to the financial sector alone. For many observers, therefore, it seems plain that creditor solidarity has been successfully maintained for the most fundamental of reasons — an instinct for self-preservation.

A closer look, however, raises doubts about this simple explanation, since it is evident that not all creditors have actually been threatened with failure by the debt crisis.

Public creditors, certainly, can take a hit on their Third World loans and survive. The viability of national govern ments is a matter of politics, not mere financial profit and loss; and the same is true ultimately of the Fund and Bank a well, because of their legal backing by the 'full faith and credit' of their respective sovereign members. Only private creditors have been directly at risk; and of these, the only truly threatened institutions have been those whose exposure was and continues to be high relative to their own capital - which clearly means just the biggest of the commercial bank active in LDC lending (see Table 7.1). For the large numbe of smaller institutions involved, with holdings well below the level of their own capital, widespread defaults would be pain ful but not disastrous. For the major international lenders on the other hand — the two or three dozen giants at the peak of the global banking industry — the result could well be technical insolvency (unless abridged by a modification o traditional accounting regulations). In reality, it is only thes giants that have had any serious reason to worry about self preservation.

This suggests that more is actually at work here than appears at first glance. Since it is the giants that have stood to lose the most from any concessions to debtors, it is thei interests that have been served most directly by the contain ment strategy in force since 1982. In effect, therefore, it i they who have called the tune — even where others on the creditor side, with other mixes of interests, might well have preferred a different drummer. Creditor solidarity has been maintained by a decision-making process dominated, in formally if not formally, by the needs and preferences o the biggest international lenders. In the words of Jeffrey Sachs and Harry Huizinga: 'The debt management strategy pursued . . . since 1982 has been geared toward the protec tion of the larger commercial banks, at least on a short-run accounting basis'.[43] The dominance of the giants may be rather less than perfect — indeed, has been quite imperfec at times — but it has been strikingly effective for all that

In practice, the giants have called the tune, however im perfectly, by exploiting two basic features of their overal institutional environment. One is the distinctly oligopolistic nd hierarchical structure of the international banking community, which in the industry as a whole gives larger intermediaries disproportionate influence over the behaviour of their smaller rivals. The other is the distinctly fragmented and dispersed structure of policy assignments within national governments, which in the capital-market countries as a whole gives banks generally disproportionate influence over official attitudes on the debt problem. In each case, coordination problems have been suppressed to the extent possible by formation of implicit transnational coalitions. Diversity of interests has been accommodated, again to the extent possible, by the usual tactics of side-payments or sanctions.

The importance of the oligopolistic structure of the international banking community in this respect has been emphasized in a number of recent analyses.[44, 45] Diversity of interests within the industry is inevitable, given the nature of the LDC loan market. Banks differ among themselves not only in terms of their exposure (absolute or relative to capital) but in a variety of other respects as well, e.g. the degree of their commitment to foreign business in general, the extent of their commercial ties to developing nations in particular, and the geographic distribution of their Third World activity. Yet for the most part divergences have been successfully suppressed by the industry's giants, using the leverage provided them by the dependence of smaller institutions on them for correspondent relationships or other financial services. Local and regional banks can be bribed by, for example, offers of privileged access to inter-bank credit lines or possible participation in lucrative new lending syndicates. They can also be coerced by threats of exclusion from traditional industry networks — 'peer pressure', as it is politely known in the trade. In effect, bankers play two games simultaneously: one collectively with LDC borrowers, the other separately among themselves. The largest banks, organized in so-called steering groups or advisory committees (one separately for each debtor country), negotiate terms with each other and with LDC governments, and then gain the ratification of smaller institutions through effective exploitation of asymmetries and hierarchy in intra-industry interdependence.

Reinforcing this position of influence, in turn, is the fragmented nature of governmental policy assignments in the capital-market countries, which typically tends to bias official attitudes on debt in favour of support for the giants of the banking industry. In all the capital-market countries, primary responsibility for LDC debt issues has been entrusted to finance ministries and/or central banks rather than to, say, foreign ministries and/or industry or trade-oriented agencies. The result, not surprisingly, has been to accord highest priority to the purely financial aspects of the problem, rather than to, say, diplomatic or commercial implications. Relatively little weight has been attached to possible threats of political disruption or lost export opportunities in the Third World. Public policy in practice has reflected most clearly fears for the safety and soundness of financial institutions — and since it has been the largest institutions that have been most at risk, it is their interests that have naturally tended to receive the most attention. The intensity of links between big banks and their home governments, as we know, tends to vary considerably, from extremely close ties in countries like Japan or France to rather more distant relations in Britain or the USA.[46,47,48] Yet even in the USA it is evident that official decision making on LDC debt has been most directly conditioned by concerns for the preservation and health of the nation's largest financial intermediaries.[43] It is hardly necessary to invoke some kind of conspiracy theory to account for the tacit alliances that have tended to coalesce in this issue area between the big international lenders and their respective home governments.

Creditor solidarity has thus been maintained, despite intra-industry differences and coordination problems, by a quite singular alignment of underlying political forces — a configuration of power centred, above all, on the joint preferences of a small number of large banks backed by an equally small number of public institutions. And within this configuration of power, no actors have been more influential in shaping creditors' collective behaviour than those of the USA: the main money-centre banks of New York, Chicago and California, together with the Federal Reserve and, most importantly, the Department of the Treasury.

Other players on the creditor side generally tend to defer to US leadership in dealing with Third World debt problems.[41] This reflects not only the key role of the dollar as the currency of denomination for most LDC paper (making the Federal Reserve, in effect, the *de facto* lender of last resort in the event of a debt-induced banking crisis). Even more to the point, it reflects the dominant market share of US lenders in the most prominent of the troubled debtor nations (e.g. Latin America and the Philippines). Bank advisory committees, by tradition, tend to comprise at most a dozen or so of a country's largest creditors. This has given America's big money-centre intermediaries, backed by the Treasury, by far the greatest influence in formulating and managing the prevailing containment strategy. It is no accident that the strategy was first articulated by a US Treasury Secretary back in 1982.[49] Nor is it an accident that all significant adjustments of the strategy since then have also emanated from Washington, e.g. the celebrated Baker Plan of 1985 or the later 'menu-of-options' approach of 1987.[50] The tune that has been called since 1982 has had a distinctly American ring to it.

The key question is: will other players on the creditor side continue to follow this tune? Or, alternatively, might any endogenous changes in political alignments be anticipated that could result in a significant revision of the effective ordering of creditor preferences? The answer is not immediately apparent. On the one hand, it is clear that growing distributional struggles among banks, and between them and other interested parties in the capital-market countries, are exacerbating intra-industry strains and co-ordination problems. Alignments on the creditor side are becoming distinctly more fluid. On the other hand, it is not at all clear that out of this increased fluidity any powerful new coalition of forces is soon likely to emerge that might decisively challenge the current dominance of the largest commercial lenders, led from the USA. Here too, as on the debtor side of the equation, change is indeed occurring — but, once again, not necessarily to a degree sufficient to fundamentally alter the terms of the game.

The signs of increasing strains on the creditor side are

everywhere. Consider, for example, relations between the big
banks and their smaller brethren. Local and regional banks
have always resented the strong-arm tactics of the giants of
the industry, which have compelled them to go along with
each successive rescheduling of outstanding syndicated loans
and even to participate on a *pro rata* basis in negotiated new
credits to troubled debtors (so-called concerted, or 'involuntary', lending). Now, however, as the prospect of *de facto*
insolvency persistently rises for many countries, growing
numbers of smaller creditors seem prepared to break ranks
despite the peer pressure that has been applied to them.
Many, especially those with only limited Third World exposure and few other commercial ties to LDCs are simply
getting out, by selling off their paper in the secondary market
or by refusing to participate in new reschedulings (thus
forcing larger banks to take over their shares).[51] Others,
more dramatically, are writing off large portions of their
portfolios or working out their own separate deals with
debtor governments.[52] The ability of the major banks to
effectively suppress intra-industry differences is clearly in
decline.

Indeed, even among the big banks themselves, divergences
of interests and priorities appear to be widening significantly.
Certainly this is evident in the changing attitude of the continental European banks, which have long chafed under the
status quo strategy of rescheduling plus concerted lending
favoured by the big US institutions (and the Treasury). With
their different regulations, the Europeans would find it less
costly to capitalize interest arrears rather than keep lending
LDCs new money with which to service old debt. With their
more substantial loan-loss reserves (mostly well hidden), they
are also less hesitant to contemplate the idea of outright debt
relief. Now, more and more, they too seem prepared to break
ranks with the Americans — or, at least, to talk publicly
about the possibility of new approaches.[53] US leadership no
longer receives quite the same degree of deference that it
once did.

Divergences among the big banks are also evident within
the ranks of the Americans themselves. One example can be
seen in Citicorp's dramatic — and unilateral — decision to add

to its loan-loss reserves in May 1987. As indicated, that initiative was quite unexpected; and while it is true that the action was soon emulated by other US lenders, it was also clearly resented by those money-centre banks less well positioned than Citicorp (either because of lower profitability or greater exposure) to meet what from that time became the new 25 per cent minimum standard for provisions. Tensions over the issue were further exacerbated near the end of 1987 by a second round of reserve increases, to an even higher standard of 50 per cent or more of exposure, begun by the Bank of Boston and some other large regionals around the country.[54] By the end of January 1988, a distinct cleavage had developed between the big New York institutions (together with the Bank of America) on the one hand, which refused to add yet again to their LDC provisions; and, on the other hand, the remaining money-centre banks of California and Chicago, as well as most regional institutions, all of which voluntarily opted for the new higher standard.[55] Evidence suggests that at least some of the big New York banks would have been extremely hard-pressed to find the requisite resources had they tried to go along.[56]

Another example of divergences within the American ranks could be seen in the deal negotiated secretly by Morgan Guaranty Bank with the Mexican Government and announced at the end of December 1987. Under that proposal, Mexico hoped to be able to swap at a discount a sizeable portion of its existing bank debt for newly issued marketable Mexican securities, which in turn would be backed by US Treasury bonds bought with cash reserves by the Mexican Government.[57] The deal was initially hailed by many as a breakthrough in coping with Third World debt problems, particularly in so far as it would enable the Mexicans (and possibly other countries) to retire some of their bank credits at less than par — in effect, to 'capture the discount' prevailing in the secondary market. For precisely that reason, however, Morgan's plan was greeted with rather less than wholehearted enthusiasm by most other US money-centre institutions, still reluctant to accept formal losses on their LDC portfolios[58] and none chose to participate when the plan was implemented two months later, causing final

results to fall far short of aspirations.[59] Increasingly, relation
among America's major banks appear to be dominated less b
thoughts of preserving industry solidarity than by sentiment
of *sauve qui peut*.

Finally, other parties *outside* the financial community
with their own interests in debtor countries, are now begin
ning to be heard more in opposition to the prevailing
containment strategy. This is especially true of key con
stituencies in the export sector, in the USA and elsewhere, a
awareness grows of the extent to which the 'low-growth
high-debt-service trap' has cut into traditional sales volume
in developing nations. Exporters have clearly had their
consciousness raised in recent years. In the words of an
executive of the General Electric Corporation: 'Over th
last ten years, our exports to Latin America have dropped
dramatically . . . . Resolving debt problems is clearly a critica
element on the export front'.[60] Anger is directed in
particular at the Treasury for its bias in favour of financia
interests. Notes one former Department official: 'Treasury
actions have catered to the short-term profit of large
American banks, but increasingly at the expense of workers
businesses, and farmers who have lost Third World markets'.[61]
More and more, calls are being made to accord higher priority
to commercial and even diplomatic considerations, rathe
than to focus mainly on financial concerns, in framing public
policy on LDC debt. Pressures are visibly growing to loosen
the close, albeit tacit, bank–government alliances that have
previously dominated decision making in this area.

Despite all these signs of strain on the creditor side, how
ever, no change can be expected in the effective ordering of
creditor preferences unless existing coalitions are supplanted
by new and even stronger alignments of forces, implicit if not
explicit, in the capital-market countries. Increased fluidity
among the players is not enough: resentments and frustrations must be translated into effective collective action
if the political equation is to be significantly altered. The
big banks, backed by finance ministries and central banks, are
unlikely to abandon their resistance to the idea of debt relief
without a struggle, since it is they who stand to lose the
most. In the absence of sufficient leverage from the debtor

ide, that resistance can be diminished or overcome only by
a superior use of power from within the creditor side — new
tactics of side-payments or sanctions to replace those
previously exercised by the industry giants. And this can be
accomplished only by some degree of political organization
among other players inside the financial community and/or
outside of it.

Unfortunately, little evidence exists to suggest that such
organization is likely to occur spontaneously. Inside the
financial community, barriers to alternative alignments will
remain high so long as the industry remains as oligopolistic
and hierarchical as it is. Outside, other interested parties will
continue to have difficulty influencing official attitudes so
long as finance ministries and central banks retain primary
policy responsibility for the debt issue. And any coalescence
of links between selected elements of the financial community (e.g. the smaller banks) and other actors (e.g.
exporters) will continue to be hampered by a lack of either
a tradition or an institutional base for effective collective
action. More realistically, therefore, we must admit that here
too, as on the debtor side, the probabilities involved are
simply too low to inspire any confidence in an endogenous
solution to the problem along these lines. Here too, the odds
are unlikely to shorten sufficiently to be able to declare
categorically *les jeux sont faits*.

CONCLUSION AND IMPLICATIONS

The message of this discussion is clear. It is that much as we
might wish for it, a genuinely cooperative solution of the
debt problem is quite unlikely to emerge spontaneously.
Even if all concerned could in fact be persuaded that the
game is not zero-sum, there seems little reason to anticipate
that the dynamics of the game by itself might suffice to
persuade players — in particular, creditors — to take the
necessary risks for cooperation. The effective ordering of
creditor preferences is not likely to be reshaped much by an
endogenous change of values and belief systems. Nor is the
underlying political equation apt to be altered significantly

in the near term despite the evidence of a growing flow of momentum to the debtor side on the one hand, and an increasing fluidity of alignments among creditors on the other. The probabilities at all three levels of analysis — cognitive, unit, and system — simply appear too low to be convincing.

From this conclusion, the implication follows that if the second of the two necessary conditions for cooperation is to be satisfied, it will have to be *promoted*. That is, if existing obstacles to cooperation are to be reduced or eliminated, an appropriate mechanism or incentive structure will have to be *designed*, not just hoped for. In short, activism will indeed be required.

NOTES AND REFERENCES

1. See, for instance, the record of remarks at the 1987 annual IMF/ World Bank annual meeting, conveniently summarized in *IMF Survey*, 19 October 1987. According to Michel Camdessus, managing director of the IMF, 'In our [debt] strategy, a fundamental element . . . must be preserved at all cost: the principle of shared responsibility and its corollary, the duty to work cooperatively' (p. 296). Added US President Ronald Reagan: 'A cooperative solution to the debt problem is the only answer. It involves a partnership among developing countries, commercial banks, and international financial institutions.' (p. 300). Similar sentiments were also expressed by Barber Conable, president of the World Bank, and in the communiqués of the IMF's influential Interim Committee and the joint IMF/World Bank Development Committee.

2. Cohen, Benjamin J., 'LDC Debt: Is There an Unexploited Opportunity for Joint Gain?' (processed), 1988.

3. Cohen, Benjamin J., 'LDC Debt: Toward a Genuinely Cooperative Solution' (processed), 1988.

4. For illustrative purposes, alternative games may be described in terms of elementary two-player pay-off structures, where from the point of view of each player individually only four combinations of strategies are available: mutual cooperation (CC), mutual defection (DD), unilateral cooperation (CD), and unilateral defection (DC). In Deadlock, players have a preference ordering of

DC > DD > CC > CD. In Chicken, the preference ordering is DC > CC > CD > DD.

5. Dornbusch, Rudiger, 'International Debt and Economic Instability', *Federal Reserve Bank of Kansas City Economic Review*, January 1987, pp. 15-32.

6. Cohen, Benjamin J., *In Whose Interest? International Banking and American Foreign Policy*, New Haven, CN: Yale University Press for the Council on Foreign Relations, 1986, p. 221.

7. Kuczynski, Pedro-Pablo, 'The Outlook for Latin American Debt', *Foreign Affairs*, vol. 66, no. 1, Fall 1987, p. 129.

8. Krueger, Anne O., 'Debt, Capital Flows, and LDC Growth', *American Economic Review*, vol. 77, no. 2, May 1987, pp. 159-64.

9. See, for example, Simon, Herbert A., *Models of Bounded Rationality*, Cambridge, MA: MIT Press, 1982.

10. Axelrod, Robert and Keohane, Robert O., 'Achieving Cooperation Under Anarchy: Strategies and Institutions', in Kenneth A. Oye (ed.), *Cooperation Under Anarchy*, Princeton, NJ: Princeton University Press, 1986, p. 247.

11. Including this observer. See Cohen, Benjamin J., 'Global Debt: Why is Cooperation so Difficult?', in Paolo Guerrieri and Pier Carlo Padoan (eds), *The Political Economy of International Co-operation*, London: Croom Helm, 1988, pp. 91-111. This paper was first presented at an international conference held in Rome, Italy, in March 1986.

12. Gourevitch, Peter, *Politics in Hard Times: Comparative Responses to International Economic Crises*, Ithaca, NY: Cornell University Press, 1986, p. 17.

13. Kaletsky, Anatole, *The Costs of Default*, New York: Twentieth Century Fund, 1985.

14. A considerable scholarly literature has developed in recent years attempting to formally model the complex bargaining relationship between international creditors and debtors. For useful surveys, see Eaton, Jonathan, Gersovitz, Mark and Stiglitz, Joseph E., 'The Pure Theory of Country Risk', *European Economic Review*, vol. 30, no. 3, June 1986, pp. 481-513; Glick, Reuven, *Economic Perspectives on Foreign Borrowing and Debt Repudiation: An Analytical Literature Review*, Monograph Series in Finance and Economics, no. 4, New York: New York University Graduate School of Business Administration, 1986; and Crawford, Vincent P., *International Lending, Long-Term Credit Relationships, and Dynamic Contract Theory*, Studies in International Finance, no. 59, Princeton, NJ: International Finance Section, March 1987.

15. See, for example, *The New York Times*, 12 August 1987.
16. International Bank for Reconstruction and Development, *World Debt Tables: External Debt of Developing Countries*, Volume I: Analysis and Summary Tables, Washington, January 1988, p. xv.
17. See *The Economist*, 8 August 1987, p. 13. It may be noted that, in the aggregate, there has been a sizeable run-off of short-term trade credits for Peru. But that began as early as 1982 and was largely completed by the time Mr Garcia took office in mid-1985. See Alexander, Lewis S., *Three Essays on Sovereign Default and International Lending*, PhD dissertation, Yale University, May 1987, p. 46.
18. *The Economist*, 20 February 1988, p. 90.
19. Brazil agreed in a provisional accord with creditors to pay $700 million out of its own reserves to bring 1988 interest up to date, though some $3 billion remained in arrears for interest due in 1987.
20. *The New York Times*, 29 February 1988, p. D1.
21. Central to the debate among lawyers are two traditional tenets of international law — the principle of foreign sovereign immunity and the act of state doctrine — and the extent to which either, or both, may constrain the legal remedies available to lenders to foreign sovereigns. Neither recent legislation (e.g. the US, Foreign Sovereign Immunities Act of 1976) nor court rulings (involving countries as diverse as Costa Rica, Cuba, and Iran) have succeeded in clarifying the juridical issues or risks involved. For a sample of opinion, see Mayer, Frank D. and Odorizzi, Michele, 'Foreign Government Deposits: Attachment and Set-Off', *University of Illinois Law Review*, no. 1, 1982, pp. 289–304; Reisner, Ralph, 'Default by Sovereign Debtors: An Introductory Perspective', *University of Illinois Law Review*, no. 1, 1982; Nichols, Bruce W., 'Sovereign Debtors Under U.S. Immunity Law', in Gruson, Michael and Reisner, Ralph (eds), *Sovereign Lending: Managing Legal Risk*, London: Euromoney Publications, 1984, pp. 81–7; Patrikis, Ernest T., 'Immunity of Central Bank Assets Under U.S. Law', in Gruson, Michael and Reisner, Ralph (eds), *Sovereign Lending: Managing Legal Risk*, London: Euromoney Publications, 1984, pp. 89–101; McCormick, Caitlin, 'The Commercial Activity Exception to Foreign Sovereign Immunity and the Act of State Doctrine', *Law and Policy in International Business*, vol. 16, no. 2, November 1984, pp. 477–538; Potter, Stuart *et al.*, 'Thinking the Unthinkable: Attaching a State's Assets', *International Financial Law Review*, vol. 3, no. 10, October 1984, pp. 15–21; and Alexander (note 17), chapter 2.

22. See, for example, *The New York Times*, 17 April 1987, p. D1. Despite their success in forcing new talks, however, the Filipinos in the end felt compelled to accept the 14/16 rate that had been originally negotiated. See *The New York Times*, 26 December 1987, p. 29.

23. Feldstein, Martin, 'Latin America's Debt: Muddling Through Can Be Just Fine', *The Economist*, 27 June 1987, pp. 21–5.

24. Lindert, Peter H. and Morton, Peter J., 'How Sovereign Debt Has Worked', Working Paper Series, No. 45, Research Program in Applied Macroeconomics and Macro Policy, University of California – Davis, August 1987, pp. 24–6.

25. One is reminded of the notorious quote by Yogi Berra: 'It's *deja vu* all over again.'

26. *The Wall Street Journal*, 20 July 1987, p. 2.

27. At least three motivations for Citicorp's action, other than a desire to strengthen bargaining leverage *vis-à-vis* debtors, have been suggested by various commentators: (1) to position the bank to 'reliquefy' its LDC portfolio by enabling it to take selective charges against its new reserves in the future; (2) to improve Citicorp's competitive position in relation to less profitable or more heavily exposed commercial banking rivals; or (3) to exploit certain tax advantages before their termination under the tax reform law passed in 1986. The four motivations, of course, are not mutually exclusive.

28. Rockefeller, David, 'Let's Not Write Off Latin America', *The New York Times*, 5 July 1987, Section 4, p. E15.

29. As quoted in *The Wall Street Journal*, 20 May 1987.

30. *Fortune*, 22 June 1987, p. 26.

31. This does not apply to banks in continental European countries, such as Germany or Switzerland, where loan-loss reserves have customarily been maintained at levels well above the 25 per cent figure; but it does apply to banks in Britain and Canada as well as the USA, and above all to banks in Japan (where provisions still amount to less than 5 per cent of LDC exposure). See, for example, *The Economist*, 30 May 1987, p. 75.

    Many bankers object to the use of quotations in the secondary market as a guide to the true long-term value of LDC paper: it is an extremely thin market where discounts, in effect, reflect 'fire-sale' prices. The market is, however, the best guide available – and is certainly more indicative of true value than the bankers' own practice of carrying all these loans on their books at 100 cents on the dollar.

32. *The Economist*, 25 July 1987, p. 69.

33. Friedman, Irving S., *Toward World Prosperity: Reshaping the Global Monetary System*, Lexington, MA: D.C. Heath, 1987.

34. See, for example, Bailey, Norman A. and Cohen, Richard, *The Mexican Time Bomb*, New York: Twentieth Century Fund, 1987.

35. Frieden, Jeffry A., *Banking on the World: The Politics of American International Finance*, New York: Harper and Row, pp. 146-7.

36. For informed discussions of these and other possible technical innovations, see: Cline, William R., *Mobilizing Bank Lending to Debtor Countries*, Policy Analyses in International Economics No. 18, Washington, DC: Institute for International Economics, June 1987; Watson, Maxwell, Mathieson, Donald, Kincaid, Russell, Folkerts-Landau, David, Regling, Klaus and Atkinson Caroline, *International Capital Markets: Developments and Prospects*, Washington: International Monetary Fund, January 1988 chapter 4; and Regling, Klaus P., 'New Financing Approaches in the Debt Strategy', *Finance and Development*, vol. 25, no. 1, March 1988, pp. 6-9.

37. Argentina, Brazil, Colombia, Mexico, Panama, Peru, Uruguay, and Venezuela. The Group of Eight grew out of earlier Latin American efforts to bring about a negotiated settlement of on going military conflicts in Central America. Four of the members (Colombia, Mexico, Panama, and Venezuela) were responsible for the original Contadora peace plan, drawn up in 1983; the others were members of the so-called support group, organized two years later.

38. See, for example, *The New York Times*, 28 November 1987, p. D1

39. As quoted in *IMF Survey*, 14 December 1987, p. 376.

40. Cline, William R., *International Debt and the Stability of the World Economy*, Policy Analyses in International Economics No. 4, Washington, DC: Institute for International Economics September 1983, pp. 91-2.

41. Aggarwal, Vinod K., *International Debt Threat: Bargaining Among Creditors and Debtors in the 1980s*, Policy Papers in International Affairs, No. 29, Berkeley, CA: Institute of International Studies, 1987, chapter 4.

42. Feinberg, Richard E., 'Latin American Debt: Renegotiating the Debt Burden', *Columbia Journal of World Business*, vol. 21 no. 3, Fall 1986, pp. 22-3.

43. Sachs, Jeffrey and Huizinga, Harry, 'U.S. Commercial Banks and the Developing-Country Debt Crisis', *Brookings Papers on Economic Activity*, No. 2, 1987, p. 557.

44. See especially Lipson, Charles, 'Bankers' Dilemmas: Private Co-operation in Rescheduling Sovereign Debts', in Oye, Kenneth A. (ed.), *Cooperation Under Anarchy*, Princeton, NJ: Princeton University Press 1986, pp. 200–25.

45. See Aggarwal (note 41), chapter 3.

46. Spindler, J. Andrew, *The Politics of International Credit: Private Finance and Foreign Policy in Germany and Japan*, Washington: Brookings Institution, 1984.

47. Wellons, Philip A., 'International Debt: The Behavior of Banks in a Politicized Environment', in Kahler, Miles (ed.), *The Politics of International Debt*, Ithaca, NY: Cornell University Press 1986, pp. 95–125.

48. Wellons, Philip A., *Passing the Buck: Banks, Governments, and Third World Debt*, Boston: Harvard Business School Press, 1987.

49. Regan, Donald T., 'Statement', *International Financial Markets and Related Matters*, Hearings before the House Committee on Banking, Finance and Urban Affairs, 21 December 1982, pp. 34–9.

50. For more on these initiatives, see Cline (note 36).

51. For example, of the 494 banks that were supposed to participate in the major rescheduling of Mexican debt negotiated in the fall of 1986, no fewer than 139 refused to do so. See Cline (note 36), p. 6.

52. Some prominent examples in 1987–88: (a) in January 1987, the Republic Bank of New York (the eighteenth largest lender to Mexico) revealed that it has unilaterally written down a substantial portion of its Mexican public-sector debt (*The New York Times*, 15 January 1987, p. D1); (b) in September 1987, Britain's Midland Bank and America's First Interstate separately struck bilateral deals with Peru accepting quantities of primary commodities in lieu of cash as part payment of debt service in arrears (*The New York Times*, 17 September 1987, National Edition, p. 25; *California Business*, December 1987, p. 18); (c) in December 1987, the Bank of Boston (America's thirteenth largest bank) wrote off $200 million of its $1 billion in loans to Latin America, quickly followed by two other important regional banks, Riggs National of Washington, DC, and Banc One of Ohio (*The New York Times*, 15 December 1987, National Edition, p. 1; 19 December 1987, National Edition, p. 21); (d) in January 1988, American Express Bank wrote off all its private-sector loans to Latin America, amounting to some $62 million (*The New York Times*, 13 January 1987, p. D1).

53. See, for example, *The Economist*, 8 October 1987, p. 85.

54. See *The New York Times*, 15 December 1987 and 19 December 1987, National Edition, p. 21.

55. *The New York Times*, 20 January 1988, p. D1.

56. See *The Economist*, 23 January 1988, p. 70. Evidence also suggests that the united front of the New York banks on this issue was a direct result of intervention by the Federal Reserve Bank of New York. The stronger New York banks (e.g. Bankers Trust and Morgan Guaranty) were confidentially urged not to go to the new 50 per cent standard, for fear of the damage it might do to public perceptions of the soundness of some of their weaker brethren (e.g. Chemical Bank or Manufacturers Hanover). See *The New York Times*, 22 January 1988, p. D1.

57. *The Wall Street Journal*, 30 December 1987, p. 1.

58. *The New York Times*, 12 January 1988, p. D5.

59. The hope at first had been that the Mexican government could swap up to $20 billion of bank debt at a discount of as much as 50 per cent. In the end, only $3.67 billion of debt was traded for $2.56 billion of new securities, representing an average discount of just over 30 per cent. Instead of cutting foreign liabilities by $10 billion, Mexico managed a net reduction of only $1.1 billion (*The New York Times*, 5 March 1988, p. 35).

60. As quoted in *The New York Times*, 6 December 1987, section 3, p. 1F.

61. Broad, Robin, 'How About a Real Solution to Third World Debt?', *The New York Times*, 28 September 1987, National Edition, p. 27.

8 Future financing for developing countries

Ingrid Iversen

THE CURRENT DEBATE

The debate on the prospects for LDCs and the debt problem is now increasingly focused on the issue of whether the 'muddling through' approach, with rescheduling of principal and injections of new money is viable, or if some form of debt relief is needed. The much wider discussion of the possibility and even the desirability of debt relief is the result of two developments.

First, the increased levels of provisioning against 'bad' loans by banks during 1987 which both recognizes and enables banks to accept that loans to LDCs are worth less than their face value. And second, a greater reluctance by both debtors and creditors to take part in long drawn out negotiations over new money and rescheduling. For debtor countries, the economic programmes, which they have followed in return for the financing of current account deficits, are becoming politically less acceptable, while for the banks, involuntary lending is often unpalatable as their business strategies change. The World Bank in their recent[1] study of debt summed up this situation well, with the phrase 'debt fatigue'.

There is therefore a general acceptance that new approaches are needed to deal with the debt and financing needs of LDCs. However, there is *not* agreement over whether these changes should be aimed at improving the current mechanisms or whether a more fundamental change is needed.

This chapter examines the current situation in the context of the experience of the debtor countries and their creditors since 1982. The objective is to highlight the potential risks to the present strategy and to point to possible alternative approaches. Finally the chapter discusses 'non-traditional' sources of future financing for developing countries.

EXTERNAL AND DOMESTIC ADJUSTMENT

External results

External adjustment by debtor countries since 1982, when voluntary new financing all but ceased, has been remarkable. Imports have been sharply cut and policies of export promotion have resulted in much higher earnings. The success of this restructuring was borne out by the resilience of oil-exporting Mexico in 1986 despite the collapse in oil prices and more generally by the shrinking current account deficits and even surpluses, now being registered by the main debtors (see Table 8.1).

Significantly, the countries that have been most successful in reducing their current account deficits are those where finance has been less available. The four largest debtors have seen much slower rates of growth in their debt than the average, and have generally made sharper adjustments (see Tables 8.2 and 8.3).

These improvements have reduced the borrowing pattern to more sustainable levels. For the Baker 15 countries[2] the total current account deficit in 1985–87 was only one-tenth of its level in 1980–82, reflected in the slowing rate of growth in debt (10 per cent per annum in 1982–84 compared with 5 per cent per annum in 1985–87).

Domestic results

The counterpart to improvements in the external accounts is sharp cuts in domestic spending, both for consumption and investment. While it was widely recognized that many debtor LDCs needed to adjust their spending patterns in line with

Table 8.1 External indicators

	Exports	Imports	Current account US $ million Annual averages	
	Growth %			
	1982–87		1980–82	1985–87
Argentina	-16.0	1.9	-3,946	-2,573
Bolivia	-45.7	33.1	-215	-479
Brazil	29.9	-22.1	-13,623	-2,200
Chile	40.9	9.0	-3,003	-1,073
Colombia	75.5	-26.7	-1,740	-450
Côte d'Ivoire	17.1	-9.1*	-1,418	-32
Ecuador	-13.6	-3.5	-969	-588
Mexico	7.9	-16.9	-9,426	+1,389
Morocco	35.8	9.8	-1,711	-552*
Nigeria	-28.9	-72.5*	-2,819	+815*
Peru	-20.5	-22.9	-1,146	-756
Philippines	13.9	-12.1	-2,388	+489*
Uruguay	-8.4	-1.7	-468	-84
Venezuela	-36.9	39.9	-1,494	+300
Yugoslavia	11.9	1.0	-1,249	+1,167

*1985–86

Sources: International Financial Statistics (IMF); own estimates.

Table 8.2 Growth in debt

	1980–82	1982–84	1984–86	1986–87e
Argentina	26.9	3.4	2.0	5.8
Brazil	14.0	7.2	2.5	9.2
Chile	19.6	7.2	2.0	-6.4
Mexico	23.3	4.9	2.5	4.0
Venezuela	4.4	6.3	-3.0	-0.4
Nigeria	20.4	2.4	8.2	n.a.
Philippines	18.3	0.5	7.2	n.a.
Ecuador	14.5	3.4	3.0	6.1
Peru	11.4	3.0	8.2	5.8
Colombia	22.1	9.1	9.1	4.7
Côte d'Ivoire	16.6	1.5	14.5	n.a.
Yugoslavia	3.9	-0.5	3.9	n.a.
Morocco	14.9	7.2	17.9	n.a.
Bolivia	8.2	10.0	9.5	4.3
Uruguay	26.1	11.4	7.2	7.8

Sources: World Debt Tables (World Bank); own estimates.

Table 8.3   GDP growth

% p.a.	1978–82	1982–84	1984–87
Argentina	-1.5	2.4	1.7
Bolivia	-1.8	-2.6	-1.2
Brazil	2.5	1.4	7.3
Chile	0.0	2.0	4.2
Colombia	3.0	1.8	1.4
Côte d'Ivoire	4.6	-5.2	7.2*
Ecuador	2.6	0.0	1.4
Mexico	4.6	-0.2	0.2
Morocco	2.5	1.6	5.6*
Nigeria	-1.1	-4.9	1.4*
Peru	5.5	-5.2	6.5
Philippines	4.0	-3.7	-1.2*
Uruguay	0.8	-6.3	5.0
Venezuela	-0.7	-3.5	3.0
Yugoslavia	1.8	0.0	2.0

*1984–86.

Sources: International Financial Statistics (IMF); own estimates.

Table 8.4   Investment as a percentage of GDP

	1980	1986
Yugoslavia	39.9	38.4
Ecuador	26.3	20.3
Venezuela	24.7	20.3
Morocco	22.7	20.3
Peru	27.5	19.7
Mexico	29.1	19.2
Brazil	24.8	18.3
Colombia	19.1	17.6
Chile	21.0	14.6
Argentina	26.4	13.3
Philippines	30.6	13.2
Côte d'Ivoire	26.5	11.8
Nigeria	24.0	11.6
Uruguay	17.3	8.7
Bolivia	15.0	8.2

Sources: International Financial Statistics (IMF); own estimates.

1e rapidly emerging external constraint, the speed at which
1is has had to be achieved has had serious adverse effects.

Slow growth has been characterized by falling investment;
; a percentage of GDP it is now only around 15 per cent in
atin America compared with levels of 25 per cent in the
1rly 1980s. In some countries where the recession has been
articularly deep this ratio has fallen as low as 10 per cent
ee Table 8.4).

The reduction in domestic spending to service the debt has
it private consumption but much more significant for long-
:rm development has been the fall in investment spending,
oth private and public. While consumption has been main-
.ined as a percentage of GDP in the 1980s (around 77 per
:nt for the Baker 15) investment has fallen from 25 per cent
1 1978-80 to 23 per cent in 1981-82 to a low of 18 per cent
1 1984-87 (see Table 8.5). The private sector has been
1ueezed by the financing needs of the public sector through
ght monetary policy and high interest rates. Inflation has
:en rapid, creating uncertainty and slow growth has
1mpened confidence.

able 8.5   *Investment, consumption and saving*
            1973-87: the Baker 15 (as % of GDP)

	1973-77	1978-80	1981-82	1983-87
vestment	25.5	25.5	23.4	17.8
nsumption	71.9	74.7	77.3	77.7
ving	23.6	22.1	18.1	16.5

urce: *World Economic Outlook* (IMF, April 1988).

Public investment has also fallen. Governments are faced
ith the need to cut spending and it is politically easier to
1t capital expenditure rather than current expenditure
hich would impact on jobs, subsidies and social spending.
.so a large component in current spending is debt servicing
1ich is difficult to cut.

Attempts to address the problem of domestic imbalances

have not always been successful. Argentina and Brazil, recognizing that inflation was both a cause and result of domestic
deficits introduced 'shock' plans[3] but the failure to reduce
the deficit, needed to ensure the success of the policies has
led to the resurgence of inflation. In Mexico, inflation is
being brought down by controlling prices, allowing some re
valuation of the exchange rate and most importantly a
reduction in the public sector deficit. It is clear that this
policy has been made possible by the success of the external
sector with healthy levels of reserves giving Mexico more
freedom in pursuing a policy aimed at domestic adjustment
less constrained by the need to produce a surplus for export

However, while there has been a return to modest growth
in the last few years, the continuing high net resource out
flows have kept this growth below politically, and arguably
economically acceptable levels (see Table 8.3).

Slow growth, and the switch to exports and growing trade
surpluses have also resulted in sharp falls in real wages which
are having far-reaching political implications. Per capita GDP
has fallen by 6 per cent since 1980 in Latin America as a
whole; in some countries this contraction has been much
larger. There are signs that some debtor countries' governments will face increasing domestic opposition to the
imposition of continuing austerity – a significant risk to
the 'muddling-through' process.

EXTERNAL FINANCING AND RELATIONS
WITH COMMERCIAL CREDITORS

Despite the external adjustment, debt burdens are still high
accounting for 50 per cent of GDP and 390 per cent of
exports in Latin America. Servicing the debt is also a problem
with interest export ratios well above 20 per cent in most
countries (see Table 8.6).

At the same time there has been a growing reluctance
among the commercial banks to continue lending to re
scheduling LDCs. What was a temporary solution to the
liquidity crises of 1982–83 has become a regular event with
few signs of any easing, with major debtors likely to need

Table 8.6 Debt indicators: 1987

	Total debt	Debt to banks	Interest as % exports of goods and services
	(US $ billion)		
Argentina	54.5	32.5	50
Bolivia	4.5	0.6	45
Brazil	121.0	81.3	30
Chile	20.6	13.3	26
Colombia	15.7	6.4	19
Côte d'Ivoire	9.1	3.4	29
Ecuador	9.2	5.2	30
Mexico	105.0	75.3	28
Morocco	18.3	5.3	29
Nigeria	27.0	9.9	15
Peru	16.7	5.0	22
Philippines	29.0	13.5	26
Uruguay	5.6	2.0	23
Venezuela	32.2	25.1	20
Yugoslavia	21.3	9.7	11

Source: *World Debt Tables*, Bank for International Settlements, own estimates.

substantial new money for the foreseeable future (see Appendix 1). There have been some improvements in the process, most notably in the adoption of a menu of options for creditors. This has allowed greater choice for banks but still boils down to continued commitment on their part. The key issue for creditors in ensuring the continuance of the present strategy is to somehow give more choice — the fact that lending has become 'involuntary' is a big obstacle. Thus the 'menus' that have been concocted have concentrated on items which allow participation through different instruments; and provide ways of exiting or selling off debt.

However, in reality it has been necessary for all banks to continue to participate in full and debt reduction has been minimal. Exit bonds, in the case of Argentina, were unattractively priced, and debt conversions have been limited in volume by domestic policy concerns.

The proposed 1988 Brazil package can now be seen as the state of the art with more 'bells and whistles' than ever. The 5.2 billion package gives a long list of choices to banks.

They can participate through new money bonds up to the value of $1 billion, which will have the same maturity and terms as other new money but it is hoped that they will be more liquid. There is also speculation that the bonds can be treated differently in banks' balance sheets, therefore not requiring further provisions, but this will have to be tested. It is also implied that the bonds have seniority in debt servicing. In general the attractiveness of this form of participation will be determined by whether a reasonable market for the bonds develops. Likewise the demand for exit bonds, which potentially can retire up to $5 billion in debt, will reflect their marketability. The Brazil menu includes further enhancements, including co-financing with the World Bank, on-lending and a 'special investment feature' which will allow banks to invest some of the new money at face value in the Brazilian economy.[4] There are also opportunities for trade finance.

The menu has in many cases eased the negotiating process and has been particularly valuable in offering options for the smaller creditors. However where they have taken advantage of this the group of creditors who now carry the burden has shrunk.

RISKS TO THE PRESENT 'STRATEGY'

Those who argue strongly that there is no need for debt relief base this on a belief that ultimately most if not all countries can service their debt and that banks recognize and will continue to lend to cover 'liquidity crises'. There is concern that it is difficult to give debt relief to some countries and not others. Some banks are less able than others to write off large proportions of LDC debt and therefore have a strong interest in the process continuing.

However with no change in the process and continuing outflows of capital there is little prospect of a return to healthy growth and a recovery in investment for the LDCs. There is therefore a growing risk that the situation becomes politically unacceptable and that action is taken to reduce the debt-servicing burden. A 'debtors' menu' including options such as partial and total moratorium on debt repayments is increasingly being discussed.[5] (See Appendix 2.)

The risk of breakdown in the present strategy would be exacerbated by a world slow-down which would further reduce the capacity of these countries to service their debt. Debt servicing over the last 5–6 years has been facilitated by growing world trade and falling world interest rates as well as sharp domestic adjustments. The capacity of countries to adjust to any further external shock has been reduced and it is unlikely that a rise in world interest rates, for example, could be absorbed by the LDCs. The cost would be felt in lower net transfers from the LDCs, i.e. reduced debt servicing.

As has been mentioned earlier in this chapter the growing reluctance by many banks to continue with the strategy also poses a risk; the issue of the 'free rider' has yet to be properly addressed and resolved.

The risks to 'muddling through' have led to the search for other more radical solutions. The belief that debt relief is coming one way or another has led to the quest for a framework within which this can be done in the way best for all parties. The need for debt relief should not be argued from a moral standpoint but should be based on economic reality. Commercial banks no longer want to be forced to continue to lend to countries and at the same time want to maximize the value of existing debt, while the countries are trapped in a cycle of slow growth and growing debt which they need to break out of.

ALTERNATIVES

Enhancement of the menu

This best characterizes the current situation, as discussed at some length earlier in this chapter with reference to the 1988 Brazil package. Official US government statements[6] have pointed out that banks should 'take a more creative leadership role in efforts to solve the problem' by providing 'diversified financial support' and using 'imaginative financing

techniques'. However this alternative implies that the strategy
is in principle workable.

Debt relief

Proposals for debt relief have come in various forms, includ
ing interest payment reduction, outright forgiveness and the
creation of an entity that would 'reorganize' debt. The real
strength of the argument for debt relief lies in:

- unless the debt burden is reduced, economic and
  political pressure in the LDCs, exacerbated by a world
  slow-down, could well result in default and therefor
  it is in the interest of creditors to act now to preserv
  the value of their loans, albeit at less than 100 per
  cent; and
- a lowering of debt-servicing requirements combined
  with further structural adjustment will allow growth
  which in turn will make these countries attractive to
  investors, both domestic and external. It can help to
  put them back into a virtuous circle of growth and
  investment.

A comprehensive proposal for debt relief has been put
forward by American Express Chairman James Robinson.
Central to the proposal is 'The Institution for International
Debt and Development' which is designed to serve two main
purposes.

First, it would address the asymmetry which currently
exists between the level of debt which the countries have
to service and the 'discount' implied by the price of LDC
debts in the secondary market and levels of banks' provisions
Most banks are now 20–30 per cent provisioned yet countries
are feeling none of the benefits. The recognition that the
debt cannot be expected to be serviced in full in the short to
medium term should be applied to countries' servicing
requirements.

Second, it would offer banks greater certainty. Once the
discount had been passed on to the countries the value of
the debt would be assured. The banks could then write off
the debt over a number of years.

The Institution would purchase LDC debt from banks at a discount determined by the countries' ability to pay,[8] and in return the banks would receive I2D2 consols and preferred stock, i.e. a share in the Institution. Governments would be involved through the financial support of a reserve fund. The preferred stock would pay dividends based on LDC's debt service to I2D2 where it exceeded I2D2's own debt service obligations.

I2D2 would then reorganize countries' debts on a case-by-case basis according to some measure of debt-servicing capacity.[8] In return the countries would be required to undertake structural reforms aimed at improving the working of the market in their economies and generally removing rigidities, thus making them more attractive to domestic and external investors. The relief should take into account a number of factors but would be primarily based on debt-servicing capacity consistent with sustainable economic growth. It is conceivable that some countries would need very little relief and only temporarily thus enabling the Institution to give significant relief where it is most needed.

However there is opposition to debt relief which comes from two quarters.

First, the banks themselves will not be happy to give relief in any event but at the very least would want to ensure that the relief given increases the quality of the remaining assets. In other words the relief should reduce the debt to a level which countries can service. However, preliminary calculations suggest that in some cases this would require very substantial relief.

Second, any comprehensive scheme which requires funding by creditor governments (especially the USA) is being met with adamant opposition on the grounds that it represents a cost to taxpayers. While the current approach continues to work, any involvement by governments is seen as inappropriate and unnecessary. Instead pressure is being put on banks to find ways of enhancing the menu so that the present strategy survives.

Debt relief as an option within the menu

Debt relief could become an item on the menu which bank
could choose. Banks that are keen to sell off some or all o
their exposure would do so and the discount would be passe
on in relief to the country. The cost would primarily b
borne by the selling banks but there would also be a cost t
the remaining banks as the burden of maintaining the valu
of their assets would be spread more thinly. The internationa
financial institutions, such as the IMF and World Bank, coul
take on the role of managing such relief. The agency con
cerned would buy debt from banks at a discount and pas
this on to the countries in the form of relief (some fundin;
would be required). Where countries have their own reserve
they could buy-back debt themselves in agreement with al
creditors.

THE OUTLOOK FOR FUTURE FINANCING

One objective of solutions is to bring in new commercia
flows, most frequently taken as shorthand for new banl
lending. However it is questionable whether this is a realisti
objective even if it were desirable. Banks are no longe
interested in cross-border lending to LDCs; their interest.
have shifted away from country risk. Also the nature of banl
lending is unsuited to development finance. However ther
is a need for some form of capital inflows.

Bearing this in mind, I2D2 does make some attempt a
improving the attractiveness of countries to external creditor;
by subordinating old debt to any new lending. This effec
tively reduces a country's debt to zero for the purposes o
servicing the new loans and so should attract new flows. I
is designed however as a temporary measure to overcome
liquidity problems. If I2D2's loans were subordinated fo
any length of time it would be very costly for the Institution
There would also have to be some control over new
financing, maybe linked to what a country needs.

The importance of giving some seniority to new loans has
been recognized in the waiver that banks have given to Chile[9]

which allows existing debt to be subordinated to a limited amount of new borrowing.

Other sources of new financing

There are other sources of external finance although none are yet significant in volume terms. The key characteristic determining new flows should be the quality of capital rather than the quantity.

Direct foreign investment

A prime example, and potentially one of the most important, is direct foreign investment (DFI). DFI differs from bank finance in that a foreign concern makes a direct investment into a project or company rather than lending to a domestic intermediary who then uses the funds. Remittances are determined by the profitability of the investment, unlike a debt which has to be serviced regardless of the income stream which it has generated. DFI is also more likely to go into investment than consumption thereby providing a better basis for growth. Bank loans in the past have financed consumption as well as investment.

DFI also brings with it new technology and management expertise that LDCs would find expensive to provide themselves. This enables them to compete internationally as well as produce goods for domestic use which are good substitutes for imports. Many companies investing will already have an international market to which the LDC gains access.[10]

The potential for DFI is great as most LDCs have not utilized this source of finance in the past, partly for political reasons but also because of the availability of other finance in the 1970s. Various measures of potential can be used.

1. If DFI reached previous high levels (peak 1975) then potential flows would be well over $20 bn, more than double the level achieved in 1986 ($9.7 bn).
2. Had DFI kept pace with GDP growth it would have been $17 bn in 1986.
3. Taking countries that have successfully maintained

foreign investment flows and assuming that half this level
can be achieved by other countries puts potential annual
flows in the region of $16–25 bn (depending on whether
one uses DFI as a per cent of total investment or as a per
cent of GDP as the benchmark).[11]

However, to some extent there is a limited amount of DFI
which countries compete for, especially on a regional basis

To make it significant however domestic economic policies
have to be favourable and there has to be a degree of stability
and certainty that they will be maintained. The problem of
repatriation of capital, often cited as a reason for LDC reluctance to allow DFI occurs when conditions deteriorate.[12]

Equity funds

Another form of foreign investment which is gaining
popularity, in large part because of the support of the International Finance Corporation (IFC), is the equity fund. A
group of investors participate in a fund, which is then in-
vested in the stock market of the recipient country. As well
as providing foreign exchange inflows, usually from a
different set of investors than would normally invest in an
LDC, the funds can prove very valuable in enabling the stock
market to develop.

The attraction of equity funds is that investments will be
made on the basis of expected earnings and so it will
generally be the competitive well-run sectors of the economy
which will benefit. It is of course a form of financing only
available to the private sector although in some cases it may
provide the opportunity for foreign involvement in the
privatization process. (The development of the stock market
is a prerequisite for a successful privatization programme.)
The enhancement of local stock markets through improving
the legal and administrative infrastructure will be beneficial
as will improved company accounting. Quoted companies
will find it easier to borrow abroad and at home.

The development of domestic stock markets is valuable in
opening up a new source of investment finance. It could
prove to be important in attracting flight capital as well as

unds from a country's emigrants. It is recognized that the
overriding need in boosting investment is for higher savings,
vhether domestic or external; developing the stock markets
can be one element in achieving this.

CONCLUSIONS

Banks are not going to be willing to lend on a voluntary basis
for balance of payments support in the future. They may
vell provide important trade and project finance but of
course this is limited to expansion of trade and viability
of projects. With traditional external financing thus constrained, it is inevitable that some form of debt relief is
coming. What is uncertain is which countries will be eligible
and how the relief will be given. LDCs have generally made
large adjustments and so the potential for further cuts in
domestic spending and increased outflows is limited.

In the immediate future the strategy will be kept going by
further enhancements of the 'menu' and there may well be
selective concessions for the more burdened debtors. In this
context interest capitalization is the most probable next step.

Given the external constraint, even after relief, the key
source of development finance in the future will have to be
domestic savings with foreign involvement seen as a bonus
and only in limited areas. Given the fall in the level of
domestic savings since 1973 there is potential for some pick-
up. However this will only occur when the heavily indebted
countries get back on the path of healthy and sustainable
growth.

Where countries use external financing quality not
quantity should be the guiding principle. Commercial bank
credit to sovereign borrowers is therefore not the appropriate
source. Direct foreign investment in its different forms
should be promoted.

NOTES AND REFERENCES

1. *World Debt Tables: External Debt of Developing Countries,*

Volume 1. Analysis and Summary Tables, The World Bank Washington DC, 1988.

2. The 'Baker 15' countries are Argentina, Bolivia, Brazil, Chile Colombia, Côte d'Ivoire, Ecuador, Mexico, Morocco, Nigeria Peru, Philippines, Uruguay, Venezuela, Yugoslavia.

3. *World Development*, vol. 15, no. 8: *The Resurgence of Inflation in Latin America*, Pergamon Press, 1987. See especially articles by L.B. Pereira and E.C. Epstein.

    A good summary of theory behind 'shock' plans is to be found in an article by Knight, Desmond McCarthy and Van Wijnberger in *Finance and Development*, December 1986.

    Also details of the 'Cruzado Plan' in *Brasil: Economic Stabilization Program*, Federative Republic of Brazil: Secretariat of Planning, 1986.

4. *Financial Times*, 23 and 24 June 1988.

5. *The Evolution of the External Debt Problem in Latin America and the Caribbean*, Economic Commission for Latin America and the Caribbean, UN, February 1988, see pp. 37–40 (and Appendix 2).

6. Speech by Assistant Secretary of the US Treasury, David C. Mulford on 27 April 1988 in Miami, Florida.

7. *A Comprehensive Agenda for LDC Debt and World Trade Growth* by James D. Robinson III, The AMEX Bank Review Special Papers, no. 13, March 1988.

8. 'Ability to pay' should be based on the level of payments relative to export earnings and GDP which is compatible with domestic growth and therefore is sustainable. The formula used will necessarily differ between countries as it takes into account the openness of the economy and the social needs which have to be met. Some work on this question has based ability to pay on what historically has been paid (net). However, given that this has not been consistent with domestic growth, this is not a useful indicator for the Latin American countries.

9. Chile has provisional agreement from its creditors to be allowed to borrow up to $500 million in the market by guaranteeing a proportion of interest payments on this new loan with export earnings. If there are enough subscribers to the new type of loan Chile will not have to come to its creditor banks for new money in 1989. It is feasible that Chile has successfully moved on from the pattern of reschedulings and forced new money.

10. For further discussion of the role of DFI, see *Foreign Private Investment in Developing Countries*, Occasional paper 33, International Monetary Fund, 1985.

1. See The AMEX Bank Review, *New Finance for LDCs. The Importance of Direct Investment*, January 1986.
2. The International Chamber of Commerce have surveyed their members as to what are the biggest problems facing foreign investors. The results are published in a report, *Promotion of Private Foreign Direct Investment in Developing Countries*, ICC, 1987. The report is based on practical examples ranging from problems with education through to marketing. The problems and recommendations are centred on 'the need for an orderly and non-discriminatory legal and administrative system'.

APPENDIX 1   OUTLOOK FOR FINANCING REQUEST 1988-89

Brazil has agreed a package with the Steering Committee of its creditor banks covering rescheduling of $61 billion loan falling due in 1987-93, and requesting $5.2 billion in new money. However, while the deal has more 'bells and whistles' than ever in the menu of options open to banks it is expected that the final signature and the conclusion of the deal is still a long way off.

Argentina faces severe liquidity problems again this year with interruptions in interest payments likely. The Argentine government is expected to begin talks with its bank creditors within the next month or so. While there will be a request for new money (in the region of $1.5-2 billion annually) it is also likely that other ways to cover the financing gap will be sought. 'Imaginative' approaches could well include interest capitalization.

Mexico still has healthy levels of reserves although the current account surplus is expected to shrink and maybe even turn into a deficit over the next year or so. It is possible that Mexico will return to the banks in 1989 asking for further financing but much more likely are further schemes on the lines of the Mexico/Morgan bond. The stated priority of the Mexican authorities is to reduce the burden of debt.

Venezuela has seen a deterioration in its external accounts which has prompted speculation that they will be seeking substantial financing in 1989. As the country is in the middle of an election campaign it is dangerous to assign too much weight to statements that Venezuela has to have more financing as they are politically motivated. However there are signs that new money will be requested over the next year.

Chile will not be coming to its creditors for involuntary new money in 1989. Instead it is likely that they will raise the necessary financing in the market. This has been made feasible by getting the agreement of its creditors to subordinate old debt to new borrowing up to a limit of $500 million. With continuing improvements in the external accounts this

mount should easily cover Chile's financing needs. The issue
; whether the priority given to the servicing of new debt will
e a sufficient inducement to lenders.

cuador failed to sign an agreement with its creditor banks
vhich was to provide the financing to clear interest arrears in
987. While domestic political factors have played a role the
tated reason is that commitments from banks fell short of
he amount agreed as many small banks were not prepared
o contribute. It is expected that the 1987 package will be
uperseded by a new agreement which will take into account
he arrears as well as financing needs for 1988-89.

APPENDIX 2   THE DEBTORS' MENU

LDCs need to reduce the net resource transfer (debt servicing less new financing). Given that this appears not to be possible under the present approach debtors are increasingly looking at alternative ways to stem the flow:

1. Selection from the market menu.
2. Full moratorium on medium-term debts. This will on the whole be conciliatory as countries are not interested generally in outright repudiation. It will be used to buy time and bargaining power.
3. Formal limits on payments. Debt servicing can be limited reflecting capacity to pay, as a percentage of exports or GDP for example.
4. Conversion of debt into bonds. This would allow the country to capture some of the discount implied by the secondary market either through a reduction in the face value of debt or interest reduction.
5. Interest bonds. Selective capitalization of interest.
6. General capitalization. Countries would capitalize some interest unilaterally, over a certain level, for example.
7. Payments in kind. Goods rather than foreign exchange used for payments.
8. Coordination with other debtors. A joint approach to negotiations.

Paraphrased from *The Evolution of the External Debt Problem in Latin America and the Caribbean*, ECLAC, 1988.

9 Strategic plans or muddling through: the generics of Third World debt policy

Graham Bird

The Third World debt problem has generated so much interest amongst politicians, academics and the media that it is hardly surprising that an apparently never-ending stream of proposals has been put forward for dealing with it. However, the temptation is rejected here of providing a detailed catalogue of the various schemes that have been suggested. Instead, this chapter sets out to identify the basic principles underlying reform; to discuss, in broad and generic terms, some approaches to dealing with debt; and to assess each of these approaches in terms of the basic principles identified. This assessment does, however, lead to some tentative conclusions.

As part of this review, a distinction is drawn between the extremes which, at one end, envisage a planned approach resting on the official creation of a new debt discounting agency, and, at the other end, rely on market-driven reforms. This distinction highlights the importance of the political economy of debt reform.

A further distinction is drawn between those approaches which ambitiously set out to solve the debt problem, and those which, more modestly, merely try to alleviate its worst aspects. Of course, an intriguing problem in this context relates to what is meant by 'a solution' — but this question is largely ignored in this chapter.

THE ECONOMICS OF DEBT RELIEF

Much of the analysis conducted earlier in this book suggests that the problem of Third World debt will not be adequately managed in the future by using those techniques that have been used since 1982, i.e. adjustment in the debtors and rescheduling. In searching for an alternative approach, certain basic questions have to be addressed.

Perhaps the prime question is whether relief should be offered to debtors — where this is defined as a reduction in the present value of their outstanding debt obligations — at this stage in the evolution of the debt problem. The granting of relief on existing debt has become a more significant issue as the prospects for new money inflows have diminished. As with most issues of economic policy, there are arguments both for and against, and any conclusion reached rests on weighing up the relative strengths of these arguments. An assessment of the arguments is, however, made difficult by the fact that it is often impossible to introduce any degree of precise quantification, with much depending on behavioural responses that are uncertain or unknown.

The case for relief covers both equity and efficiency. From the point of view of equity, it is argued that relief represents an effective transfer of resources from rich to poor countries. Moreover, in as much as the debtor countries have certainly not been totally responsible for the problems they are encountering, contracts should be revised to share more evenly between debtors and creditors the distribution of the costs of a deteriorating international economic environment.

From an efficiency point of view, the arguments for relief are essentially as follows. First, by reducing their debt burden, it would raise debtors' creditworthiness. Second, if relief is not offered, other measures which are more damaging to global economic welfare — in particular default — will evolve. Third, without relief there will be little incentive for debtors to adjust, since the domestic marginal returns will be low. Fourth, the debt problem is becoming more difficult and intractable as 'debt fatigue' sets in, reducing the incentive for debtors to carry on servicing their obligations and for creditors to put up new money or reschedule debt. A new initiative, such as would be provided by debt relief, is needed to restore progress.

The case against debt relief also incorporates equity and efficiency arguments.

The equity argument is that the countries benefiting most from relief would be those that are most heavily indebted. These countries are not amongst the *least* developed nations of the world. If concessionary assistance is to be made available should this not go to the poorest countries? Extending the equity argument, it is maintained that relief would reward the profligate and not the prudent. Critics maintain that it would be difficult to offer selective relief and that there would therefore be a 'free rider' problem.

These equity concerns also have efficiency aspects to them since, if relief is provided to those encountering debt problems, will this not encourage countries to take on more debt than they have the capacity to service, precisely to gain access to the additional resources that relief implies: is there not a moral hazard involved with granting relief, even in circumstances where this is granted *ex post*?

Apart from discouraging appropriate adjustment policy, the argument against relief also suggests that it will *reduce* debtor countries' creditworthiness and will therefore impair their access to finance in the future and will also reduce their lines of trade credit thereby inflicting an anti-trade effect. According to these arguments, relief is not in the interests of the debtors any more than it is in the interests of the creditors, global equity or efficiency.

Although, as noted above, there are grounds for disagreement on these issues, there is perhaps a reasonable presumption that events since the mid-1980s have strengthened the relative case for some form of debt relief. Creditworthiness amongst the debtors is already so low that it is difficult to see how relief could have a significantly adverse effect on their market access, which is at present poor in any case. Meanwhile flexibility in the nature of the relief given, as well as the appendage of policy conditionality could, in principle, deal with the problems of inequity, free riders, and moral hazard.

While, in this fashion, the arguments against relief can be

neutralized, the positive case for it seems particularly strong
at a stage in the debt problem when alternative measures have
been tried and have largely failed, and when pressures may be
mounting for inferior policy responses. Although it is easy to
model the global conditions necessary for a resolution of the
problem, these conditions seem unlikely to hold in the foreseeable future. The growth of developing countries' exports
seems likely to be insufficiently high and the level of world
interest rates to be insufficiently low to allow an inactive
approach to Third World debt to be warranted.

But if there is a systemic case for debt relief should this be
provided by the banks or by the official sector?

If it can reasonably be argued that the debt problem is as
much to do with historical overlending by the banks as it is
to do with overborrowing by the debtors, then there may be
some moral obligation upon the banks to accept a share of
the costs of adjustment. Similarly, to the extent that debt
difficulties have been caused by external factors which were
unseen by debtors and creditors alike, this may be used
as an argument for sharing the burden of adjustment between
all participants. However, whatever the merits of such
arguments, it is unlikely that the banks will be much influenced by them. They are only likely to consider the
provision of debt relief if they deem it to be to their own
advantage.

Assuming that banks set out to maximize their expected
profits, a concept which involves both return and risk, debt
relief will be perceived by the banks as being self-serving if
it increases the probability that countries will continue to
service their remaining obligations or, in other words, reduces
the probability of debtor default, thus increasing the secondary market value of remaining debt.

Of course, in one sense, the banks might be encouraged to
offer relief to debtors if they believed that this would be well
received by the market and would increase their own stock
market value. This indeed could be a powerful incentive for
providing debt relief.

With recent moves in terms of provisioning and of limited
debt sales at discounted prices, the banks have, in a sense,
conceded that they are unlikely to receive the full repayment

of their loans, although defence of their bargaining position discourages bankers from saying as much publicly. The key issue relates to the optimal distribution of the discount on the debt and the extent to which this should be allocated to the debtor countries. The banks, having cleared their balance sheet constraints on the provision of relief, have to weigh up the relative likelihood of the alternative responses that relief (and non-relief) will generate. Will relief bring forth greater resolution and effort on the part of the debtors to meet remaining obligations, and will it make a significant contribution to financing domestic investment and relaxing the foreign exchange constraint on economic development? After all the best chance the banks have of getting their money back is for the debtor countries to enjoy a period of sustained growth.

Or, on the other hand, will relief for some countries spill over into relief for all, and will it encourage countries to relax in their efforts to keep up with remaining obligations in the belief that further relief will be forthcoming? In a sense this reduces to the question of whether failure to service obligations reflects an inability or unwillingness to do so. If inability is the decisive factor the banks might be more prepared to offer relief.

Moreover, unless banks believe that relief provision will increase their own market strength, there will be little incentive for any individual bank to take independent action. While joint action might not be against the interests of banks as a whole, independent action could be against the interests of the bank undertaking it.

Different banks may, of course, have different views about debt relief depending on the size of the developing country debt they hold, since although large absolute costs could be counterbalanced by larger absolute benefits, the uncertainties surrounding the response of debtors would mean that larger risks would be carried by those banks with larger amounts of developing country exposure. Debt relief might be expected to have a more heavily adverse effect on the short-run profits of highly exposed banks.[1] Having said this, the generalization of provisioning amongst the banks has made it more likely that, if they are to continue to offer assistance, they will do so in the form of relief as opposed to new money. Moreover, if banks believe that relief is more likely to induce the pursuit of appropriate macroeconomic policies in the debtors than is new money which increases indebtedness, then it may again be in their interests to switch the emphasis towards granting more relief.

The practicalities of the debt problem are that an extension of debt relief by the banks is now more likely than before. Historically the resolution of debt crises has usually involved either creditors providing some form of relief or debtors defaulting; and it is difficult to see how the banks would gain by the latter course of events.

On top of this, the strength of the relative bargaining positions of debtors and creditors has been changing. For reasons mentioned earlier in this book, the pressures for debtor countries to default have been increasing while the costs of relief to the banks, as they have diversified away from developing country debt, have been falling.[2] The banks are now in a stronger position to withstand the granting of relief than they were during 1983–86. This, in itself, reduces the chance that default would result in a huge international financial crisis during which developing country exports would be seriously threatened, and thereby strengthens the debtors' bargaining position *vis-à-vis* the banks. Moreover, the way in which provisioning was introduced served to weaken the solidarity of the banks and may, for this reason, have strengthened the bargaining position of the debtors.[3]

Of course, decisions of the banks relating to relief could be influenced by the official sector. Just as the banks have been under pressure to put in new money, they have also been exposed to pressure to grant relief. Banks might also be encouraged to offer relief through tax incentives; relief granted by the banks could be subsidized from the public purse. If there are systemic, public good-type efficiency gains from debt relief, as well as gains in terms of equity, then a subsidy might be legitimate. Alternatively, additional finance could be made available to the debtors through the multilateral institutions, particularly the IMF and the World Bank.

The problems with such a policy are twofold. First, to reduce the costs to the banks of inappropriate lending decisions might be inefficient, since it could, in principle, encourage an inappropriately high level of lending in future. Yet, as noted earlier in the book, the medium-term scenario is at present one of sub-optimal bank lending, and a measure which encouraged more lending might therefore be seen as increasing efficiency. Second, if official money is to be provided in an attempt to alleviate the problems faced by debtors, should this not go to the low-income countries of Africa and Asia rather than the middle-income developing countries of Latin America? This is an important consideration. The provision of assistance for highly indebted countries should not be arranged in a way that crowds out aid for the poorest countries of the world.

To offset these arguments, however, it may be countered that, if it were government policy in the industrialized countries which caused or at least contributed to the debt problem, by means of forcing up world interest rates and forcing down the export receipts of indebted countries, it is legitimate that the same governments should now make a contribution towards solving the problem either directly or indirectly through the provision of subsidies on bank-based debt relief and the financing of the multilateral institutions.

THE PRINCIPLES BEHIND REFORM

The above discussion seems to suggest that there is a growing case for debt relief of one form or another. Moreover, various criteria also suggest that this relief should be provided by both the official sector, in the guise of the multilateral institutions as well as governments in the industrialized countries, and the private sector, in the guise of the commercial banks.

In attempting to design a revamped approach to debt, which incorporates a larger element of relief, the following issues need to be considered. The first relates to the appropriate *blend* of adjustment and financing, and to the choice of the appropriate *type* of adjustment. Where the type of adjustment is inappropriate and the blend of adjustment and financing policies is sub-optimal global welfare will not be maximized. It needs to be recognized, however, that the selection of an approach involving, say, a slower pace of adjustment brings with it a need for more financing.

The second issue then relates to the *source* of this extra financing. If the private sector is unwilling to lend, can the official sector be relied upon to fill the financing gap and can the finance be provided through debt relief? Either way, at a time when financing is likely to be in short supply, any approach needs to ensure that available finance is used efficiently.

Reform should not, however, be completely preoccupied with considerations of efficiency. International equity is the third issue which has to be tackled. Just because the problems of one group of countries are particularly visible, it does not follow that the problems of other countries can be ignored. Even in terms of efficiency, debt policy needs to allow for the fact that what is appropriate in one country may be inappropriate in another.

The fourth issue relates to the institutional arrangements through which a preferred approach may be operated. What is the appropriate role for existing institutions? Are new institutions required? What is the proper division of labour between the official and private sectors and between different institutions within these sectors? The institutional arrangements also have to involve an incentive structure that encourages the debtors to act in a desirable way. Problems of moral hazard have to be avoided.

Finally, to maximize the chances that the approach will actually be implemented, the political economy of the issues it raises needs to be considered. There is little practical point in advocating reform which requires massive amounts of additional funds, or which is perceived to be of little benefit to those constituencies whose support is vital; unless, of course, the mere advocacy of such reform enables negotiators to compromise on alternative and less ambitious plans which might otherwise have been deemed unacceptable. Linked to the question of political economy is the distribution of the costs and benefits of reform. Actors in the debt game are hardly likely to support measures which they perceive as conferring benefits on others while imposing costs on themselves.

Bearing in mind the above issues and the aspects of the current Third World debt situation discussed earlier, what reforms might offer a chance of providing a long-term solution?

GENERIC OPTIONS

An international debt facility (IDF)

As with most generic reforms, there are a number of variants on the theme of an international debt facility from which to choose. However, the basic ideas behind an IDF are common to all proposals and look for an agency to be established which would buy debt from current holders — largely the banks — paying a price lower than the face value. The agency would then restructure the debt and offer debtors liberalized terms which might include: a reduced contractual value of the debt; a lower interest rate; and a longer repayment period. However, in return, the IDF would expect, or indeed compel, the debtor to accept conditions relating to the conduct of domestic economic policy over an agreed period of time.[4]

Proposals of this genus differ in terms of the purchase price of the debt, the amount of debt purchased, and the way in which purchases by the agency are financed; with variations in these elements influencing the distribution of the costs and benefits, as well as the feasibility of the scheme. However, while acknowledging such differences, it may still be useful to try to assess the proposals for an IDF in terms of the principles identified in the previous section.

As far as the blend between adjustment and financing is concerned, the scheme would not provide new money but would reduce debtors' existing obligations. It would, therefore, make a larger proportion of foreign exchange earnings available to finance imports. The financing effect would depend on the price paid by the agency for the debt acquired and the extent to which the discount is passed on to the debtors. The lower the price paid and the greater the pass-on, the greater the financing benefit to debtors.

The provision of financial relief would, however, be institutionally tied to adjustment through policy conditionality, in an attempt to avoid the moral hazard problem of encouraging countries to engineer debt problems to gain relief. At first sight it might be supposed that conditionality would be implemented through the IMF, with its appropriateness therefore depending on the appropriateness of Fund conditionality. But, since the degree of maturity transformation brought about by the agency could be significant with, for example, the liberal use of grace periods, the conditions attached could be allowed to relate more heavily to structural adjustment. If this is what is required in many debtor countries, it follows that IDF conditionality would be of a more appropriate type than IMF conditionality, allowing debtors more easily to escape from the high debt/low growth equilibrium trap.

Although an IDF would bring immediate financial relief to debtors, the longer-term implications for financing also need to be considered. There are a number of relevant factors in this context, although they do not all point in the same direction. First, it may be argued that it has only been the overhang of debt that has encouraged banks to put up new money. With an IDF taking over this overhang, the incentive for banks to lend more would be removed and new inflows would dry up. Of course, to the extent that new money has all but dried up in any case, the financial gains to debtors from relief provided by an IDF would represent a net gain. Second, inasmuch as the restructuring of debt conducted by the IDF increases the probability of debtors being able to service their remaining obligations to the banks, this could reduce the discount on such debt and could, in principle, make the debtor appear more creditworthy. However, unless this effect were to be sufficiently strong such that it all but eliminated the discount, it is difficult to see how there could be a significant impact on new financial inflows.

Third, if the existence of an IDF were perceived by private lenders as reducing the risks associated with future lending to highly indebted countries, this would clearly tend to increase their propensity to lend, and this would be of benefit to the debtors.

As far as equity is concerned, there is no reason, in principle, why an IDF should not discriminate between debtors in terms of the size and type of relief offered. Greater relief could be provided to the least developed countries. However, it is not only the debtors that would gain from the operations of an IDF. To the extent that its activities raised the secondary market value of remaining debt, the private international banks would also benefit. Indeed, it is in the nature of the scheme that risk is transferred from the banks to the IDF. Since participation by the banks in a debt rediscounting operation is envisaged as being voluntary, it is reasonable to assume that the discount on the debt which they would accept would be lower than the value of the gain from the reduced risk of their loan portfolios. It is, in this regard, that the IDF is seen as a means of baling out the banks.

Connected with the view that it would be the facility, or in other words the official sector, that would carry most of the risks, there is the argument that an IDF could be too expensive to operate. Less comprehensive schemes would clearly cost less but would not make significant inroads into solving the debt problem. Even if the necessary finance were to be raised from the private sector through bond issues by the IDF, the question remains as to whether the financing of an IDF is either the most efficient or most equitable use of such resources. Doubts in this area probably make the scheme unfeasible, and certainly this genus of reforms has received little support from either the official or the private sector. Even debtors show some reluctance to accept the formalized write-down of their debt that would be a central component of the IDF.[5]

SDR allocation and loan insurance

While the purpose of an international debt restructuring agency is to provide financial assistance to debtors through the provision of relief orchestrated by the official sector, an alternative genus of reform is to use the official sector as a means of either directly generating or indirectly facilitating additional financial flows to indebted countries. Additional finance could be provided directly by an additional allocation of special drawing rights, while it could be facilitated by the provision of loan insurance for the private sector.

SDR allocation

There are strong arguments for a new allocation of SDRs irrespective of the international debt problem.[6] Many indicators point to a global inadequacy of SDRs. First, although the international community has accepted that the SDR should be established as the principal reserve asset, the SDR's importance relative to that of other reserves has declined rather than increased. Second, published statistics suggest that international reserves did not increase very much during the early 1980s, and that in real terms they declined. Third, but in conjunction with this, the global ratio between reserves and imports has also declined. Fourth, various symptoms of reserve inadequacy both in terms of the performance of key economic variables, such as output, unemployment, and interest rates, and in terms of the conduct of economic policy, have become more marked in recent years.

Of course, these indicators are highly imperfect, and a number of legitimate questions may be asked about them. For example, how should reserves be measured? Is the quantity of reserves not in fact determined by the demand for them, i.e. by endogenous rather than exogenous factors? Is not the quantity of liquidity more important than the quantity of reserves? Does the reserve–import ratio really tell us much about the adequacy of reserves, particularly where the nature of the exchange rate regime changes and where the trend in deficits may not match that in the level of trade? And is not the symptomatic approach subject to numerous theoretical and practical shortcomings?[7]

Although each of these questions, and the implied criticisms of the measurement of reserve adequacy, has a great deal of truth in it, the fact remains that, for the early 1980s, the indicators tend to point in the same direction. They therefore need to be taken seriously.

In addition to the case made above, however, there is the

argument that a new allocation of SDRs would be particularly appropriate in the context of the Third World debt problem.

First, such an allocation would increase the owned reserves of the major borrowing countries and would enable them to pursue adjustment policies which are more gradualist in nature. Although there certainly are instances where shock treatment is required (largely where expectations have to be changed), for many debtor countries these circumstances do not exist and a strategy of adjustment with growth is preferable to one of adjustment with contraction. Indeed it may be suggested that the latter approach does not involve 'adjustment' at all but rather 'stabilization'. The major debtors are experiencing a particularly marked inadequacy of reserves relative to developed countries. Although the two groups of countries have similar reserve–import ratios, the latter group tend to make greater use of their exchange rates and tend to have easier access to private international capital markets; they therefore require relatively fewer reserves. The major debtor developing countries, on the other hand, face an availability constraint in terms of the supply of credit. An allocation of SDRs to them would help overcome this constraint, not only directly providing them with more owned reserves but also indirectly by raising their creditworthiness in the eyes of private lenders.[8] There would therefore be a form of multiplier at work, with an SDR allocation acting as a catalyst for other financial flows.

By maintaining the market-related interest rate on the net use of SDRs the concessionary element to the major borrowers would be limited. Similarly, concern that the SDRs might be used to support policies which would not enhance the capacity of the recipients to service debt in the future, could be dealt with by making the receipt of the SDRs at least partially dependent on the negotiation of a programme of policies with the IMF. Alternatively, the extra SDRs could be channelled through the lending facilities of the IMF. In this case they would go only to countries with balance of payments problems; they would, depending on the specific facility under which the country was drawing from the IMF, involve a degree of conditionality; and they would be repayable over time. Of course, where SDRs are

channelled through IMF lending windows, the benefit of a
new allocation to the major debtors will depend on the
appropriateness of Fund conditionality.[9]

A second reason why a new allocation of SDRs is
particularly relevant in the current debt situation is that
it would also assist in resolving the debt problems of the
least developed countries. In their case, however, there might
be an argument for subsidizing interest payments on net use
and for avoiding allocational arrangements which would involve repayment.[10]

The extent to which different countries benefit from a
new allocation of SDRs depends on the distribution formula
used. The debt problem faced by the developing world
enhances the case for some form of 'link' between the
allocation of SDRs and the provision of development assistance. It might be anticipated that the traditional hostility
towards the link on the grounds that it would be destabilizing
and inflationary would be more muted in conditions where
the debt problem is already destabilizing, and where global
inflation rates are low and unemployment levels high.

In any case there is now a strong body of theoretical and
empirical evidence to support the view that even a substantial allocation of SDRs, combined with the introduction
of a 'link', would result in, at worst, only a very insignificant
acceleration in world inflation.[11] Indeed, as a means of
defusing the debt problem, the developed world might be
persuaded that a 'linked' allocation of SDRs offers something
for them as well as for the recipient developing countries.
For any given overall allocation, the higher the proportion
that goes to the developing countries, the greater the
generally beneficial impact on the problem of global debt.

Fear of the consequences of a debt crisis may therefore
persuade industrial countries to support an additional allocation of 'linked' SDRs.

How does the proposal for a new and preferably 'linked'
allocation of SDRs stand up to the questions and issues
raised earlier in this chapter? First, the allocation would tend
to shift the blend of adjustment and financing towards the
latter.

Second, the additional financing would come from the

official sector, though it might be anticipated that some additional voluntary private financing would thereby be encouraged. The public finance might not be seen by developed countries as having adverse financial consequences for their own economies since, unlike some other forms of financial assistance, it would not raise the public sector borrowing requirement in the donor countries. Even so, the perceived cost is likely to remain that of inflation, although, as noted above, this is largely ill-conceived.

Third, in addition to being efficient, an SDR allocation could help deal with problems of international inequity, and be to the significant advantage of the least developed countries. However, it would not only be the debtors that would benefit. The banks would also gain from any reform that allowed indebted countries to meet their outstanding debt obligations.

Fourth, the reform would require no fundamental institutional reforms. Though some modifications to existing institutional arrangements might be needed, these would depend on the precise nature of the SDR allocation and, in particular, on the means through which the SDRs were distributed.

Before moving on, another aspect of an SDR allocation may be noted. If some developed countries cannot be persuaded to expand their economies and to reduce their surpluses, it will be impossible for debtor-deficit countries to eliminate their deficits — something that the resolution of their debt problems requires them to do. Adjustment at the global level will not take place, and attempts to achieve it will result in a demand-inflationary bias. In such an environment there is a still stronger case for providing additional finance to indebted countries through the creation of SDRs, to allow them to finance deficits at an acceptable level of economic activity and domestic investment.

Loan insurance

An important impediment to lending arises from perceptions of the default risk involved. If the official sector can reduce such risk it can thereby influence the willingness of private creditors to lend. Risk could be reduced by applying the principle of insurance. Under normal insurance schemes individuals or companies buy certainty for the price of a premium plus (usually) a deductible. The insurance company takes on the exposure but reduces its overall risk through the application of the law of large numbers. The principles involved here could be applied to private lending, such as bank lending to developing countries, with creditors (or indeed debtors) taking out insurance against country risk. Under such schemes the lenders would benefit from the reduced risk, with the benefits clearly outweighing the costs of the insurance cover, and the borrowers would gain from the enhanced flow of lending.[12]

Of course, the possibility exists that banks would attempt to recapture the cost of insurance by increasing the spread on their loans, but to the extent that existing spreads already incorporate a risk element which would now be passed on to the insurer, this need not cause great concern. Indeed, if private insurance is a more efficient way of covering risk than syndicated lending, spreads might even fall.

Doubts about private insurance arise more from the likely lack of depth of the market on the supply side. If, however insurance would benefit borrowers and lenders, and would encourage additional flows of capital to developing countries with benefits for the world economy as well, there may be 'public good' arguments for providing the insurance through an official agency such as the World Bank or the IMF.

However, official insurance or guarantees would involve a number of problems, associated with the principles outlined in the previous section. First, there is the worry that the provision of insurance would create a 'moral hazard' both for the lenders, who might be encouraged to be less careful in their country risk analysis, and for the borrowers, who might feel that the costs of default have been reduced. But the payment of the premium and deductible should offset the moral hazard as far as the lenders are concerned, while, if an insurance claim were to be linked to the requirement that the country involved accepted IMF or World Bank conditionality, this should deal with the moral hazard as applied to borrowers. Moreover, default would no doubt raise the

:ost of insurance cover on the defaulter and, since this might
)e expected to reduce the quantity of future loans, this
vould also act as an incentive for countries to avoid default
vhere possible.

A second problem is that while an insurance scheme
hould be self-financing or even profit-making, once estab-
ished, in the short run it will cost something to set up.
There might also be a learning period needed to find the
.ppropriate insurance rates for this kind of business. The
cheme would need to have sufficient resources to provide
onfidence that claims would be honoured. It would clearly
iot be necessary to hold 100 per cent backing but there
vould be a significant initial cost. The difficulty in meeting
his cost from official sources is not only that the money
nay not be available, but also that to use scarce official
esources in this way would deflect them away from other
.ses. Important distributional issues therefore arise. Should
upport of lending to better-off developing countries by the
Vorld Bank or IMF receive priority over lending to the least
.eveloped countries?

An alternative would be for the World Bank or IMF to
·orrow directly from the private capital markets to provide
he initial financing. No doubt this would be possible, but
ven this method of financing raises the question of whether
ie provision of guarantees would absorb resources that
·ould otherwise have been lent directly to developing
ountries. However, given the current situation where new
)ans are not forthcoming, this anxiety may be overstated.
he insurance cover could be offered only on new loans and
ould, in effect, be shared between the agency involved and
ie banks by applying only to a *portfolio* of loans rather than
) *individual* loans.

Insurance schemes of the type described above have a clear
:lationship to many of the issues raised earlier in this
iapter. The role of the official sector would be enhanced
ot only as a provider of resources but also as a catalyst for
·rivate flows. Total financial flows substantially in excess of
fficial funds might be expected to result. Through con-
itionality the IMF and the Bank would make an extended
)ntribution to ensuring the appropriate blend between

financing and adjustment. Although some degree of institutional modification would be required, no large institutional changes would be needed.

While most of the benefits would be derived by the better-off developing countries, the private lenders would also gain from being able to secure a preferred combination of return and risk. Other reforms such as an SDR link would need to address the problems of the least developed countries.

Export and interest rate compensation

While an additional allocation of SDRs would, at present, increase the reserve holdings of indebted countries on the basis of a formula which rests only indirectly on the state of their balance of payments, an alternative approach would be to make additional finance available to indebted countries to compensate for shortfalls in export receipts or excesses in interest payments which push their balance of payments into deficit. To the extent that debt problems are caused by unforeseen falls in export receipts or increases in interest rates which are beyond the control of debtor countries, a scheme of compensation would protect vulnerable countries from a deteriorating world economic environment. Moreover, where the deterioration is temporary and a cause of short-term illiquidity for debtors rather than of long-term insolvency, an approach which provides short-term financing assistance might be seen as working on the root cause of the problem.

This is not the place to undertake a full review either of the IMF's compensatory financing facility or of the proposal to introduce an interest rate compensation facility within the Fund.[13] However, it may be useful to see briefly how a generic approach of financial compensation against exogenous events would perform in terms of the principles identified earlier.

With regard to the blend between adjustment and financing, it would tend to raise the contribution of the latter. In one sense this could be argued to be entirely appropriate, if indeed the problem is nothing to do with domestic economic mismanagement, and is temporary. Yet even here, concern over the ease with which it is possible to redict just how temporary a problem is *ex ante*, over whether appropriate domestic adjustment will be made to deteriorating world environment, along with difficulties in disentangling in real life the degree of exogeneity in any specific balance of payments problem — with this itself raising the problem of moral hazard — seems likely to ensure that compensatory finance is made conditional on the implementation of adjustment policies. In this regard, it is relevant to note how the CFF has been modified over recent years to contain a much more highly conditional element.[14]

Conditionality would, then, be one way of dealing with any perverse incentive structure that might be associated with compensatory schemes, but it would do little to deal with a potential equity problem. This arises from the fact that it would be the largest debtors that would tend to gain most from compensation schemes along, of course, with the banks which would benefit from the improved ability of debtors to meet their outstanding debt obligations. To some extent it is unsurprising that, other things being constant, larger trading economies will tend to receive greater amounts of export and interest rate compensation. But, with interest rate compensation, there is the problem that debtors, although not responsible for increasing world interest rates, may have been responsible for the extent to which they are vulnerable to them through overborrowing in the past. Even with respect to export compensation, governments may have pursued policies that have been hostile or unhelpful to export expansion and diversification. Again, it is probably unrealistic to assume that adjustment would fail to feature as an integral part of compensation schemes. This would cloud the question of the degree of responsibility a country has for its debt problems and could be a further source of inequity.

Given that compensation schemes would carry with them a financial cost, they would involve a transfer of official finance to debtors and ultimately to private creditors. Apart from the equity aspects of such redistribution, and the question of whether it represents an efficient use of official finance, there is the further question of how the finance will be raised in the first place. Although compensatory schemes do not encounter significant impediments in terms

of institutional structure, they may simply be budget
constrained. For both this reason and that of internationa
equity, it may be argued that interest rate compensatior
would be more appropriately provided by the private bank
themselves rather than by the official sector, which woulc
thereby be allowed to focus its attention on the leas
developed and poorest countries.

Market-based policy: muddling through

All the plans discussed so far envisage an expanded role fo
the official sector and involve a centrally planned approacl
to solving the Third World debt problem. A contrastin
approach is to rely more heavily on initiatives emanatin
from the market place. Here debt policy would be driven b
market forces. Examples of this genus of policy include: th
use of debt equity swaps and debt buy-backs using the secon
dary market price of the debt; exit bonds; as well as th
extended use of liberalized rescheduling to include, perhaps
some element of interest rate capping.[15]

There are, without doubt, some persuasive arguments fo
not attempting to impose a solution to the problem of Thir
World debt from above, but to be aware of and take int
account what the market will accept. Indeed, to go further
there are arguments for relying more exclusively on market
based reforms. What are they?

First, muddling through has worked from 1982 onwards i
the sense of avoiding a large international financial crisis
grandiose plans are therefore not needed. Second, and in an
case, the alternative of a planned approach is infeasibl
because of bargaining and political, as well as financial con
straints. Third, market pressures will ensure that a
appropriate amount of debt relief is provided as and whe
required. The belief here is that when the problem is in
sufficiently severe to threaten default, relief is not needed
But, when it is severe, the market will respond by providin
relief, since this will be the policy perceived as maximizin
the creditors' expected profits. The amount of relief i
indicated by the secondary price of the debt. Fourth, marke
based relief ensures that some of the burden of provision i

carried by private creditors, and therefore represents a resource transfer from private creditors to debtors. At the same time, banks may themselves benefit if their provision of relief is seen as raising the discounted present value of their future contracted receipts through the increased probability that debtors will meet these obligations. It is possible to argue in this way that market-based policy is Pareto-efficient, with all parties gaining.

Judged against the principles listed earlier in the chapter, market-based policy also has various other potential attractions. It may be used to alleviate financial pressures on debtors and may modify the blend of policy towards more financing. Yet relief can be tied to IMF and World Bank conditionality, thereby ensuring that needed adjustment is not side-stepped. Moreover, in addition to the potential equity benefits noted above, market-based policy will not require institutional reform which would be difficult to negotiate, or substantial amounts of official finance which would be difficult to raise. There is then, in summary, considerable initial appeal to the idea of leaving things mostly to the market, with the official sector only providing the conditionality input and assisting those countries which are bypassed by the market.

However, further examination reveals a number of shortcomings to the market-based prospectus.

First, although it may have avoided an international banking crisis, it has imposed significant costs on indebted developing countries. Relief has not been granted in any significant amount to such countries by market-based policy. The distribution of the costs and benefits has not been equitable. Thus, market-based reform, such as provisioning, has not conferred any relief to debtors, while buy-back schemes which would have given relief have found little favour in the market. Debt equity swaps have only granted relief to debtors to the extent that the governments of debtor countries have found ways of taxing the surplus or rent derived by participants.[16]

Second, there is considerable doubt over whether market-based policy will provide relief in future. Although the changing calculus of repudiation is putting more pressure

on banks to provide it, there remain significant impediment
that need to be surmounted.[17] If the market is inefficient
and wrongly predicts the appropriate time to offer relief
damaging international financial instability could be caused
Indeed instability would tend to be caused even if relief wer
to be provided before a crisis, since uncertainty would almos
systematically exist. Relying on the market mechanism i
therefore a high risk strategy. The market might, of course
be *relatively* efficient if it possessed superior informatior
Yet an argument can be made that the market possesse
inferior information as compared with the multilatera
agencies. Certainly the market was not efficient enough t
avoid the debt crisis in the first place. If reliance on th
market was at least a contributing factor in causing the deb
problem, can it be relied upon to produce the require
solution?

Instead, and third, there are reasons for arguing that, as
means of solving the debt problem, the market fails, not onl
because of inefficiency but also because of inequity. Marke
failure provides a vindication for government interventior
and is associated both with the externalities mentione
above, and the inability to produce a public good, in th
form of orchestrated debt relief, which would benefit a
those involved in Third World debt, but would not be in th
interests of any individual private creditor to provide.

Doubts about the ability of the market to generate a
equilibrium secondary price for debt, and about the appro
priateness of using the secondary market price as a means c
allocating debt relief, with the associated problem of mor;
hazard, further call into question the ability of the marke
unaided, to find a solution to the problem of Third Worl
debt. What the market has come up with have been, at bes
marginal reforms at a time when the problem is increasingl
fundamental. Therefore, while it is certainly unwise to ignor
the market and to fail to acknowledge market pressures, it
equally unwise to rely too heavily and too exclusively on
as the way forward.

Having said this, the essential appeal of market-base
policy remains, in the sense of not requiring much inst
tutional reform or significant amounts of public money

While a case for more public money can be made, there is little point in relying too heavily on that either. Of course, it is largely the costs of most institutional reform proposals that make them infeasible. Institutional reform which does not involve significant additional official financing might be much more acceptable.

A new negotiating framework

The basic rationale behind attempts to derive a new negotiating framework for dealing with the problem of Third World debt is to provide a coordinated approach which incorporates more structure and certainty than does the market-based approach and yet retains flexibility to deal with individual cases as appropriate. The purpose is not to impose a preselected solution but to establish a mechanism through which solutions may be negotiated between debtors and creditors. The outcome of the negotiations would almost certainly, however, involve both adjustment and financing elements. Emerging agreements would not rely exclusively on any one approach or policy option, but would include a mix of policies. Within the negotiations the following issues would be addressed: the appropriate combination of adjustment and financing; the required type of adjustment; the form of debt relief (including the grant element); and the financing of relief. As more individual cases were assessed, a stock of 'case law' would be assembled which would enable certain criteria relating to the provision of relief to be identified. In principle, such criteria could be established *ex ante* rather than *ex post* but, as a practical matter, it might be more difficult to formulate them in anything other than the most general form without specific cases to consider.

The concept of a new negotiating framework is not the same as the proposal for a new lending institution. Indeed, such an institution could make matters worse rather than better by fragmenting negotiations concerning Third World debt still further. What is needed is a greater measure of coordination between those constituencies already involved. To some extent, such coordination is beginning to happen under the IMF's structural adjustment facility, but it has yet to involve the private banks.

One idea would be to set up an agency, possibly a joint subsidiary of the Fund and the Bank, to which countries with debt difficulties could apply directly.[18] The agency would then bring together all interested parties, including the banks in an effort to agree on an appropriate and coordinated package of policies involving debt relief, extra financing, and adjustment. The policy details would vary from case to case with different blends of financing, adjustment and debt relief being offered. However, these details could be negotiated within the agency, by drawing on expertise from its various constituents. Since all the main creditors as well as the debtors would be involved in the design of the package of policies, there would be a higher level of commitment to the emergent plan.

The agency's role would be to help orchestrate an appropriate response to any individual debtor country's problems. A typical response might involve loans from the IMF under various of its existing facilities, as well as from the World Bank; debt relief from the banks, including debt equity swaps, debt-for-debt deals and interest relief; debt relief from the Paris Club; and macro/micro policy conditions jointly approved by the Fund and the Bank.[19] Experience would allow the agency to identify where specific institutional or systemic reforms were needed and it could then exert concerted pressure to get the necessary changes made. The agency could then assist in the evolution of a dynamic strategy for alleviating the Third World debt problem.

The banks might see such a new organizational structure as providing the leadership and policy conditionality they demand, and might therefore be more prepared to collaborate than they would be to carry on with existing and increasingly unsatisfactory *ad hoc* arrangements. At the same time, the structure would enhance the significance of the official sector which, through the IMF and World Bank, could act as an intermediary between the debtors and their private creditors, without requiring a massive injection of new public capital. In return for accepting policy conditions, which would, it is hoped, be designed to strengthen their capacity to service debt in the long run, the debtors would receive consistent and clearly defined support from both official and private creditors.

In essence, the new negotiating framework would provide the necessary superstructure for the emergence of appropriate debt policy. While the expectation is clearly that it would facilitate the provision of relief on a disaggregated and case-by-case basis, and would therefore provide the equivalent of extra financing, the relief would be provided in a cooperative and conciliatory fashion.[20] However, the framework would also contain a structural adjustment element. The cost of relief would be shared between both the official and private sectors, although a key argument is that such a structured solution to the Third World debt problem would allow all participants to gain in the long run. At the same time, the administrative costs would be low and the scheme should therefore be capable of securing a wide measure of support amongst debtors and creditors. The existence of a new negotiating framework could also have a beneficial effect on the future flow of funds to developing countries. The sight of debt difficulties being handled in a more organized fashion could do little other than help the restoration of creditworthiness. Furthermore the bringing together of official agencies and private banks could assist the expansion of co-financing.

CONCLUDING REMARKS

This chapter builds on the premise that the Third World debt problem will not evaporate in the heat of world economic expansion. Indeed, it assumes that a deteriorating debt situation will require a more fundamental policy response than has been forthcoming up to now.

Against this background the chapter examines, in broad terms, a range of generic policy approaches. A number of criteria are discussed against which these approaches may be assessed. The criteria include efficiency and equity. But it is also recognized that it is important to consider the feasibility, and therefore the political economy of reform.

Although it is difficult to judge proposals empirically or purely scientifically, the analysis contained in this chapter suggests that some score more highly than others. Market-based reform, although not without merit, seems unlikely to provide a solution to, or even a significant alleviation of, the problem of Third World debt. There are well established reasons for arguing that the market fails in this context. At the same time, however, grandiose schemes, that are sometimes presented as if they will solve the problem at a stroke, are seen here to be no more likely to succeed.

What is left? Rather than relying on one policy or on no policy, what seems to be required is a collection of policies which are mutually reinforcing, and which together provide a genuinely multilateral debt strategy. Some of the policy elements should relate to financing, and might include SDR allocation, export compensation, and interest rate relief, while others, essentially conditionality, should relate to adjustment. If, however, it is conceded that structural adjustment is, in many cases, needed, it follows that, because structural adjustment takes longer to achieve, additional financing is also required. According to the analysis here, additional financing should not come exclusively from the official sector, even though the official sector does warrant expansion, but should also come from the commercial banks in the form of debt relief.

It is also argued that there are relatively few reasons to believe that such a strategy will automatically emerge. A new initiative should be mounted by the multilateral agencies. Current trends in Third World debt suggest that the market, while not coming up with the strategy itself, would be receptive to a new initiative. However, any new initiative requiring fundamental institutional change and significant amounts of public money would probably prove politically unacceptable. In these circumstances, a strong case exists for establishing a new negotiating framework under which debtors and creditors can come together in an attempt to resolve the debt problem. The alternative is the high risk approach of continuing to muddle through, with largely unorchestrated debtor defaults and similarly unorchestrated creditor

esponses. Such an approach is unlikely to be either efficient
or equitable.

NOTES AND REFERENCES

1. This is one of the reasons why Benjamin Cohen, in Chapter 7, concludes that banks are unlikely, on their own, to provide debt relief. He is also doubtful that debtors will be able to exert co-ordinated pressure on the banks to offer relief. Certainly the banks that most dominate the Third World debt problem have been the ones most opposed to relief. The variations in view amongst banks are, however, nicely illustrated by the discussion of the Amex Bank proposal in Chapter 8 by Ingrid Iversen.

2. Stephany Griffith-Jones in Chapter 3 shows how the dynamics of Third World debt seem likely to bring about a change in debtors' attitudes and their approach to the problem. However, her analysis also suggests that a conciliatory approach to default rather than a conflictual one is superior. This conclusion is relevant later in this chapter when we come to talk about the need for a new negotiating framework.

3. Again see Benjamin Cohen's chapter for a more detailed discussion.

4. Early versions of this proposal were put forward by Felix Rohatyn, *Business Week*, 28 February 1983 and Peter Kenen, *New York Times*, 6 March 1983. A similar proposal has more recently been suggested by Jeffrey Sachs, *New York Times*, 9 August 1987. For a review of this generic form of policy see W. Max Corden, 'An International Debt Facility?', *IMF Working Paper*, February 1988. It is Corden's generic description of the facility as an international debt facility (IDF) that is used here; other authors have used different names.

5. But see the proposal put forward by Amex Bank described in Chapter 8 in this book by Ingrid Iversen.

6. For a clear and detailed review of the issues involved see John Williamson, *A New SDR Allocation?*, Policy Analyses in International Economics, Washington DC, Institute for International Economics, March 1984.

7. For a discussion of the problems associated with the measurement of reserve adequacy see Graham Bird, *World Finance and Adjustment: An Agenda for Reform*, London, Macmillan, 1985. In any case, to the extent that the supply of reserves is demand-determined, the issue of reserve adequacy becomes of less concern. If, however, the world can adjust to any level of reserves, this can

be used as an argument for an extra SDR allocation just as much as an argument against it.

8. Examination of country risk analysis as undertaken by the private banks shows that a country's level of reserves has a positive impact on creditworthiness. For a review of approaches to country risk see Graham Bird, 'New Approaches to Country Risk', *Lloyds Bank Review*, October 1986, as well as Chapter 2 in this book by Philip Suttle.

9. The question of the appropriateness of Fund and World Bank conditionality is reviewed in this book by Tony Killick, see Chapter 5.

10. For an attempt to estimate the benefits of SDR allocation to different groups of developing countries see Graham Bird, 'The Benefits of Special Drawing Rights for Less Developed Countries', *World Development*, March 1979, and 'SDR Distribution, Interest Rates and Aid Flows', *The World Economy*, December 1981.

11. For the arguments for and against the link and for an assessment of its impact on inflation, see Graham Bird, *The International Monetary System and the Less Developed Countries*, London, Macmillan, 1982.

12. The provision of insurance or guarantees is not a new idea. It already exists as part of the World Bank's co-financing activity, which could itself be usefully expanded.

13. For such a review see Graham Bird, *International Financial Policy and Economic Development: A Disaggregated Approach*, London, Macmillan, 1987.

14. For further discussion of this issue, see Chapter 5 in this book by Tony Killick.

15. For an analysis of debt swaps see Graham Bird, 'Debt Swapping in Developing Countries: A Preliminary Investigation', *Journal of Development Studies*, April 1988. For a review of debt buy backs see Mike Faber, 'Dissent on Debt: The Implications of Mexico's 1986 Rescheduling', *Development Policy Review*, vol. 5, 1987, and Richard Portes, 'Debt and the Market', Centre for Economic Policy Research, October 1987. The market-based approach also has something to say about what policies should be pursued by debtors domestically: in brief these are also seen as being market-based.

16. See Bird, ibid.

17. These are catalogued in Chapter 7 of this book, by Benjamin Cohen.

18. One such proposal is to set up the equivalent of a bankruptcy court, see Benjamin J. Cohen, 'Needed: An International Chapter

11', *New York Times*, 18 August 1987. For a more detailed explanation of how the scheme might work see, Benjamin J. Cohen, 'LDC Debt: Toward a Genuinely Co-operative Solution', mimeographed, April 1988.

19. The appeal of the scheme would therefore depend again on the appropriateness of such conditionality. On this topic see again Tony Killick's analysis in Chapter 5 of this book.

20. In this regard, as well as in others, the idea of a new negotiating framework is consistent with the analysis contained in Chapter 3 of this book by Stephany Griffith-Jones.

10 Beware of debtspeak

Mike Faber

WORDS ARE WEAPONS

Whenever an issue becomes large and important and complex, new words are needed to analyse and understand it; to refine and differentiate; to break it up into its component portions, so that further instruments can be designed to handle it. The Third World external debt issue is no exception, and a whole glossary of technical terms, new meanings for old terms, acronyms and euphemisms has been spawned around it.

These words, these instruments not only condition what we think, but influence our attitudes. Not only what is possible, but also what is desirable — what is moral, even — is determined by the words which we are given, and accept. Giving out the right words, putting them together in the right phrases to produce the desired effects is thus a highly strategic, highly skilled activity. In the Third World debt issue, the creditors have been much better at this activity than the debtors. The strong have appropriated the language and, at times, have perverted it further to strengthen their position.

The lexicon is large, and the phenomena worthy of our admiration are many. But the lexicon is also an armoury. And the words within it can be deployed, individually or in combinations, as weapons. The rest of this chapter provides some examples of this art.

MISLEADING DESCRIPTIONS

Voluntary borrowing

Chairman (Mr Terence L. Higgins, MP): Could I just clarify one thing? You used the expression 'voluntary borrowing' and I was not clear whether that was voluntary lending or involuntary borrowing.

Sir Jeremy Morse, KCMG: You are quite right; voluntary lending putting it away from involuntary lending, yes.

Why does this mundane exchange, which took place before the House of Commons Treasury and Civil Service Committee on 7 July 1986, hold such fascination for the student of language? Because in it the chairman of Lloyds Bank, unquestionably one of the most thoughtful and articulate of today's commercial bankers, is drawn into admitting that when as a matter of course he uses the term 'voluntary borrowing' as in 'a return to voluntary borrowing' what he is actually talking about is a return to voluntary lending. So why does he do it? I suggest a truthful answer would go something like this: because confidence is all-important in banking; and many are those amongst lenders and borrowers alike (and bankers are both) who do not say what they think, much less what they intend, but what — in the line of duty — they wish to be believed. All adjectives contain within themselves the suggestion of their own opposites. A phrase like 'a return to voluntary lending' suggests immediately that what must be going on at present is 'involuntary lending'. But bankers do not like to admit to involuntary lending. It displays a certain loss of control, and suggests further that not all the assets in the loan book are quite up to the quality that could be desired. That in turn reflects upon the appropriate value for the bank's shares and could even, if matters got further out of control, reflect upon the bank's solvency. Perish such thoughts — or better still, do not allow them to be uttered in the first place. But how to do this? Why, by transferring the 'voluntary' label, with its suggestion of involuntary action, from the creditor to his debtor.

New money

The point about 'new money' is that it isn't. What it is is the
old money recycled plus part of the interest on the old
money that is due to the creditor being added to the
principal outstanding. But 'new money' sounds better —
more positive, more generous, more altogether helpful. The
classic example can be observed in the 1982 Mexican debt
rescheduling, when dollar interest rates (that was part of the
problem) stood at 14 per cent. The banks re-lent the
principal that was owed to them and added to it half the
interest that was due; Mexico ran a balance of payments
surplus (by contracting imports) sufficient to pay the other
half of the interest due. The effects were as follows. The
banks' exposure to Mexico increased, but providing other
business increased faster, their relative exposure declined.
The assets in the banks' loan book remained 'performing'
and even the half of the interest that had to be re-lent could
be taken into the profit and loss account. The Mexican
government avoided being in default but, despite having
made a substantial net transfer of resources to the financial
institutions of the north, its total foreign debt also increased.
In addition, unless its foreign exchange earnings increased
faster than that (which usually hasn't happened) the main
ratios of its creditworthiness further declined (which usually
has happened). But, from the point of view of the banks, it
is convenient to regard all the old debt including all due
interest as having been repaid, and all the recycled loans and
what is, in effect, partly capitalized interest as 'new money'.
And if the debtor says, 'Hey, where's the new money, I seem
to be the one that is making the net transfer?', well we must
have pity on him — he obviously doesn't understand the
language of debtspeak.

Moral hazard

'Moral hazard' is a brilliant invention. It suggests throwing
your daughter out on to the streets in the almost certain
knowledge that she will sink into prostitution. Who would
want to have to admit to any such thing? Obviously it is a

course of action, a crime even, to be avoided. But what 'moral hazard' actually turns out to refer to in the current debt debate is 'forgiveness', something which the best bankers pray for on the sabbath but want to have nothing to do with for the rest of the week. The argument is that if one sinner is forgiven his debts, albeit in a situation where it is clear that through no fault of his own, he cannot repay them, that will encourage all other sinners or potential sinners to get into debt also in the confidence that they, in their turn, will be forgiven. So, by a strange quirk of appropriation, one of the leading Christian virtues gets stigmatized as a crime. But note two things about 'moral hazard'. It was never used in respect of those young persons in Citicorp etc. who promoted their careers in the 1970s through profligate and irresponsible lending to those debtor nations which are now in trouble. Nor is it generally used (at least by bankers) about forgiveness of bilateral debt by governments. After all, that suits the banks since it reduces the number of competing claims on foreign exchange earnings. It is forgiveness, and that of course is dangerous — but it is forgiveness that we approve of, so it cannot be 'moral hazard'. It merits instead a suitably obscuring euphemism. Say, what about 'retro-active terms adjustment'?

Muddling through

Sounds heroic, doesn't it? Somehow redolent of the Battle of Britain, the bulldog spirit, the eventual triumph of the determined pragmatic amateur over the wily foreign theorist. Those are the associations which the term suggests, which is doubtless why the creditor institutions have adopted it with a sort of wry pride to describe their present 'case-by-case but with no master plan' strategy for dealing with Third World debt. And it is amazing how many commentators and financial journalists (even those from the *Financial Times* where they ought to know better) have been gulled into adopting this description and going along with it. I say 'amazing' because a moment or two's thought should have revealed that 'muddling through' is in fact a dishonest pros-pectus. The term implies that you do get *through* the problem and emerge successful, or at least alive, at the other end. There is no intellectual basis whatever for presuming that the current handling of the problem will achieve for Third World debtors any such result. By the lenders' own favoured criterion of success ('the restoration to credit-worthiness'), the collectivity of debt-troubled countries are now some 40 per cent worse off than they were in 1982 as a result of the 'muddling through' strategy, despite the massive net transfers they have been making to the creditor institutions. What 'muddling through' truthfully amounts to is 'muddling on' – a very different process: *muddling on* while the banks gradually strengthen their balance sheets, as the practices of the past six years have enabled them to do, and while the Third World debtors continue to sink deeper and deeper into their quagmire of debt.

LIES, DAMN LIES, AND GDP ESTIMATES

At a recent conference an IMF representative stated that over a wide range of countries in Sub-Saharan Africa, 'official statistics show' 2 per cent per annum growth in GDP over recent years. At this same conference, I stated that over much of Sub-Saharan Africa living standards for most of their populations had deteriorated by 25 per cent. Which of us was telling the truth?

As a matter of fact, we both were. As two old pros, carefully choosing our words and our statistics, we silently acknowledged that to each other. But, how should the layman reconcile these apparently contradictory statements?

My IMF colleague was careful to preface his remark with 'official statistics show'. Strictly speaking that does not commit him to the accuracy of what they show, only to the truth of the statement that they do in fact show such growth. Some might maintain that, metaphysically speaking, GDP figures have no reality outside official publications; none the less, one must respect his caution. I was somewhat bolder, purporting to state a fact about actual living conditions but aware as I did so that the proposition – though dramatic – was so vaguely worded that it would be almost impossible of verification (or falsification). The careful listener would have detected that we were talking about different sets of people over different periods of time. Each of us, naturally, had chosen the set and the period which best substantiated his argument.

The remaining steps of reconciliation concern the concepts themselves — of 'GDP' and 'living standards'. To move from the first concept to a reasonable measure of the second requires a series of discrete operations to take account of population growth; converting from domestic to national product; moving from 'gross' to 'net'; the understated decline in the value of public services; and the conversion from nominal to real values. Let us go through these step by step.

First, GDP constitutes a measure of total gross output within a country, regardless of population changes. To arrive at GDP per head, a crude GDP growth rate would have to be adjusted for population growth. Accurately the adjustment should take the form:

$$\frac{(1 + \Delta\text{GDP})^{\sim}}{(1 + \Delta\text{pop})^{\sim}}$$

but where $n = 1$, and ΔGDP and Δpop are both small, this approximates to ΔGDP − Δpop. So if the prevailing rate of population increase is 2½ per cent p.a., the adjustment required is −2.5 per cent a year.

The next adjustment involves moving from gross *domestic* product to gross *national* product. Domestic product is defined as what is *produced within* the country. National product (or national income) is the earnings of factors of production *resident within* the country. The difference arises from taking account of factor payments paid abroad less factor payments received from abroad. The interest component of debt servicing is a factor payment, and to the extent that those payments are made, goods and services available to the domestic population are correspondingly reduced. As the interest on external debt rises to 2½ per cent of GDP, *national* product — *ceteris paribus* — is correspondingly reduced. To take account of these rising debt service obligations requires an adjustment of −0.5 per cent a year.

But it is still *gross* national product, while what is more significant for determining what is happening to welfare and living standards is *net* national product. The difference resides in whether we take account of depreciation. 'Gross' does not; 'net' attempts to do so. Yet anyone who has travelled in Sub-Saharan Africa in recent years knows that the neglect of maintenance (the physical activity which depreciation is meant to finance) is a significant factor in the deterioration of buildings, roads, factories, hospitals, schools — in short, in the effective value of a whole range of public and private services. To omit to take account of this because of national accounting conventions formulated in countries where it was assumed that maintenance and re-placement expenditures would occur as a matter of course is to close one's eyes — unwittingly — to one of the most drastic of the symptoms of economic decline. To enable GDP estimates to bring into reckoning the decline in living standards occasioned by this 'unrealized depreciation' would require a downward adjustment of about -3.0 per cent a year.

Comparable to the deteriorating infrastructure resulting from the neglect of maintenance is the decline in the real value of many government services. The causes are well known. They start with falling public revenues, an increase in domestic credit creation, and rising inflation. The government budget has to be cut — public capital formation is cut first as being easiest. Then the recurrent budget also needs trimming. This is done by cutting down on the purchase of provisions and supplies — especially imported supplies — as being politically less unpopular than cutting down the numbers in the civil service. The remaining civil servants, however, no longer have the equipment and supplies neces-sary to do their job properly. Clinics go without drugs. Extension workers cannot visit for lack of fuel. Schools run out of textbooks, and then notebooks, and then pencils. Statistics are no longer produced because the air-conditioning has broken down in the computing room. Queues lengthen. Pension payments cease arriving. The complaints department telephones have ceased to work. That's the first phase. In the second phase, domestic inflation combined with an overvalued exchange rate has eroded the value of civil servant salaries and made even local supplies unobtainable. Instead of just sitting at their desks doing very little (as in Phase 1), increasing numbers of civil servants now absent themselves from the office for long periods tending their vegetable gardens or looking after the demands of their 'second job'. Service to the public becomes a residual activity. And how is all of this familiar sequence reflected in the national accounts? It isn't. Because government departments do not normally produce a marketed output, the convention has always been that the volume of the public sector's output should be measured by the cost of its inputs. A more unrealistic assumption in times of severe economic decline, it would be difficult to imagine.

The effect of this kind of process is difficult to measure year by year but its consequences are only too obvious after a period of five or ten years. Even allowing for a decline in the real cost of civil servant salaries, it is not uncommon for the quality of public services to decline by say a quarter in little more than five years. For the purposes of our reconciliation, the required adjustment to GDP has been estimated to be –2.0 per cent a year.

Finally there comes the matter of adjusting for inflation. Important elements in the national accounts are estimated in money terms and then deflated by a price index. If the chosen price index understates the actual inflation, the drop in living standards will also be understated. It nearly always does, because it suits governments to do so; or because statisticians are instructed to ignore 'parallel market' prices, even when certain goods are only available on the parallel market. One government statistician recently told me that his investigators no longer asked the prices of certain goods for fear of being assaulted. But this problem — and government attitudes to it — are not unique to Third World debtors. During the Second World War the British government deliberately subsidized the price of candles. The consumption of candles had dropped substantially with the spread of electricity, but they were still a significant component in the basket of goods used in compiling the cost of living index. Somebody had calculated that it was cheaper for the government to subsidize candles than to have to meet the additional wage awards that an increase in the index would trigger. To take account of understated inflation requires a further downward adjustment, modestly estimated at –1.0 per cent a year.

Table 10.1 shows the sequence of downward adjustments necessary to reconcile the GDP growth estimate quoted by the IMF with our own statement of what has actually been happening to living standards.

Table 10.1 Downward adjustments

Reconciliation		Annual adjustment (%)	Cumulative after 5 years
	Selective choice of subject, population and time period	–2	
a.	Convert to GDP per capita	–2½	
b.	Convert from 'domestic' to 'national'	– ½	
c.	Convert from 'gross' to 'net'	–3	
d.	Adjust for decline in real value of public sector output	–2	
e.	Understated inflation	–1	
		–11	–68%

Summary

1. Cumulative growth of GDP at 2 per cent p.a. for 5 years = 10.5 per cent
2. Corrections (a. to e.) to arrive at actual change in living standards = –53.9 per cent
3. 5-year decline in living standards consistent with these assumptions = –43.4 per cent

At this point, I clearly owe my readers an apology. The drop in living standards to be derived from an IMF claim of 2 per cent GDP growth for five years is not 25 per cent, but something in excess of 40 per cent.

THE ART OF THE ARTIFICIAL DICHOTOMY

The art of the artificial dichotomy works like this: 'Everything is either an A or a B. The example before us is clearly a B, so it cannot be an A.' Alternatively it may sometimes be convenient to state the conclusion as: 'The example before us is clearly *not* a B, so it must be an A.'

The two most common examples of this technique in the Third World debt debate arise in arguments about whether the causes of the crisis were mainly internal or external, and about whether the solutions reside in systemic reform or in a case-by-case approach.

Rhetorical samples, which are simply variations of what we have all heard, are provided below.

Sample one

Rhetorical question: 'Has Sub-Saharan Africa's crisis been caused by external factors or by internal factors?'

First answer: 'The over-extension of the state. Discrimination against agriculture. Loss-making parastatals. Overstaffing and inefficiency in the civil service. Out of control budgetary deficits. Excessive credit creation. An overvalued domestic currency. The discouragement of enterprise. Poorly conceived policies. Extravagance, waste, nepotism, corruption. Look around you and these are what you see. Ladies and gentlemen, need I say more? Is it not obvious that internal factors have been responsible, and that those who seek to put the blame on external factors are simply trying to divert attention from their own incompetence?' And so on.

Of course a very similar speech could be given stressing the drastic consequences of the external factors.

Second answer: 'Falling commodity prices, increasing import costs, soaring interest rates, the nefarious practices of the TNCs, the disloyalty and corruption of the immigrant business community, etc. How could any small, open economy have possibly survived such hostile external influences? Critics from the capitalist world accuse us of domestic mismanagement only because they are unwilling to cease their own exploitative practices.'

The logical structure of each answer is precisely the same. The cause was A, therefore it could not have been B. Also the same is the motive for giving such an answer — an unwillingness to accept any part of the blame, matched by a reluctance to introduce modifications in one's own practices. It thus suits the intransigent forces on both sides to accept the validity of the dichotomy. In real life, the dichotomy is nearly always invalid and the language favoured in IMF letters of intent approximates the true explanation: 'inadequate policy response to adverse external developments'.

Sample two

Rhetorical question: 'Should the Third World debt problem be tackled on a case-by-case basis, or does it require a reform of the entire trading and financial system?'

Answer: 'Because circumstances in each debtor country are different, there is no alternative to the case-by-case approach.'

The cleverness in this answer is that it is convincing, and it is convincing because it is true. Indeed it is so obviously true that, said with appropriate emphasis and a tone of 'Next business, please', it distracts from asking the really important questions, which are 'But is it right to present these as alternatives?' and 'Might it not also be true that the case-by-case approach can only be successful if it is accompanied by wider, systemic reforms?'

There is really no mystery as to why the creditor institutions find these particular dichotomies so convenient.

The bankers will stress the need for (and, by implication, the adequacy of) policy reform, market liberalization and structural adjustment, i.e. all the internal factors, because to admit the existence/prevalence of external factors might lead to the conclusion that external agencies should accept some of the responsibility (and much of the cost) of dealing with the debt overhang.

OECD governments will concentrate on the need for (and, by implication, the adequacy of) the case-by-case approach, first, because their negotiating position is very much stronger if all the creditors collectively (public at the Paris Club, private at the London Club) negotiate with the debtors individually; second, because even if many senior officials might accept privately that some form of systemic approach is desirable, or even, at some stage, inevitable (if only to design new ground rules for individual application), none is confident that he knows what the new rules ought to be, or how they could be acceptably negotiated, but all are confident that — whatever they are — their own governments will not wish to meet the costs.

CONTRIBUTIONS TOWARDS AN ALTERNATIVE LEXIS

This is a guide as to what those who are intimately involved in the Third World debt debate actually mean when they use the words listed.

VOLUME ONE — LENDERS' LINGO

Securitization: the art of packaging a set of extremely insecure investments so attractively that someone else will be induced to buy them. Favoured by the Bank of England as a way of distributing the High Street banks' risks to investors at large. The resultant instruments are known as 'James Bonds' since the chance of full recovery is about 007.

Impaired asset: a loan we wish we had not made, thus a strong candidate for securitization.

Debt/equity swap: the attempt to convert potentially impaired assets into, say, a Mexican hotel, a Chilean copper mine, a Brazilian automobile factory — other suggestions please to Amex Bank.

Debt/development swaps: an offer to do what we ought to

be doing anyway, if only you'll relieve us of some of what we owe.

Write-down: usually a euphemism for right-down-and-out.

Default: not, as you might suppose, a question of the debtor not paying. Only occurs when the creditor finds it convenient to declare publicly that the debtor cannot pay, which for some reason he never does.

Salami defaults: the elimination of debt by a thousand cuts.

Moratorium: where troubled debts go to recuperate; next stop, the crematorium.

Special provisions: a belated guess as to what the mistakes of the past will cost in the future — alas, not as special as we would wish.

Matrix: distortion of Ma's tricks, thought to be a reference to the Old Lady of Threadneedle Street's hints on home provisioning.

Supply side provisioning: currently much in favour, when the level is determined by what a bank can afford to supply rather than by what the risks actually demand.

Two-tier provisioning: a Bank of England invention which results in small lenders being encouraged to make bigger provisions than the big lenders can afford.

Macho provisioning: term coined by patricians to describe muscle flexing by stronger upstarts — actually signifies 'I can't matcho your provisions . . . '.

Shared benefit provisions: provide that if one creditor gets paid out in preference to others, he is obliged to share the benefit. Fine in theory, in practice creditors find it even more difficult to collect from each other than they do from the debtors.

Transfer risk: when too many of a bank officer's loans are non-performing, he risks being transferred to another profession.

Capital flight: a secret journey across the balance sheet — as a result of which a bank's assets may also become its liabilities.

Spread: obtained by subtracting what we pay for your money from what we intend to earn from our own. Claimed to be a function of risk, but more affected by immediate market liquidity.

Floating rate: an invention which guarantees the lender a profitable income even if it sometimes bankrupts the borrower. Seemed a good idea at the time.

Negative earnings: the constructive way to look at a thumping loss.

Zero-coupon: a bond without interest but, as collateral, not necessarily uninteresting.

Syndication: whereby, for a fee, the sins of the one are visited upon the many, yea, even unto the seventh rescheduling.

Off-balance sheet financing: commitments which, if they go wrong, will hit the stockholders that way.

Ratio analysis: a procedure for assessing company risk which it was supposed could also be applied to country risk. Mistakenly.

Marking to market: valuing one's assets at what they could actually be sold for — appropriate for those we lend to, but undignified for bankers.

Bank's balance sheet: an exciting work of fiction, e.g. the books of James Hadley Chase Manhattan.

Secondary market: ranks with Shepherd's Market, so we'll

sue if you say you saw us trading there. Best to deny (or, at least, decry) its existence if your special provisions are not adequate.

Bank of America: — but for how much longer? Rumoured likely to be taken over by Robert McNomura Securities.

Clausen's dilemma: the more strongly I urge the need for confidence, the less of it I appear to have.

Illiquidity: William R. Cline's eccentric diagnosis of insolvency.

Dollarization: conduct of business in currency other than one's own — spreads rapidly as businessmen lose faith in the integrity of their domestic money.

De-dollarization: opposite of the above; spreads rapidly as businessmen lose faith in the integrity of the dollar.

Reaganomics: a main contributory cause of the above phenomenon.

Merchant banks: corruption of the french *banques méchantes,* so called because of their legendary cunning.

Abs: Dr Hermann, the father and master of LDC debt re-scheduling (Indonesia, 1970) since when comparable terms have not been achieved. Hence the expression 'Abs-ence makes the heart grow fonder'.

VOLUME TWO — THE SEARCH FOR SOLUTIONS

Stabilization: standard IMF medicine involving a severe contraction in domestic demand, strongly recommended for others but politically hazardous for application to oneself. Said by some to be what the World Bank needs.

Structural adjustment: highly controversial concept. Is it a state of grace? An eternal process? Or merely a redirection of one's economy so that more of the product can go to foreign bankers? (Even its famous motto 'Servir fit fortes ad justum' is subject to rival interpretations. Some render it 'Grow strong just so you can service your loans', others 'Adjust that you yourself may become strong'.)

Structural adjustment program (SAP): preferably, but seldom, domestically designed programme of reforms which a miscreant government presents as its proposed path to a state of grace.

Structural adjustment loan (SAL): again capable of ambiguous interpretation — the loan/bribe which the World Bank offers to enable/induce a repentant(?) government to pursue its chosen/imposed programme.

Conditionality: invented by the IMF as a form of behavioural control; now practised mainly on Third World debtors but never on that account to be described as financial neo-colonialism.

Performance criteria: a way of checking that the con-ditionality terms are adhered to, which is normally impossible.

Tranche warfare: the practice of releasing promised finance bit by bit as a way of ensuring that if the government has not in fact met its conditionalities, it has at least been wounded in the attempt.

Getting the prices right: thought to cure all ills — trouble is no two economists ever agree on what the right prices are.

Privatization: favoured in SAPs as a way of transforming public loss into private profit.

Rescheduling: normally a recognition of the inevitable. Current rules are that principal can only be rescheduled once, interest not at all. But rules themselves are likely to be rescheduled.

MYRA: short for multi-year rescheduling agreement, a lady currently much wooed by forlorn adjusters, especially at the Paris Club. Some suggest she should get together with IDA and SAL.

The Paris Club: clients visit it to discuss rescheduling and conditionality with OECD governments under the chaperonage of the IMF. Not to be confused with

The London Club: where meetings are less public, more private and often take place without a chaperone.

Inverse, reverse, perverse resource flows: all refer to the same phenomenon, but the BIS prefers the first term, UN agencies the second and debtors themselves the third.

Conciliatory debt reduction (CDR): partial default, but offered with an apologetic smile. Very much the coming game.

Capitalization with a cap: combines capitalization of interest with interest capping, but not to be confused with capitalization of interest over the cap. Unpopular with lenders.

Competitive sovereign debt tendering (CSDT): the process whereby unobliging borrowers oblige lenders to bid against each other in offering their debts back at competitive discounts. A variant of CDR likely to find increasing favour, especially amongst those suffering from the Sisyphus syndrome.

Sisyphus syndrome: the feeling — increasingly common amongst chronic debtors — that however often one reschedules one is never going to reach the top of the mountain. Line of thought is therefore: debtor nations — detonations — reduce size of mountain.

The Baker plan: no longer to be called a plan — a proposal that other people put up a lot of new money. Universally welcomed, since when everybody has been waiting for the other fellow to comply . . . .

The Lawson initiative: a proposal that governments should be willing to write off a lot of old money on the unusually realistic grounds that it is not going to be repaid anyway.

(*Note:* the difference between a plan and an initiative is this. If a plan fails, it is the planner's fault. If an initiative does not succeed, it is because others have failed to respond to it adequately.)

LIDD (low income distressed debtors): equivalent to the deserving poor of the Victorian era, i.e. to be sent to the workhouse, given an invigorating regime (see SAP), and if they have the effrontery to ask for more, to be treated to a sharp Oliver Twist.

Menu of options: generate splendid cooking-up fees for the merchant banks while distracting debtors from what they really need — a complete change of diet.

Mexican auction: ingenious but ingenuous scheme to reduce Mexico's debt by up to $10bn; heavyweight banks recognized this as an invitation they could afford to refuse.

Funarol march: journey around OECD capitals with a set of proposals which everyone knows will be rejected.

Brazilian fudge: rich concoction of subterfuges, digestible by regulators and just palatable enough to avoid the calling of defaults.

Fallacy of composition: when all debtors are advised to increase exports of identical commodities, as a result of which prices fall, debtors are worse off, but consumers in the creditor countries can import such commodities even cheaper.

Protectionism: having insisted that Third World countries repay their debts, this popular device cunningly deprives them of the means of doing so.

Index